G000109010

SMILE

You're on HAROLD'S PLANET

© 2019 Lisa Swerling & Ralph Lazar
Published by Last Lemon Productions
60 Woodside Dr. San Anselmo,
CA 94960, USA

ISBN 978-1-7332675-4-0

*All rights reserved. Artwork from this book or any portion-
thereof may not be reproduced or used in any manner what-
soever without the express written permission of the publisher
except for brief quotations/sections in printed reviews.*

First Printing, 2019

www.lastlemon.com

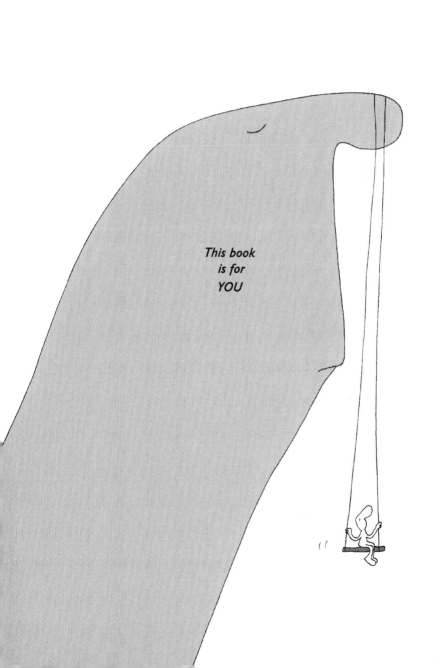

*This book
is for
YOU*

SMILE

You're on HAROLD'S PLANET

Have you met Harold? He's our bobbly-nosed, soft-footed hero, beloved to many through the Harold's Planet greeting cards (millions of which have been sold around the world since 1999) and the stream of new cartoons seen on thousands of screens every day.

Now for the first time since we began Harold's Planet twenty years ago, his world is brought alive in this book collection of our favourite cartoons.

There are still thousands of Harold's Planet cartoons and stories languishing unseen on old hard-drives. We hope to bring them to light in the near future. This is just the beginning!

In this book we also share the story of how Harold's Planet came about, and how he has endured through two decades, delighting hundreds of thousands of people around the world.

Lisa + Ralph

Lisa Swerling and Ralph Lazar

Genesis

The very first evening Ralph and I met, at Khan's Indian restaurant in London in 1998, he told me the story of Harold's Planet.

The man awoke to a sunrise sky. It was a beautiful morning and he decided to go for a walk. He whistled as he made his way across the open plain. He was so busy watching the sky that he failed to notice a hole in the ground in front of him.

The hole was deep and down he fell, for forty days and forty nights. Down and down into the depths of the planet, finally hitting the bottom with a bump.

Up on the ground meanwhile, the man's wife became concerned. Coming upon the hole, she guessed the truth, and so jumped in herself. For forty days and forty dark nights she fell, finally reaching the bottom with a bump.

He husband was overjoyed to see her.

Soon the hole was filled with the cries of newborn babies.

The years went by and the man and his wife grew old.

On their deathbed they spoke of the world above, of the open plains and misty hills. And breathing their last, they told their children of the way to reach the surface.

The children began their task. They pushed their parents' bones into the soil to make a ladder to get to the surface, and began the journey upwards.

Hours became days. Days melted into weeks, which drifted into months. Months became years, and relentlessly the group continued upwards.

It was a difficult journey and after many years there was only one left.

His name was Harold.

He continued alone. He knew he was close to the end of his journey as the tunnel was becoming lighter and lighter every day.

Finally he reached the surface.
And before him he saw the open plains...

...the plains of Harold's Planet.

It was the most moving and romantic story I had ever heard.

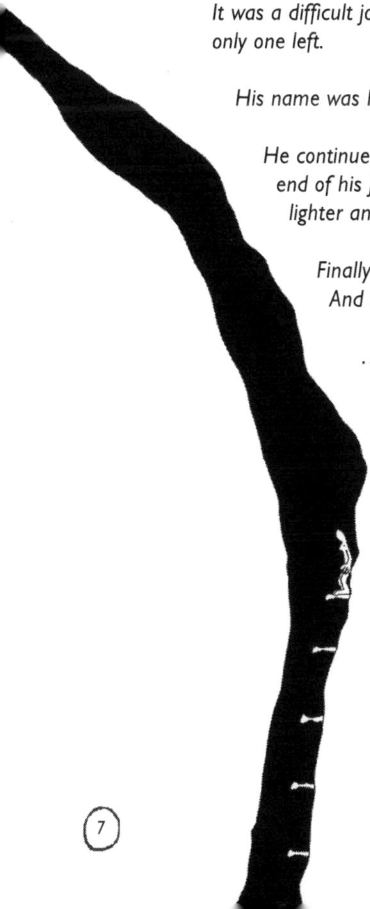

Collaboration

Ralph told me, with a twinkle in his eye, that he was looking for a 'collaborator'.

I hoped his motives were not solely creative - any which way I jumped at the chance to work with him.

In fact we both jumped - hand in hand into the deep unknown - when shortly after we gave up our day jobs and committed to developing Harold's Planet together.

The story of what happened after we jumped, continues on page 190.

The story of what happened after we jumped, continues on page 190.

Between there and here, over 350 of our favourite Harold's Planet cartoons from the last 20 years...

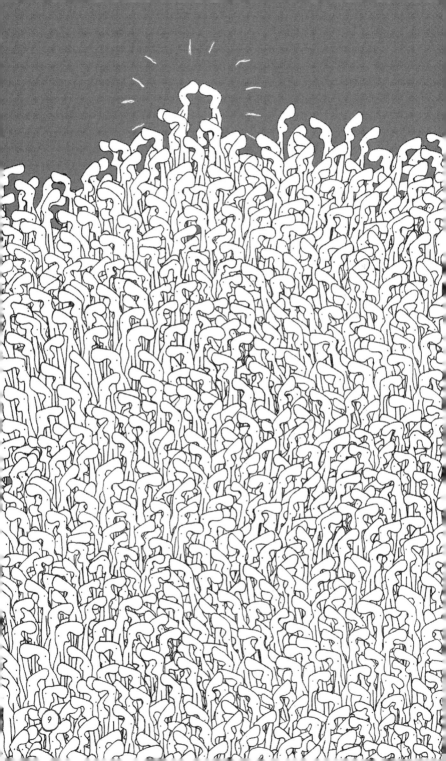

Laws of Nature # 1
There's no such thing as too many books

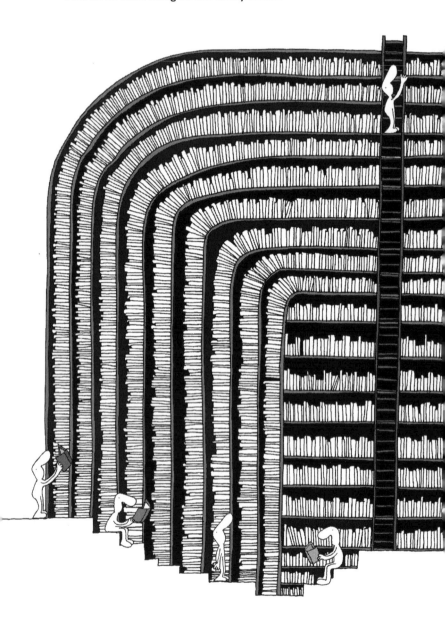

CAPITALISM
is
DEAD
How much for
the sign?

2008

GUIDE TO BASIC KNOTS

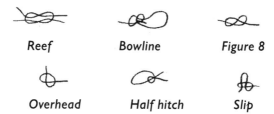

Reef
Bowline
Figure 8
Overhead
Half hitch
Slip
Life

2014

Own less, do more

2018

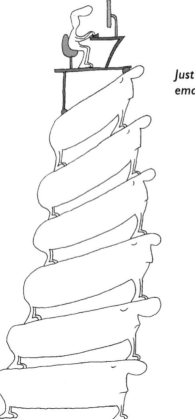

Just checking email

2011

I always carry a spoonful of sugar with me. You never know when a lovely cup of tea may come along...

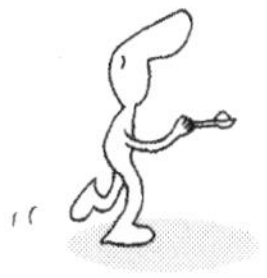

2011

Dad's camping motto:

BE PREPARED

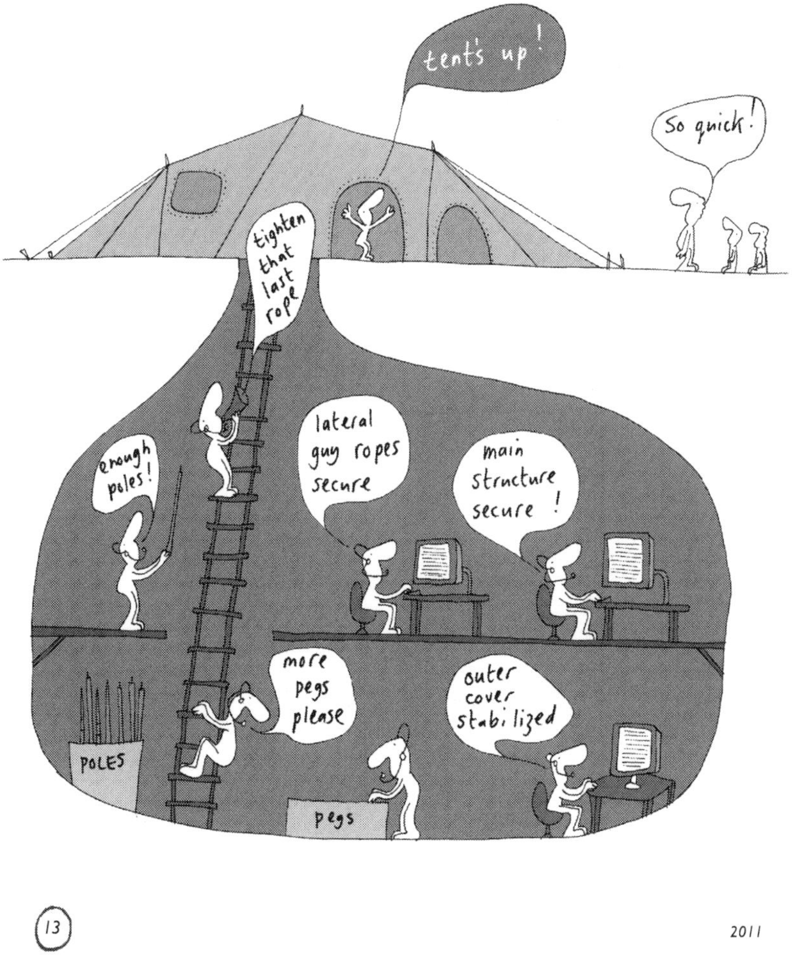
tent's up!
So quick!
tighten that last rope
enough poles!
lateral guy ropes secure
main structure secure!
more pegs please
outer cover stabilized
POLES
pegs

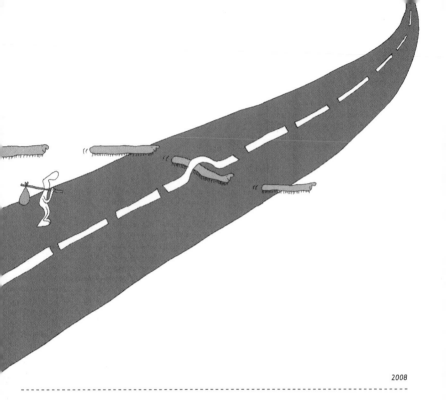

Def: ***BYEBYEMISSAMERICANPIE DROVEMYCHEVYTOTHE LEVEEBUTTHELEVEEWASDRY -OPHOBIA***

The fear of getting an annoying song stuck in your head

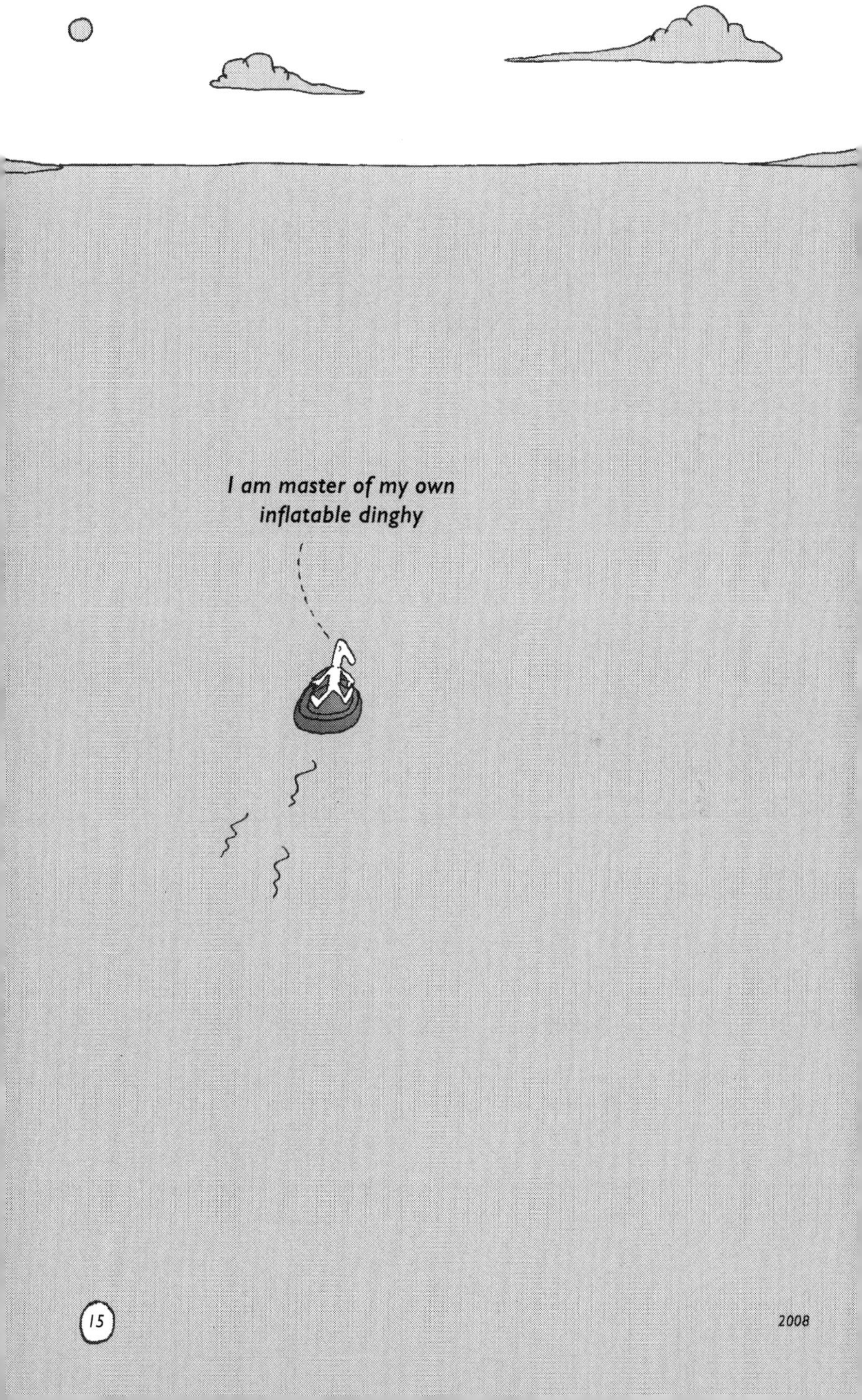
I am master of my own inflatable dinghy
15
2008

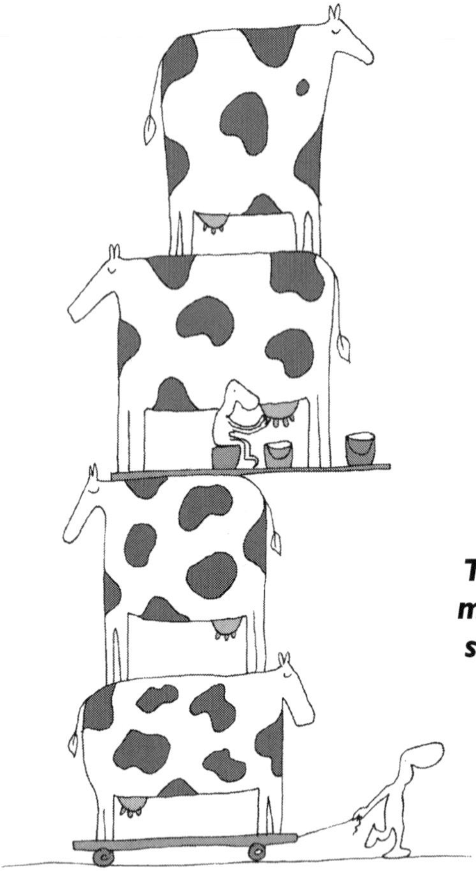

Traveling milkshake salesmen

2012

"It is one of the blessings of old friends that you can afford to be stupid with them."

-Ralph Waldo Emerson

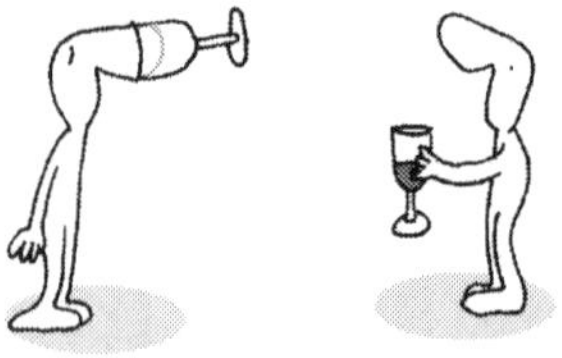

2012

HOW TO
Protect the Planet

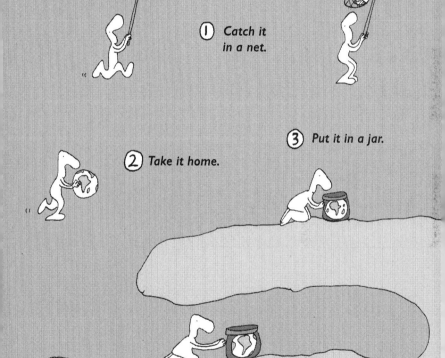

① Catch it in a net.

② Take it home.

③ Put it in a jar.

④ Hide it somewhere where humans will never find it.

HOW TO AVOID RUNNING INJURIES

Walk.

2014

A 'sock-over-my-head' kind of day

2012

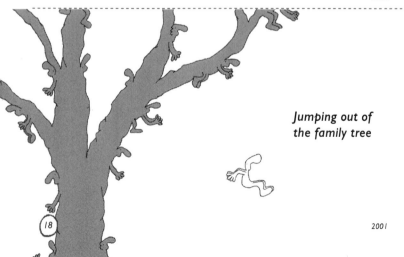

Jumping out of the family tree

2001

I'm no good at surfing but I'm exceptionaly good at standing on the beach with my surfboard, especially at sunset.

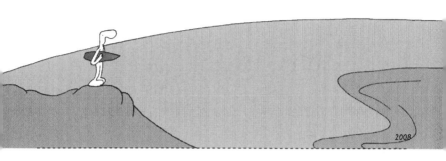

I'd do anything for you

2012

Life's simple pleasures...

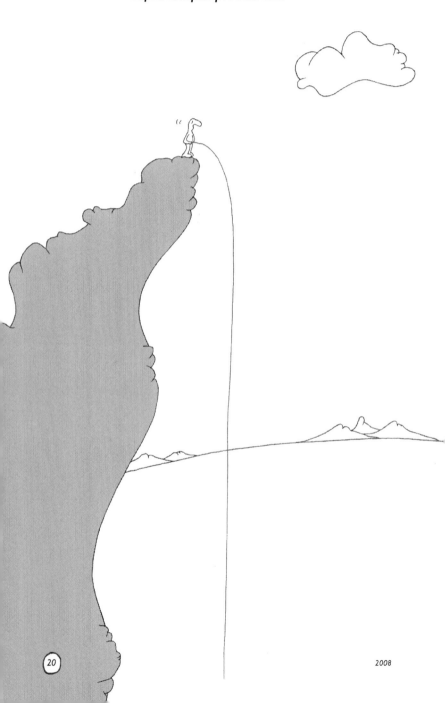

Correct Computer Posture

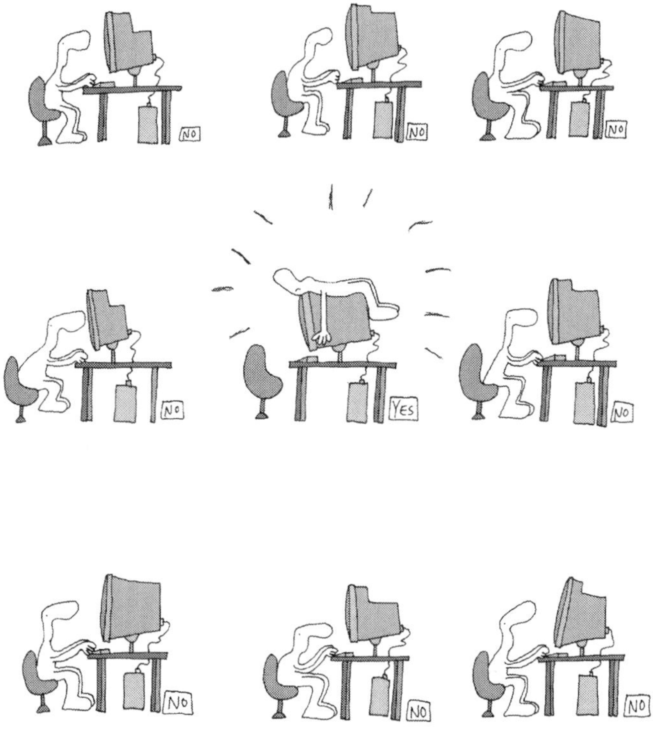
NO
NO
NO
NO
YES
NO
NO
NO
NO

2003

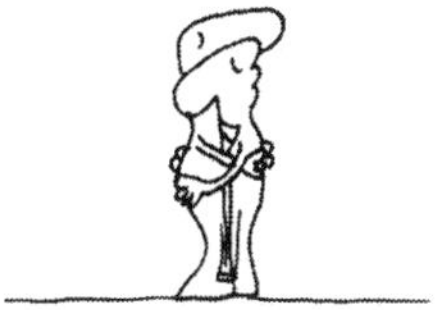

The humble hug

2012

How to go up in the world

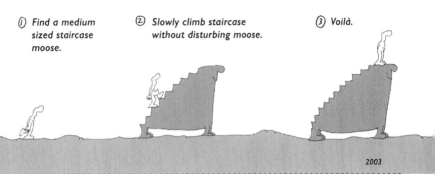

① Find a medium sized staircase moose.

② Slowly climb staircase without disturbing moose.

③ Voilà.

2003

HYNPAT?*

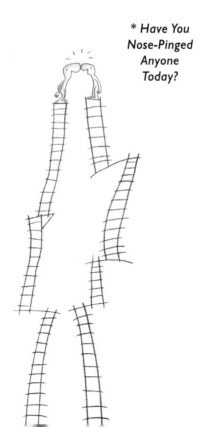

* Have You Nose-Pinged Anyone Today?

2018

Some days are NORMAL.	Others can be quite	WEIRD.

If you IGNORE the weirdness	things return to normal.	BUT if instead you GRAB on...

AMAZING
things can happen...

FONTOPHOBIA
The fear of trendy fonts

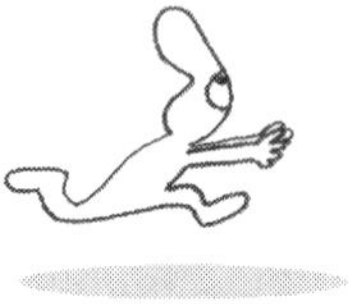

2014

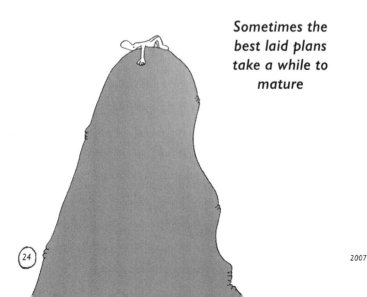

Sometimes the best laid plans take a while to mature

2007

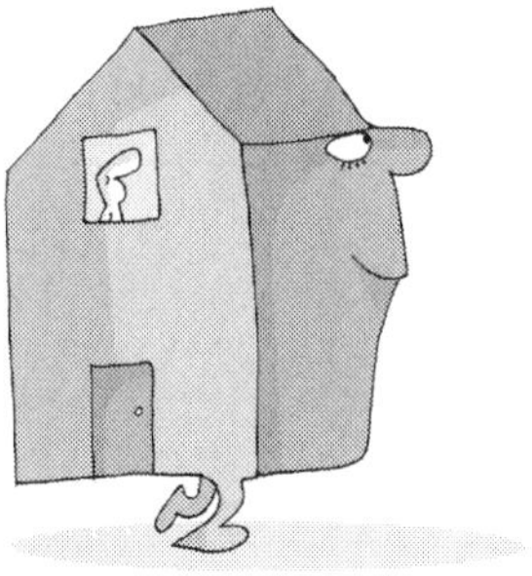

I wish our homes had legs, so we could see each other more often.

2018

Small group of middle-aged men silhouetted against a summer sky

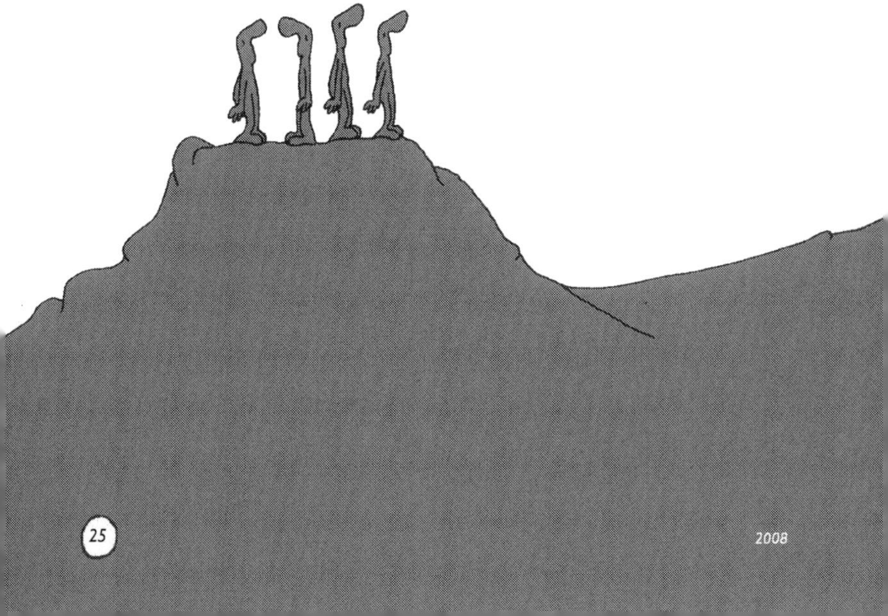

2008

True happiness
comes from within...

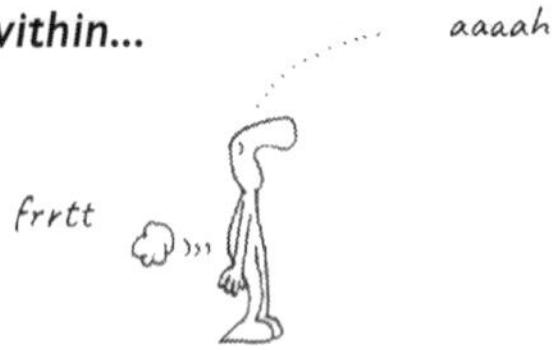
aaaah
frrtt

2008

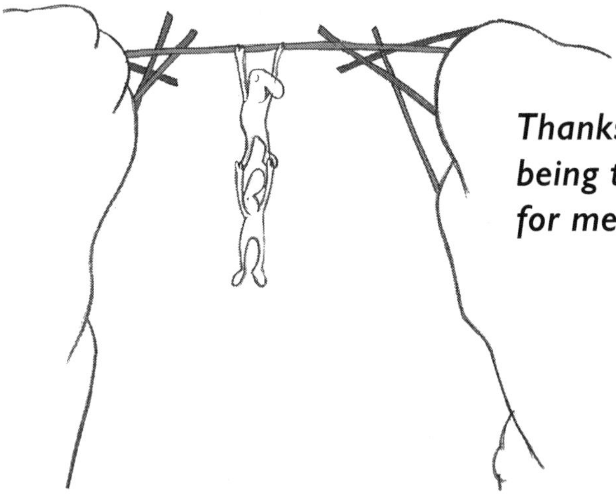

Thanks for
being there
for me...

2013

**OPTIMISTS
WITHOUT
BORDERS**

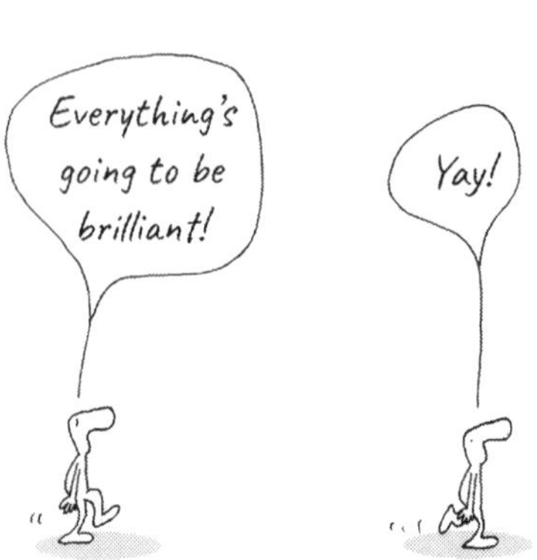
Everything's going to be brilliant!
Yay!

2010

Things to stop worrying about: #3

BEING FOLLOWED BY A SOFA

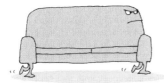

X INCORRECT
X CORRECT

2008

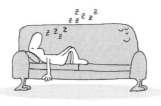

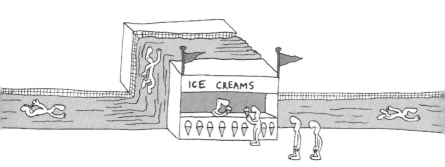

ICE CREAMS

2008

Certified:
Officially Addicted to The Internet

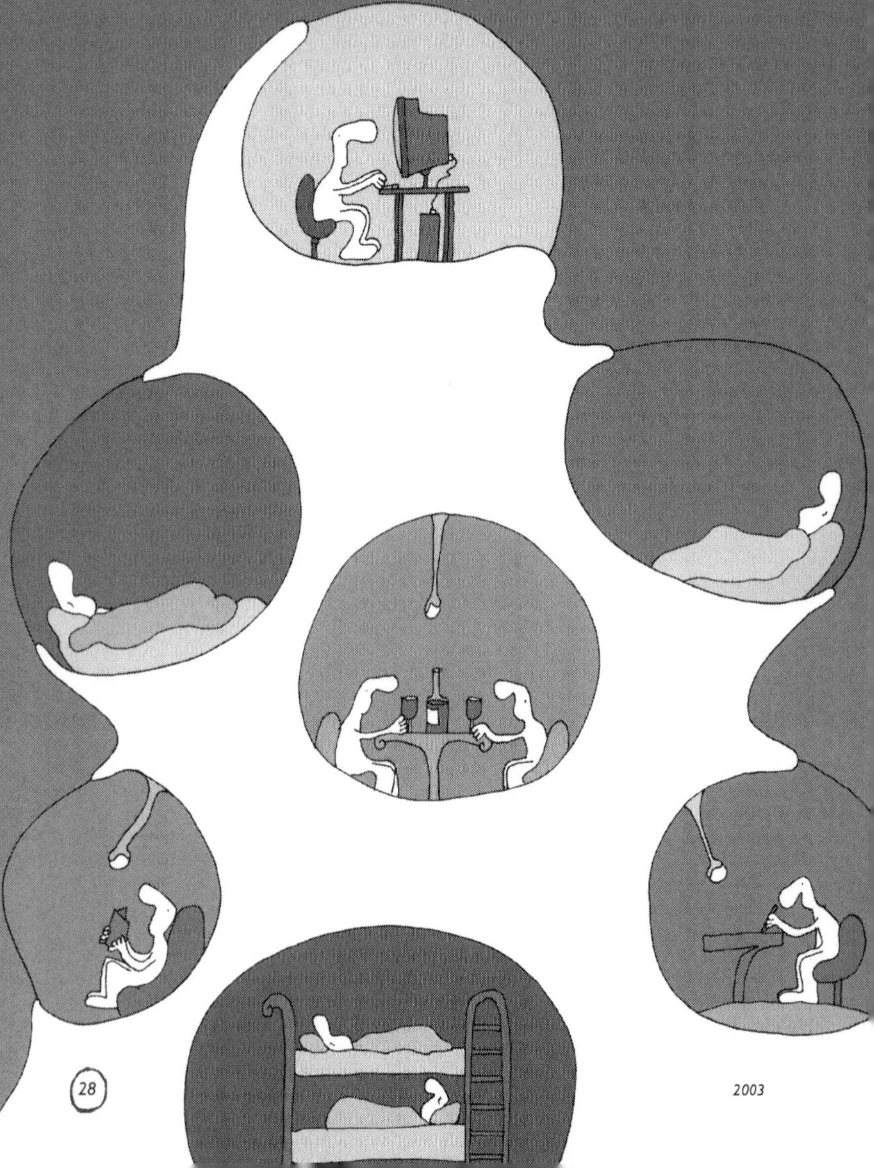

2003

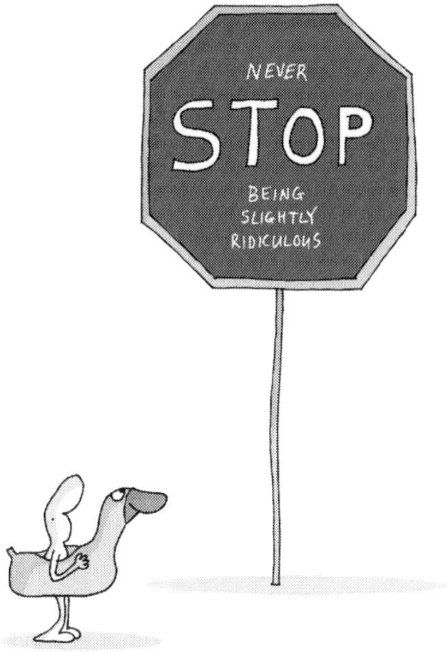
NEVER
STOP
BEING
SLIGHTLY
RIDICULOUS

2018

Think, dream, plan, make lists...

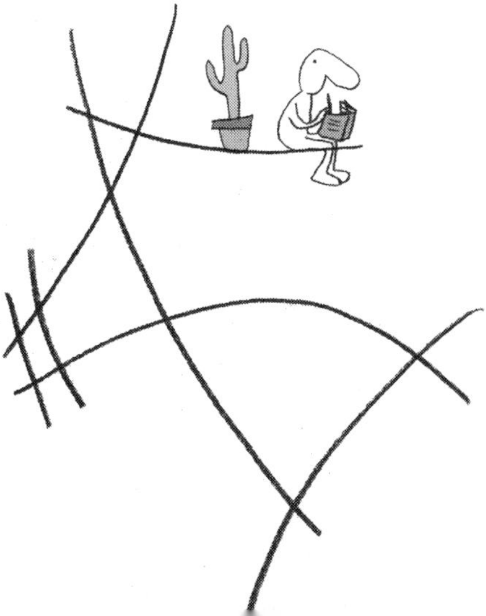

2014

Happiness is...
an empty inbox

2013

ALWAYS
PINK
THOSITIVE

2014

How to Deal with Words like **Discombobulated**

1. Establish visual contact.

2. Run off and fetch large dictionary.

3. Smack word with dictionary.

4. Voilà.

2003

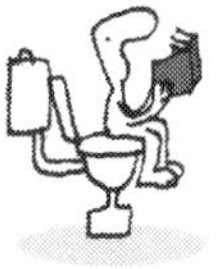

Nothing quite like a really good book.

2008

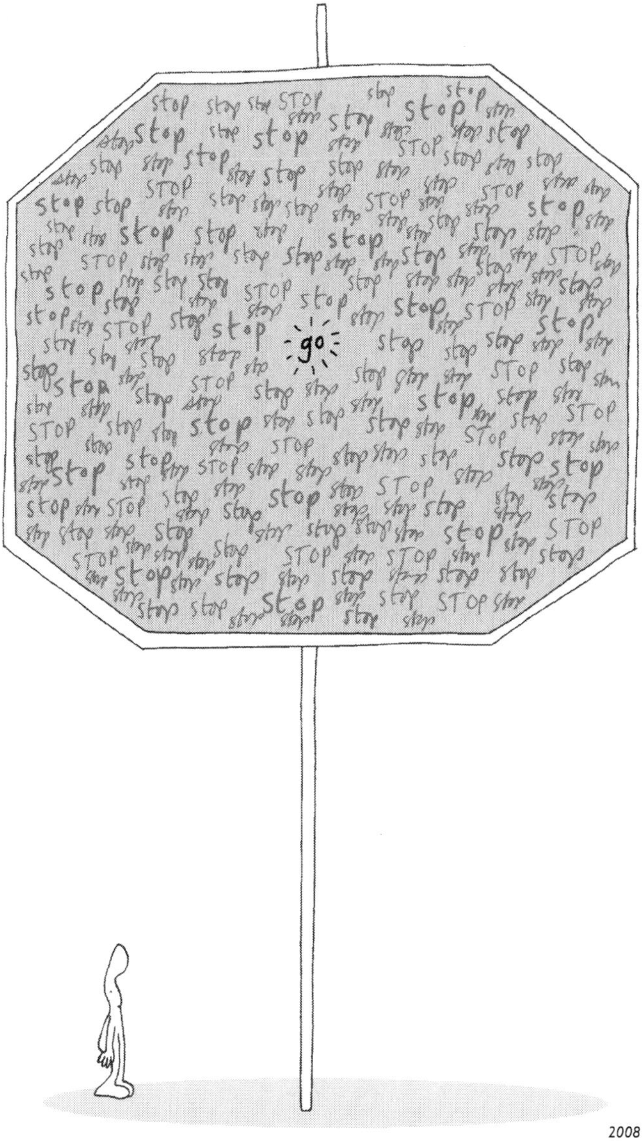
stop
go

2008

Just the four of us:
*you + me + a hot-tub
+ the night sky*

2011

The Fine Art of being a Mom

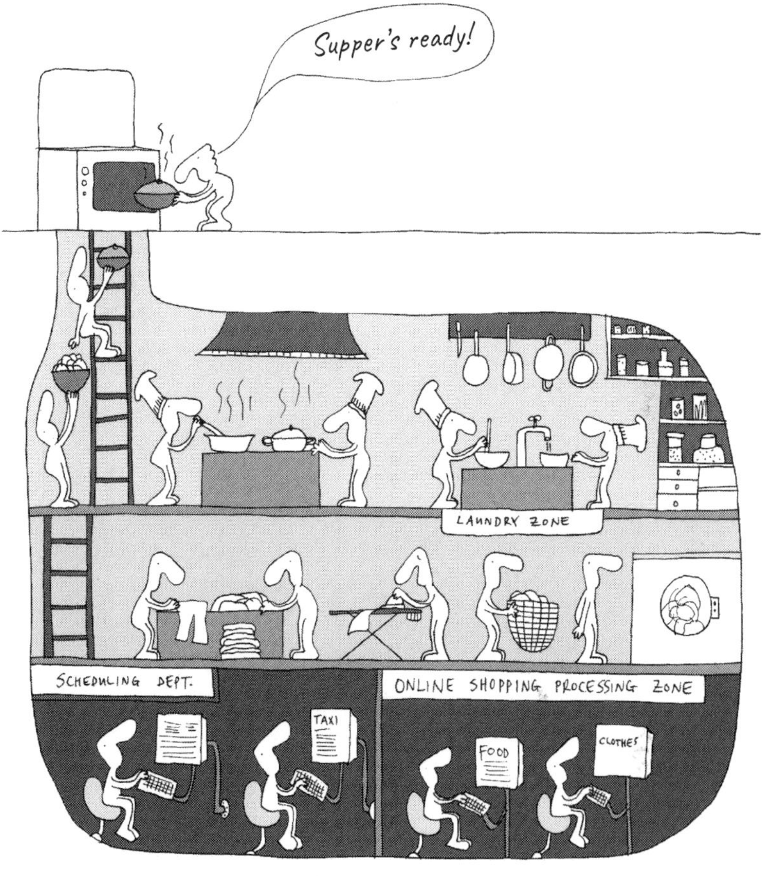
Supper's ready!
LAUNDRY ZONE
SCHEDULING DEPT.
ONLINE SHOPPING PROCESSING ZONE
TAXI
FOOD
CLOTHES

2011

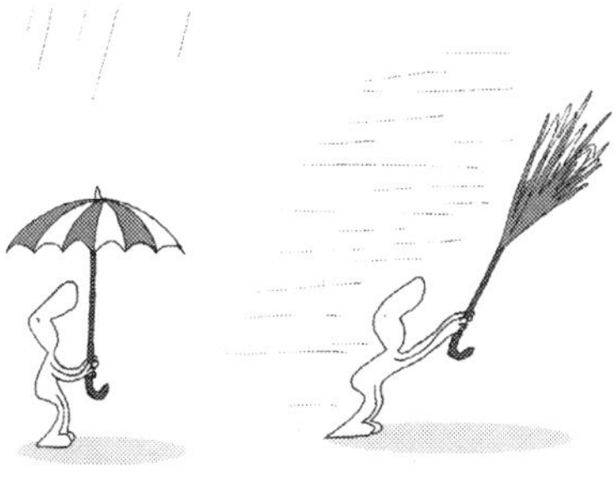

umbrella **unbrella**

2011

Def. **SPLOSHOPHOBIA**

Fear of the Splosh

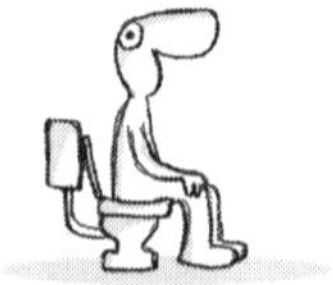

2014

Just taking Colin out for a quick walk...

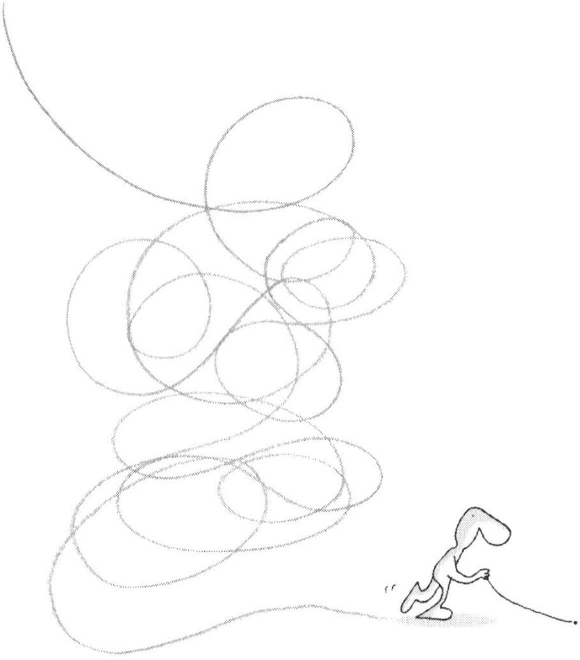

Colin is one of my ants.

2018

In my humble opinion...

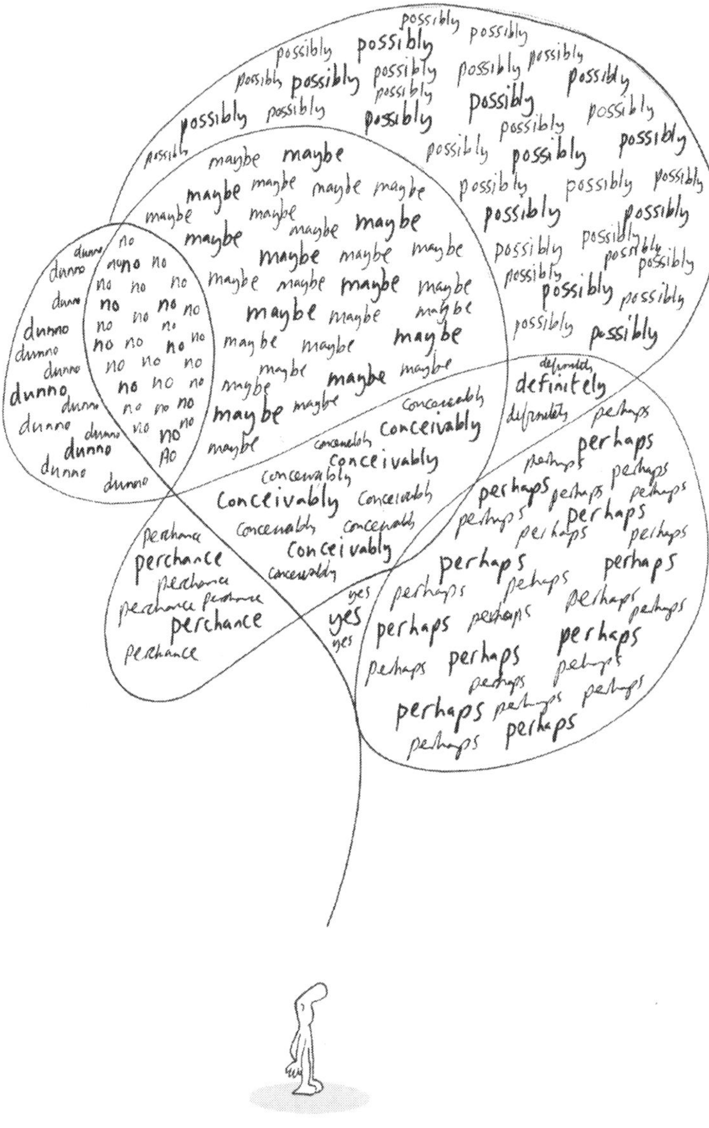
possibly possibly
possibly possibly
possibly possibly possibly possibly
possibly possibly possibly possibly possibly
possibly
possibly possibly possibly possibly possibly
possibly possibly possibly possibly
possibly possibly possibly possibly
possibly possibly possibly
possibly possibly possibly possibly
possibly possibly possibly possibly
maybe maybe
maybe maybe maybe maybe
maybe maybe maybe maybe
maybe maybe maybe maybe
maybe maybe maybe maybe
maybe maybe maybe
maybe maybe maybe
maybe maybe maybe maybe
maybe maybe maybe
maybe
no
no no no
no no no
no no no
no no no
no no no no
no no no
no no no
no no no
no no
no
dunno dunno dunno dunno dunno dunno dunno dunno dunno dunno dunno dunno dunno
definitely
definitely
definitely
conceivably
conceivably
conceivably
conceivably
conceivably
conceivably conceivably
conceivably conceivably
conceivably
conceivably
perchance
perchance
perchance
perchance perchance
perchance
perchance
yes
yes
yes
perhaps perhaps
perhaps perhaps perhaps perhaps perhaps
perhaps perhaps perhaps perhaps
perhaps perhaps perhaps
perhaps perhaps perhaps
perhaps perhaps perhaps
perhaps perhaps perhaps
perhaps perhaps perhaps
perhaps perhaps perhaps
perhaps perhaps

2008

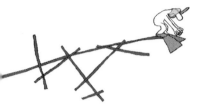

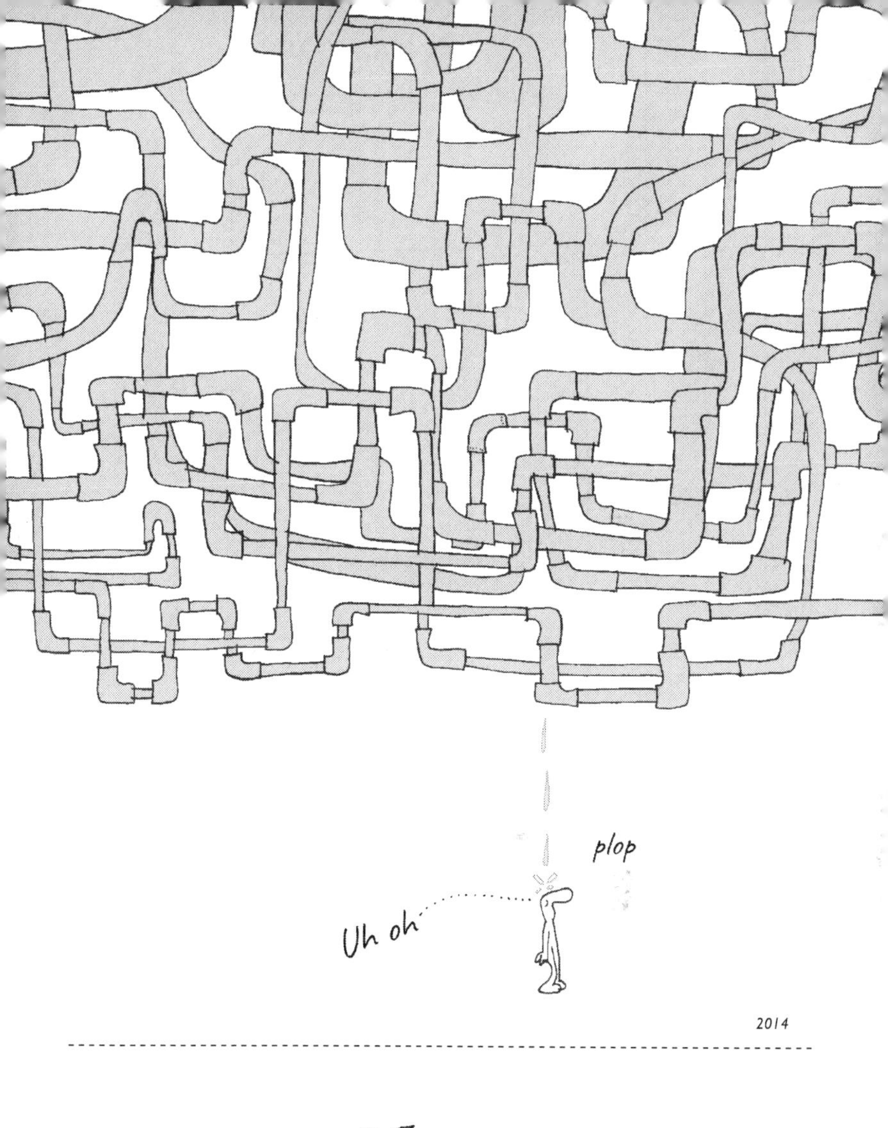
plop
Uh oh

2014

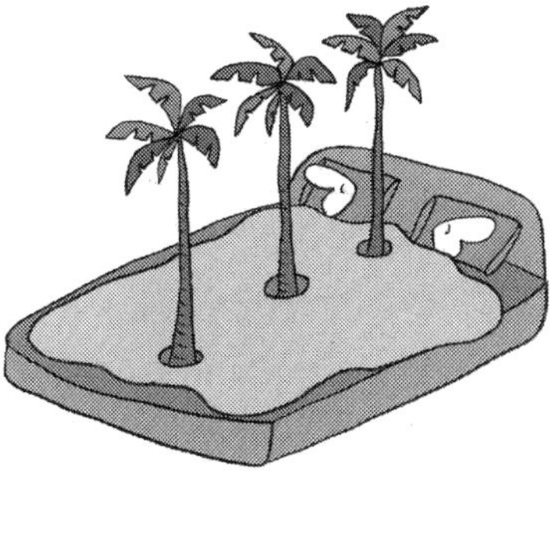

HOW TO
stop a duvet hog once and for all

2018

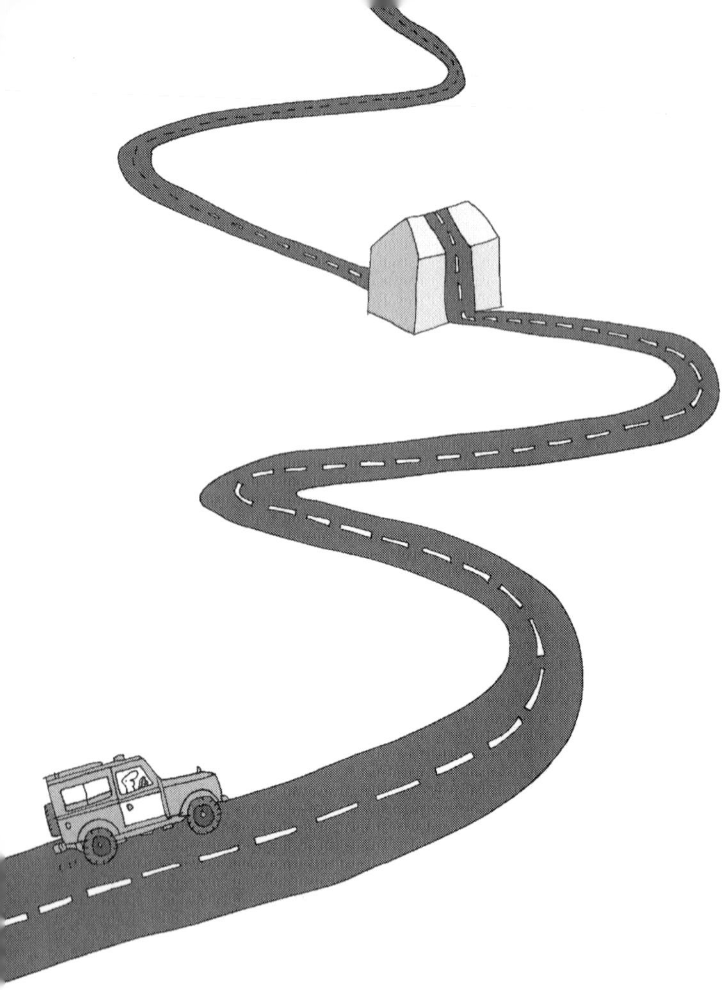

2008

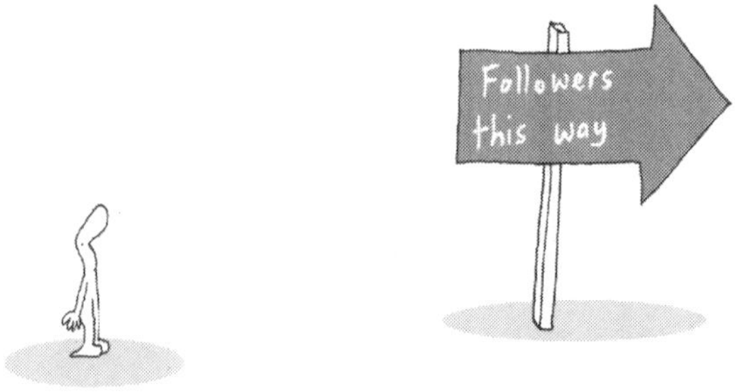
Followers
this way

2008

My life so far...

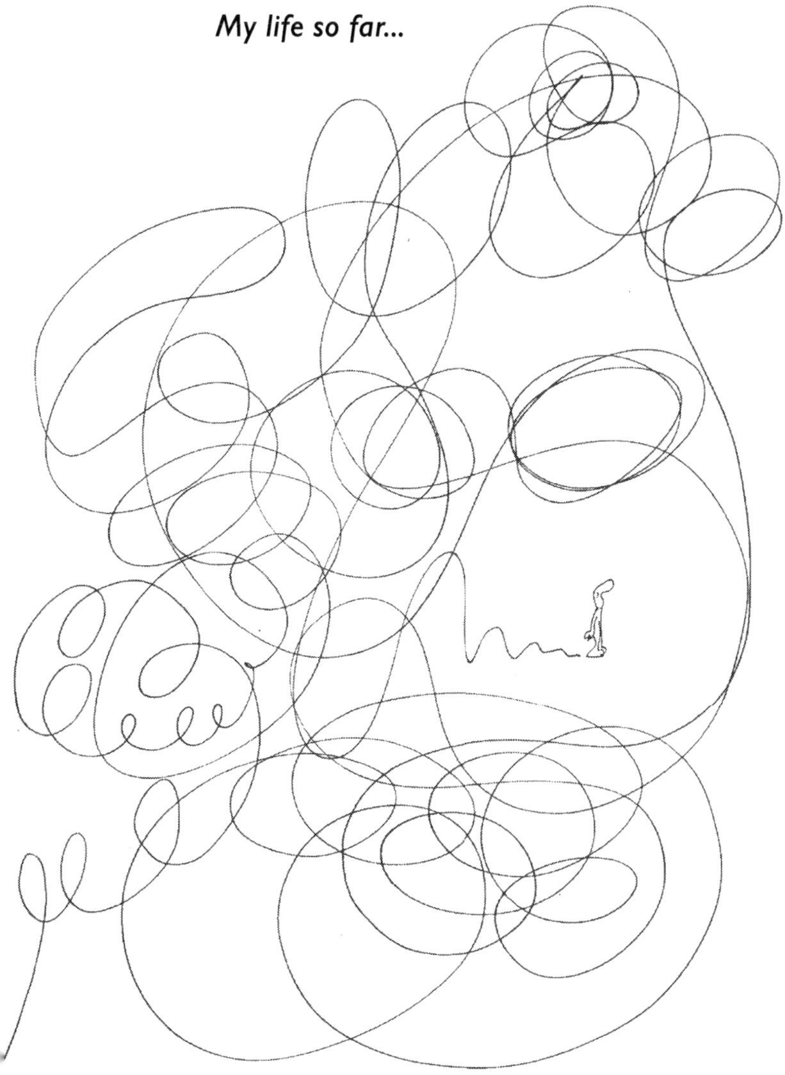

2008

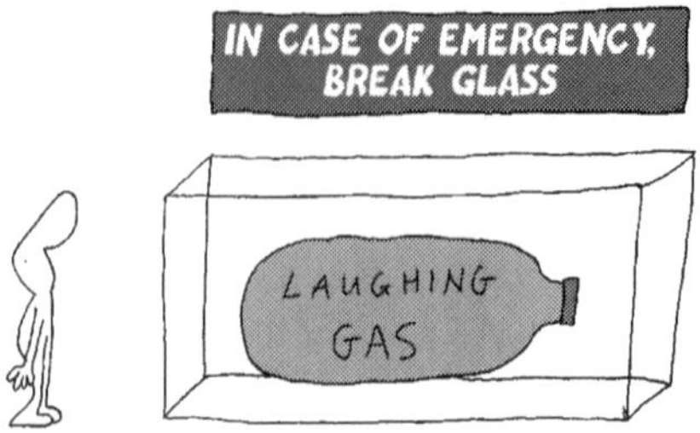
IN CASE OF EMERGENCY, BREAK GLASS
LAUGHING GAS

2012

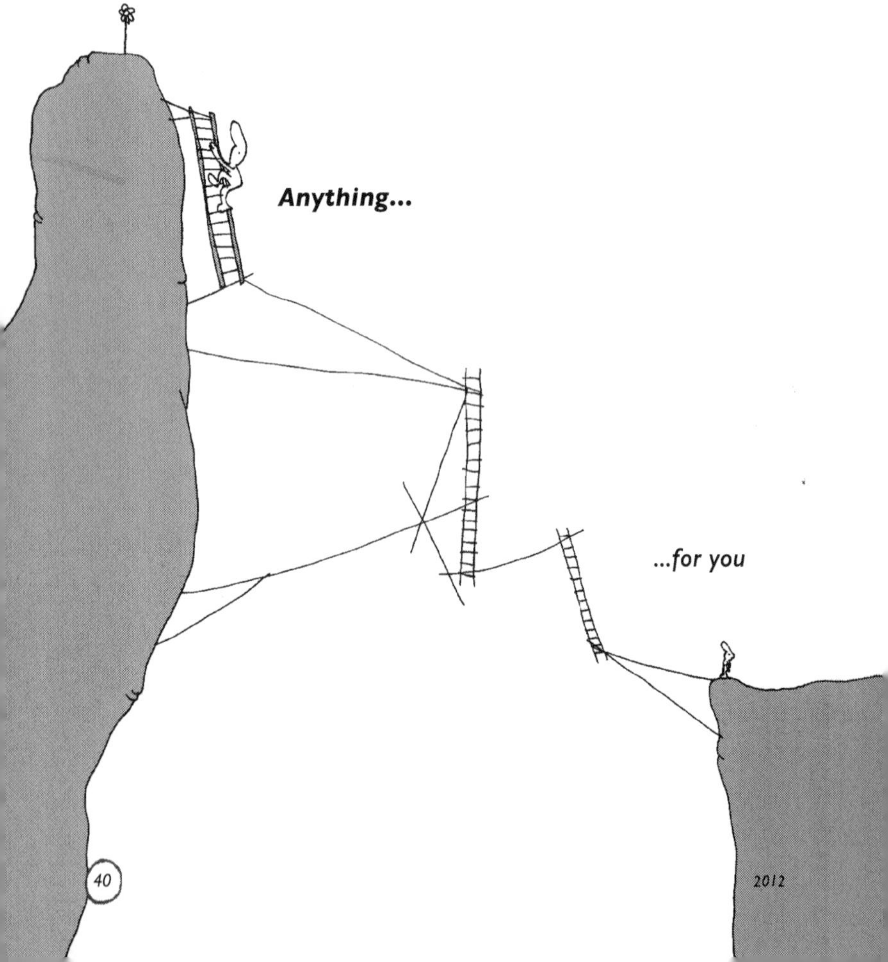
Anything...
...for you

2012

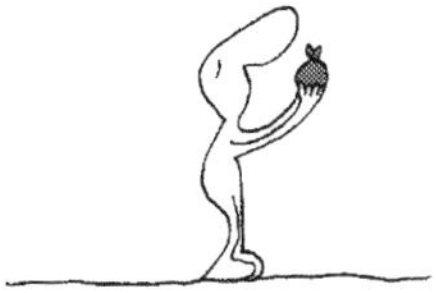

Life may be complicated,
but give me
a firm ripe tomato,
and I am happy.

2012

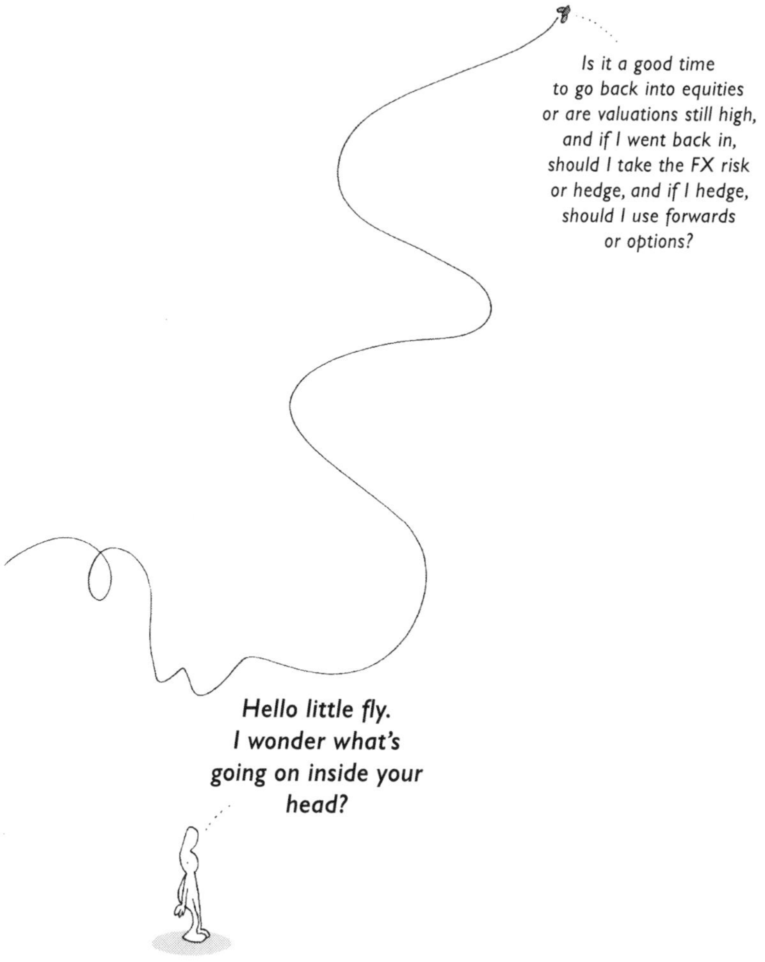
Is it a good time to go back into equities or are valuations still high, and if I went back in, should I take the FX risk or hedge, and if I hedge, should I use forwards or options?
Hello little fly. I wonder what's going on inside your head?

2009

Harnessing Wind Energy #17
Foot massages

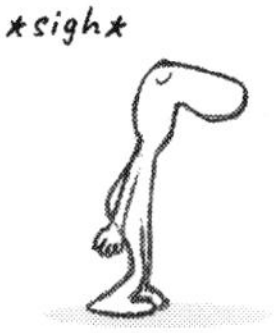
sigh

Perfectly fine to have a little sigh every now and again...

2014

Everest, 09h00

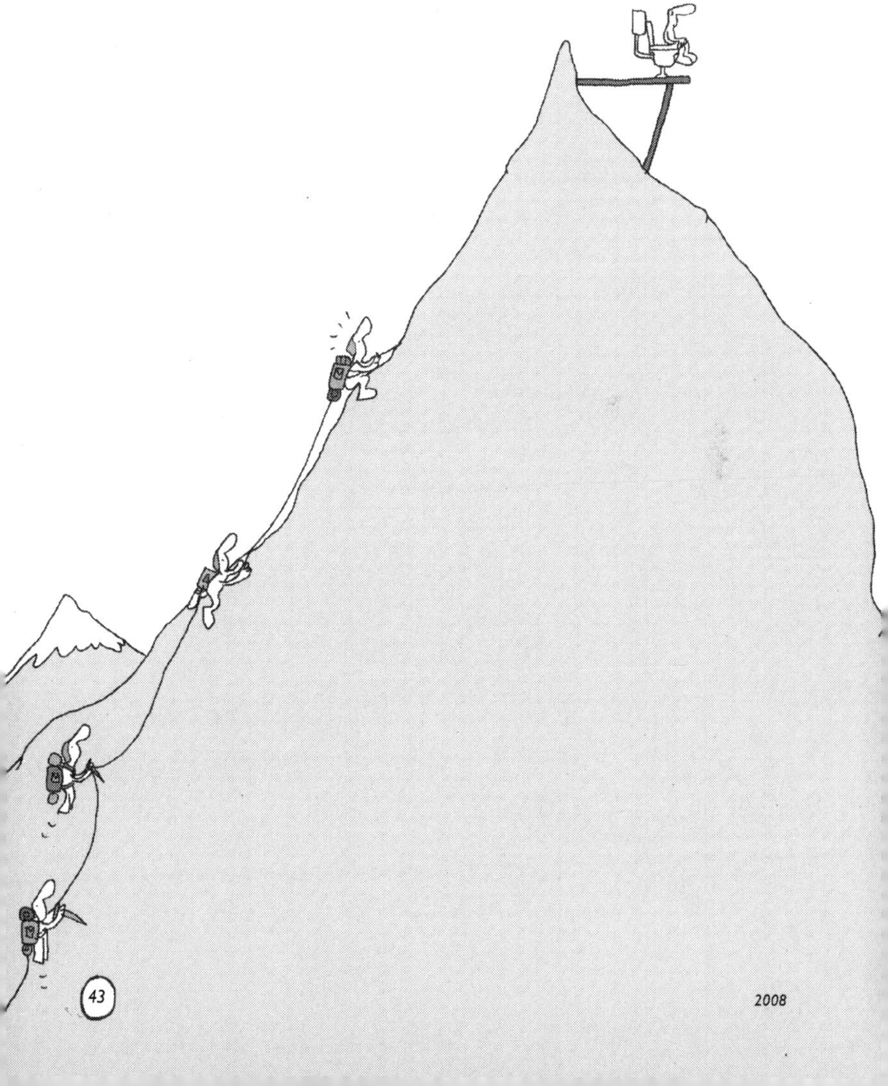

2008

Little Jack Horner,
Sat in the corner,
Checking email...

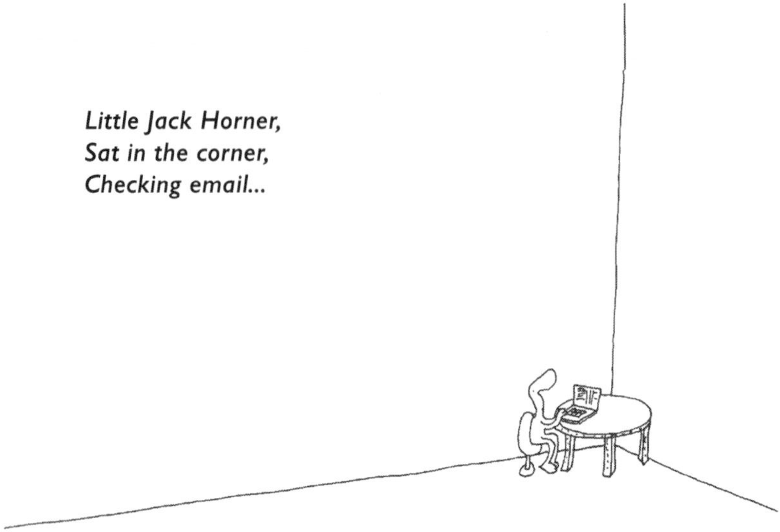

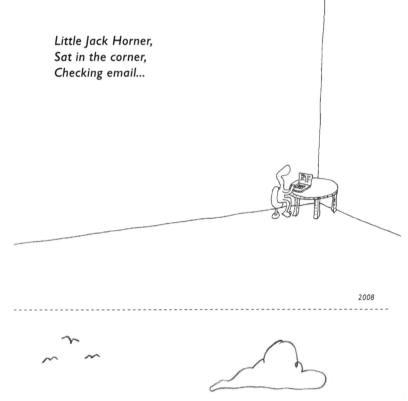

2008

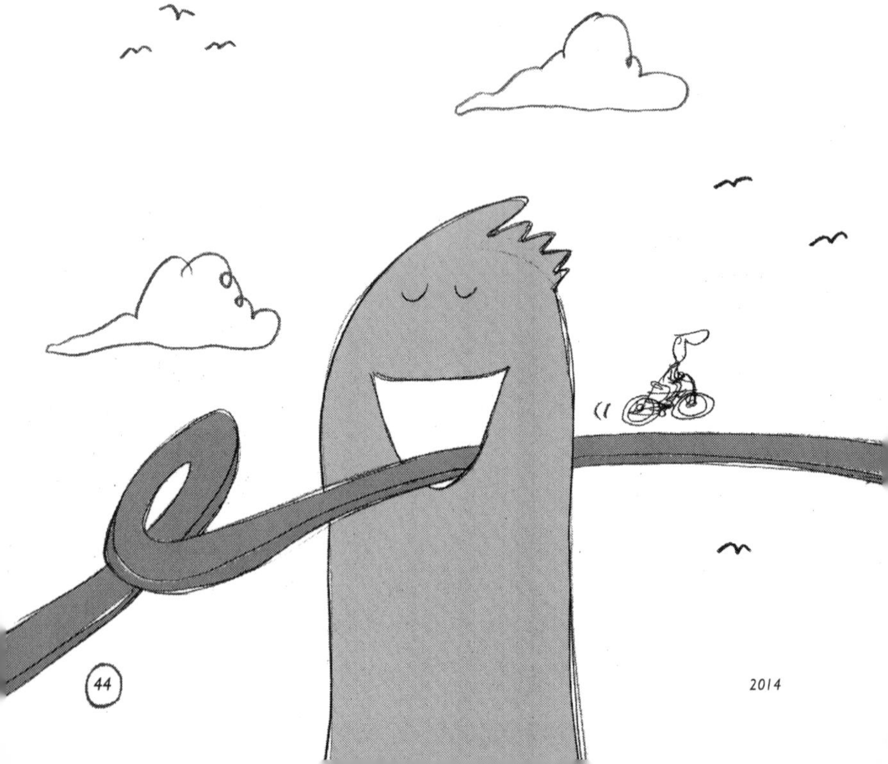

2014

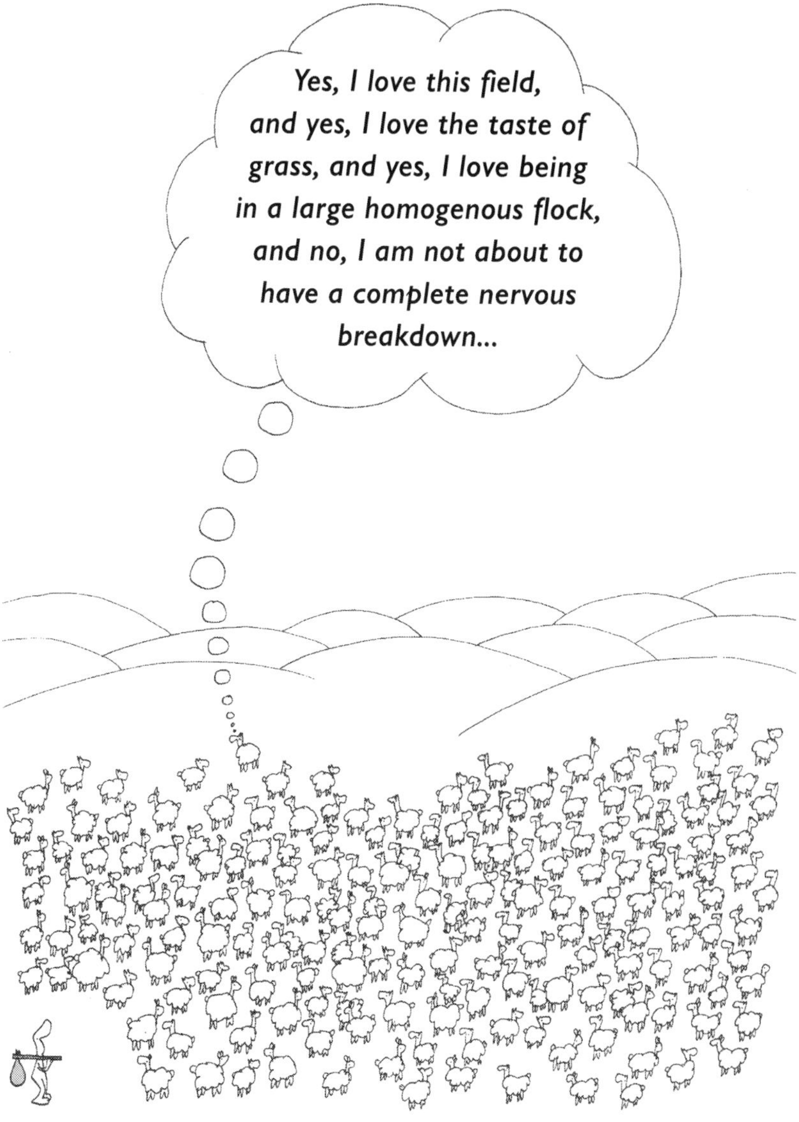
Yes, I love this field, and yes, I love the taste of grass, and yes, I love being in a large homogenous flock, and no, I am not about to have a complete nervous breakdown...

2008

Useful Gadgets #14

A machine that gently explains that the world is far too complicated for us to understand, then pours us a drink.

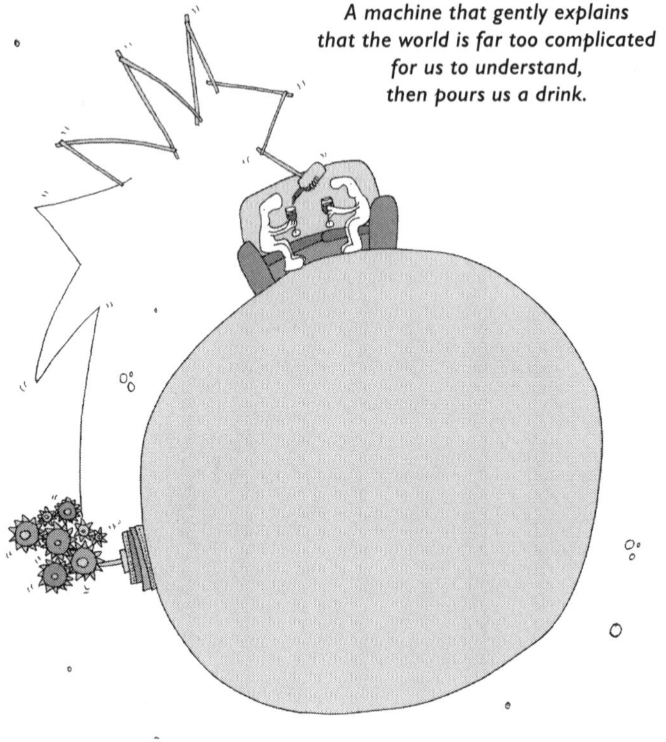

2007

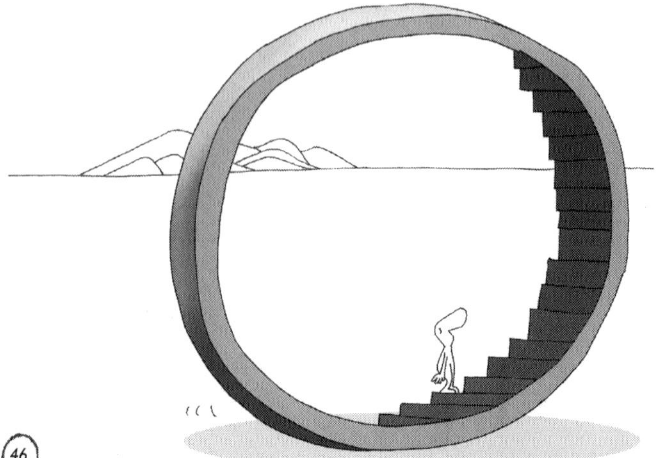

2014

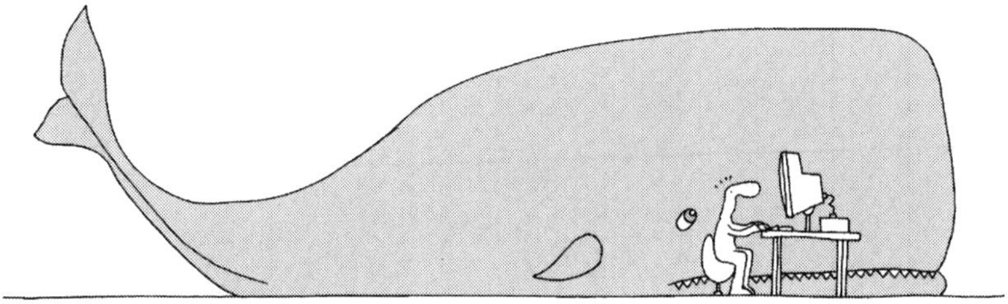

2006

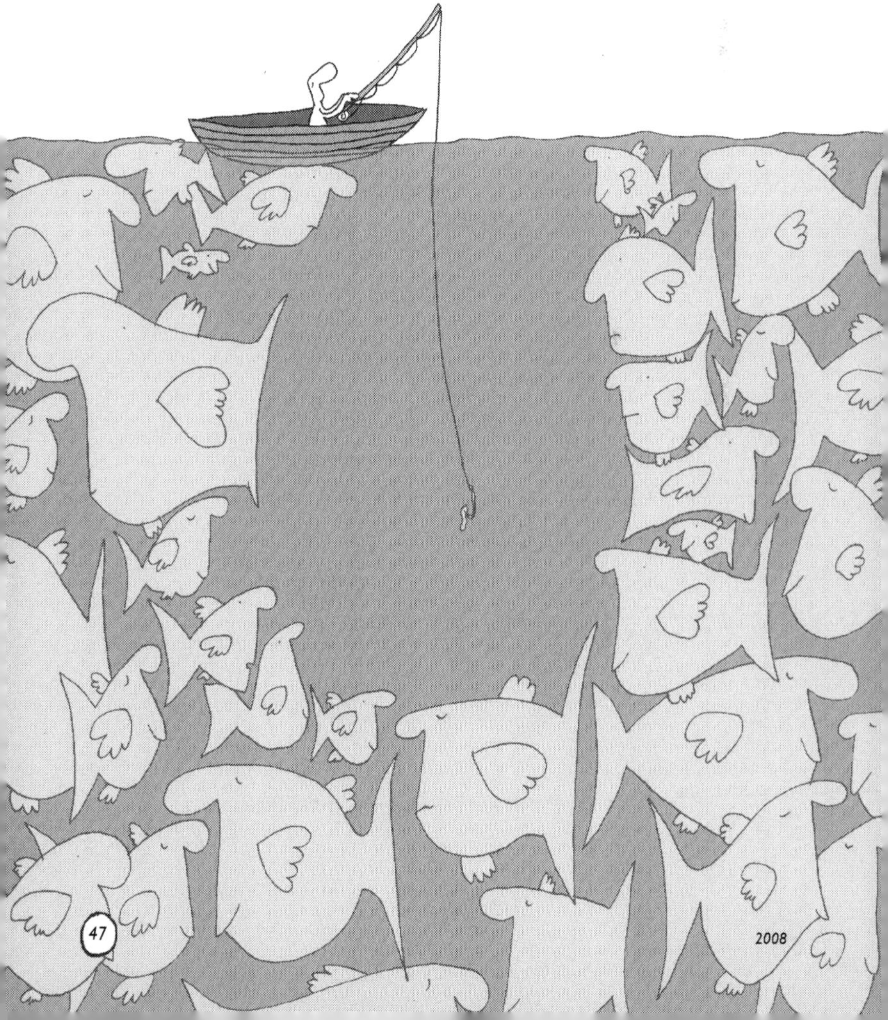

2008

How to *Avoid a Trapped Arm whilst Cuddling in Bed*

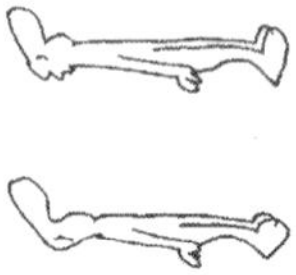

① *Commence on back.*

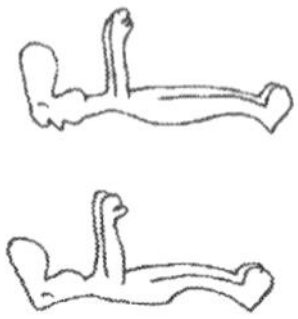

② *Raise both arms in the air.*

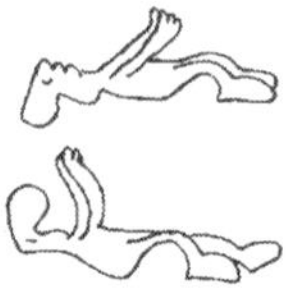

③ *Roll slightly towards cuddlee.*

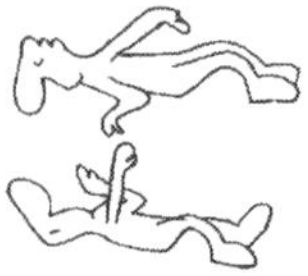

④ *Pull lower arm towards yourself.*

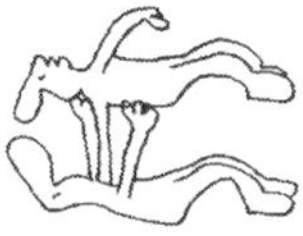

⑤ *Extend lower arm under neck of cuddlee.*

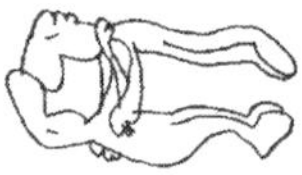

⑥ *Relax upper arm.*

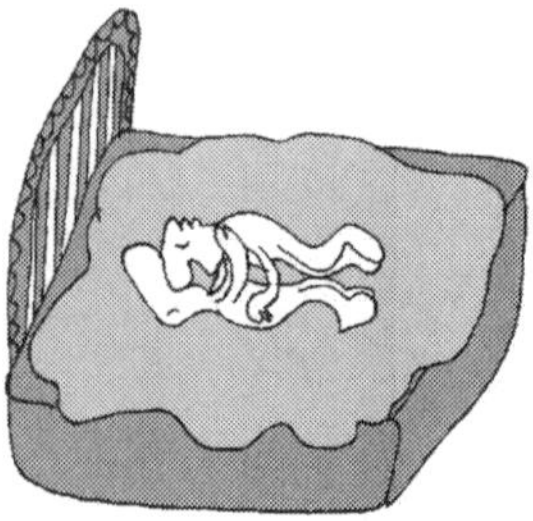

⑦ **Activate full cuddle mode.**

Things to Stop Worrying About: #1

GROWING UP

2018

---

*The day I met you
I just knew...*

2018

Dreaming the same dream

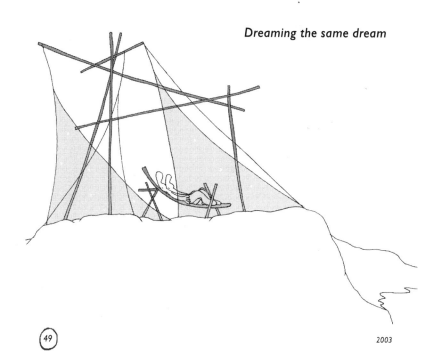

2003

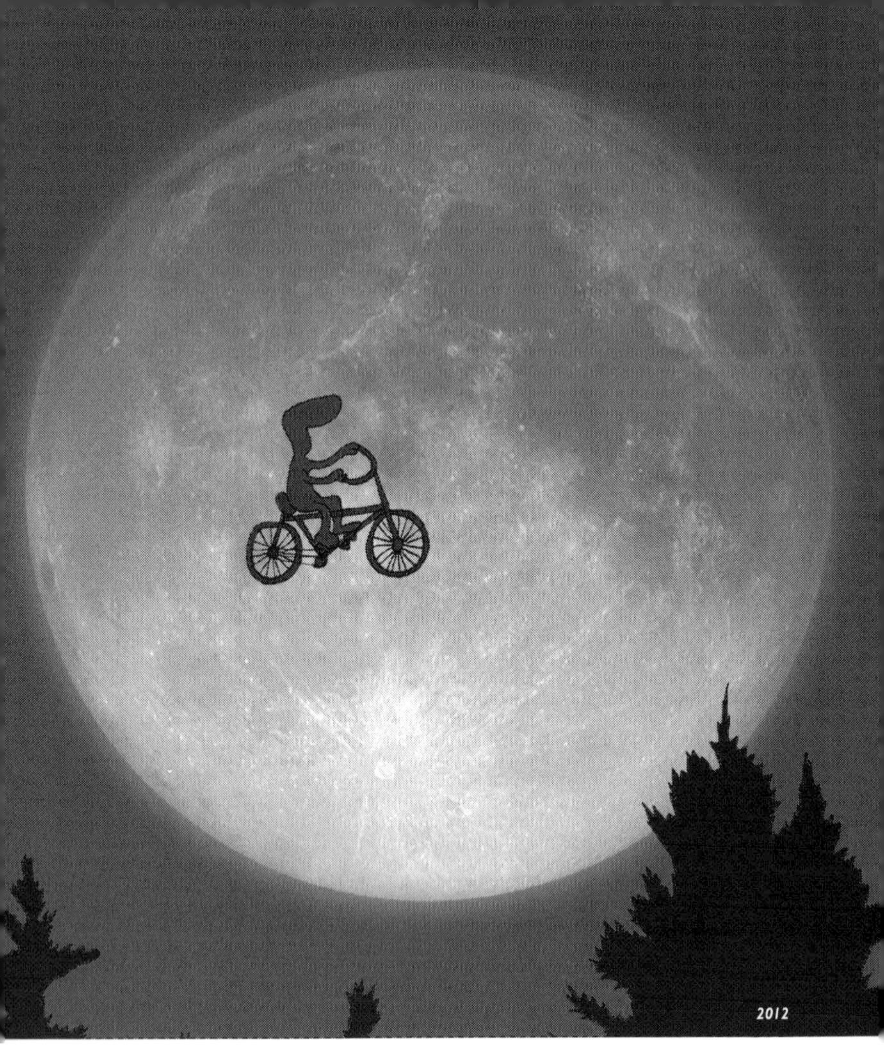
2012

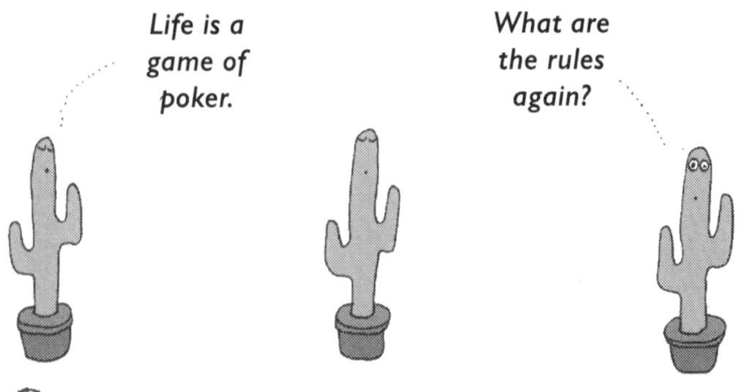
Life is a game of poker.
What are the rules again?

2008

Yoga for Wine-lovers

ALSO AN ANIMATION! **www.lastlemon.com/harolds-planet/animations**   2013

Go away,
I'm reading...

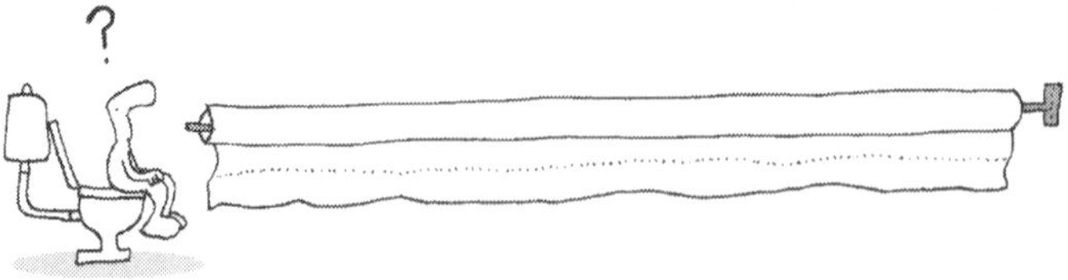
?

2007

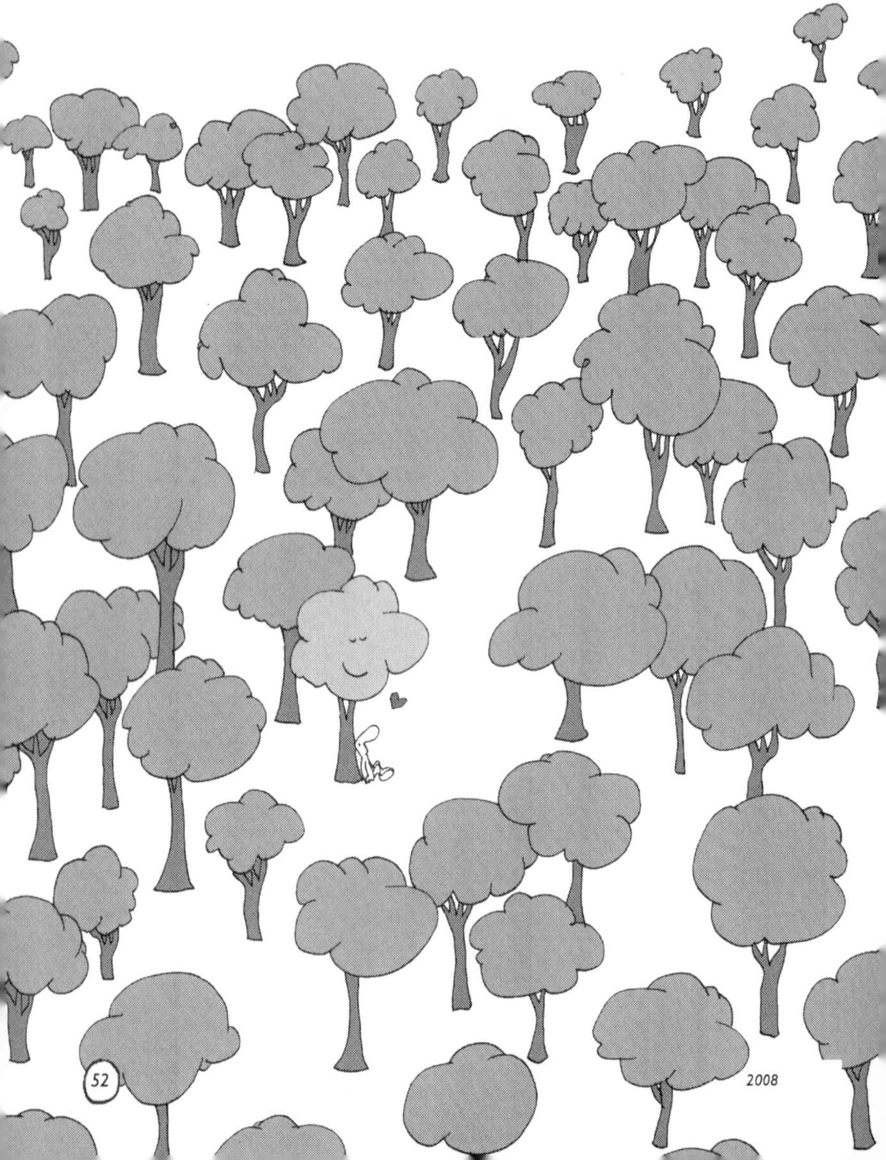

2008

① Life before Satnav

② Life after Satnav

Things to Stop Worrying About: #2

WHAT YOUR HAIR LOOKS LIKE

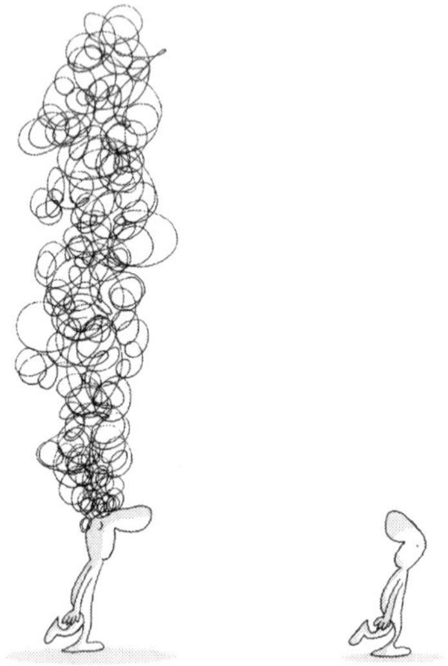

2018

HOW TO *get Rid of an Itch*

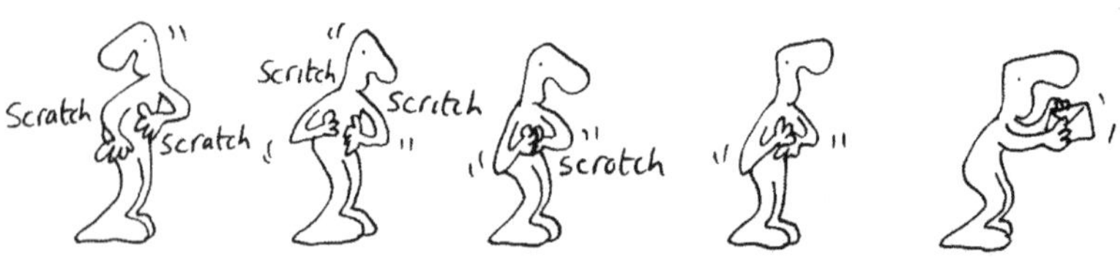
Scratch
Scratch
Scritch
Scritch
scrotch

① *Isolate itch.*

② *Trap itch.*

③ *Place in envelope.*

I love my new car

(and yes, people keep their distance)

2012

---

④ Seal envelope.

⑤ Take to postbox.

⑥ Post to an enemy.

2003

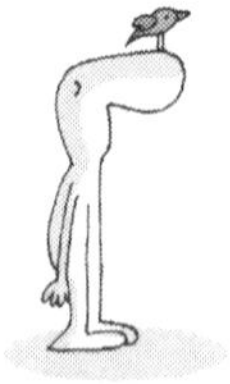

What do you like most about me?

My nose, I suppose?

2019

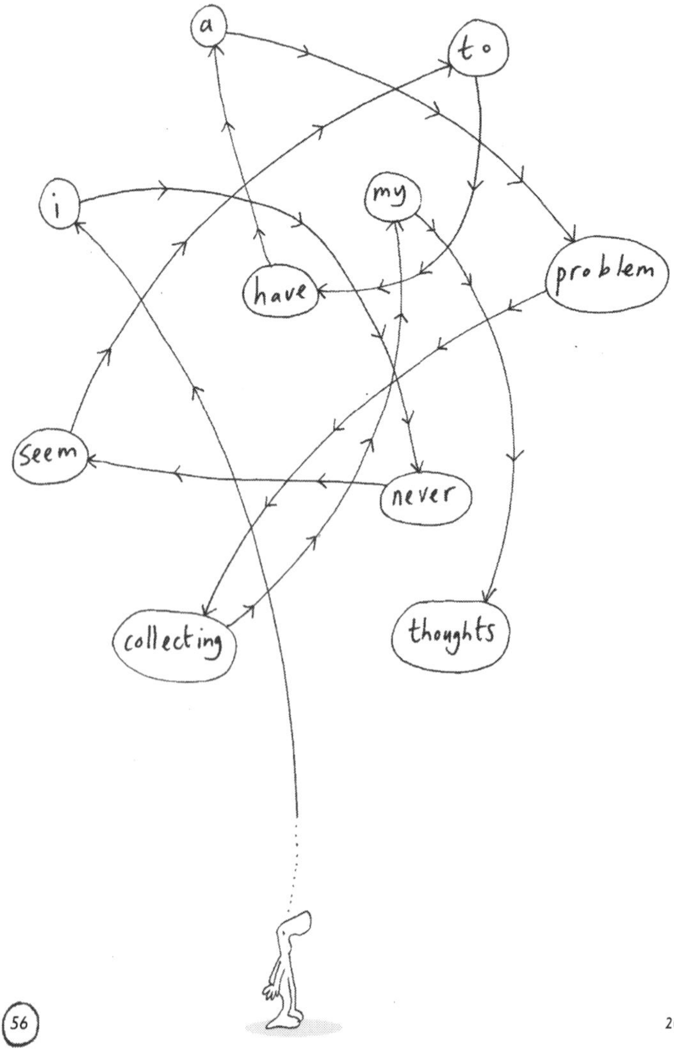
a
to
i
my
have
problem
seem
never
collecting
thoughts

2008

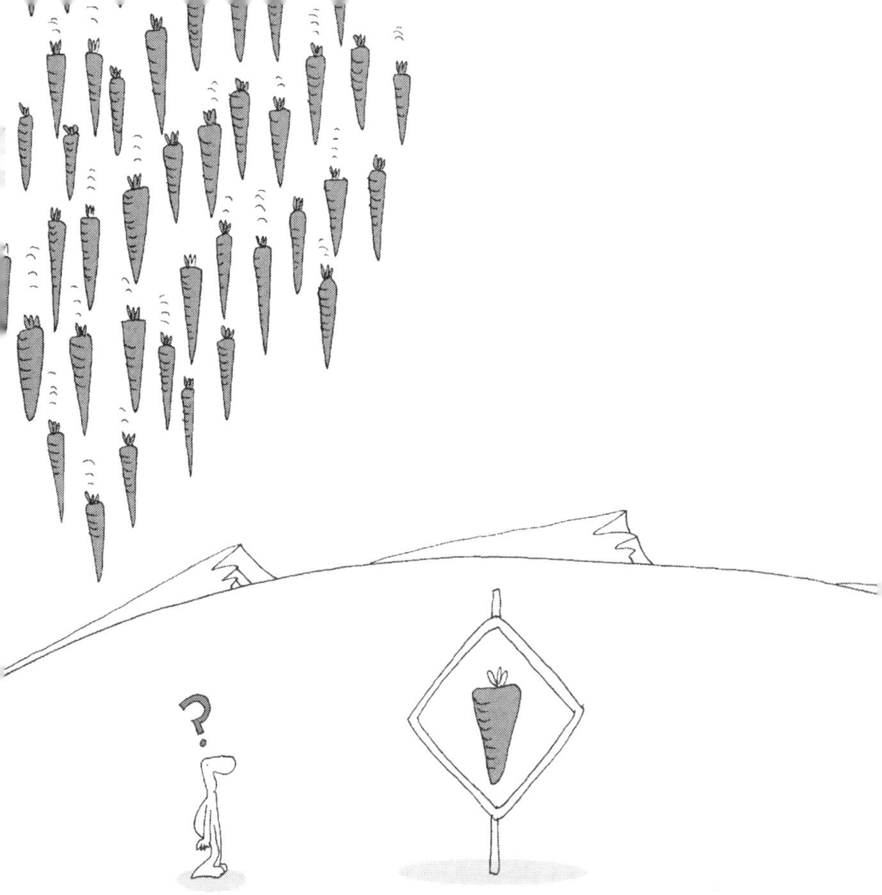
?

2008

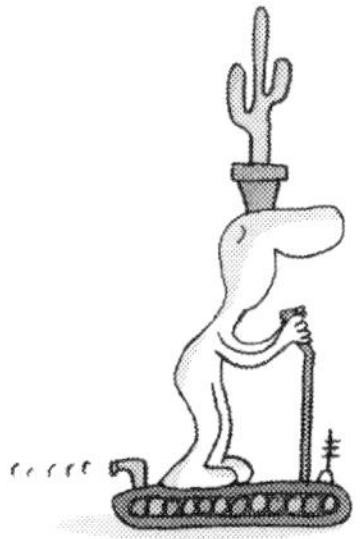

“You're only given a little spark of madness. You mustn't lose it.”

Robin Williams

2014

A chance meeting...

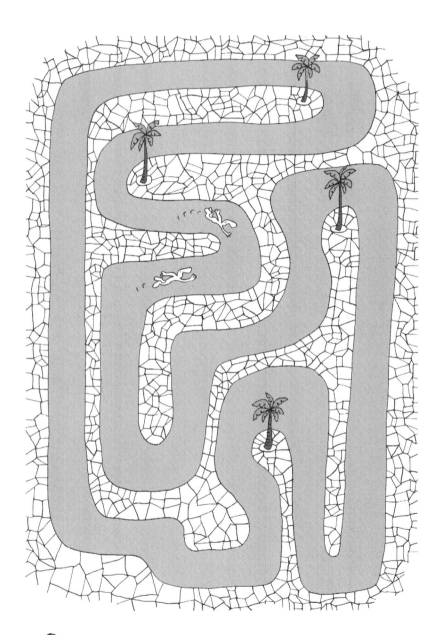

How to *Laugh in the Face of Adversity*

①   Spot adversity up ahead.

②   Laugh in
       its face.

③   Run for
       your life.

2008

Always beetroot to yourself

2015

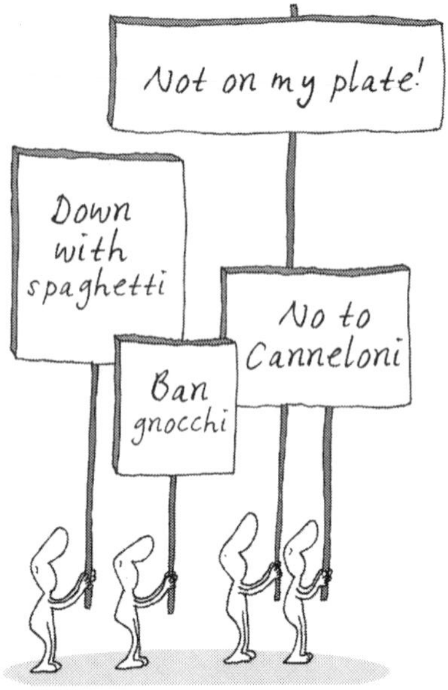
Not on my plate!
Down with spaghetti
No to Canneloni
Ban gnocchi

ANTI-PASTA

2011

You Can Do Anything

as long as you have a compass, a pen-knife, some string, cheese, wine, several credit cards, a few million dollars in your bank account, a private helicopter, and tissues...

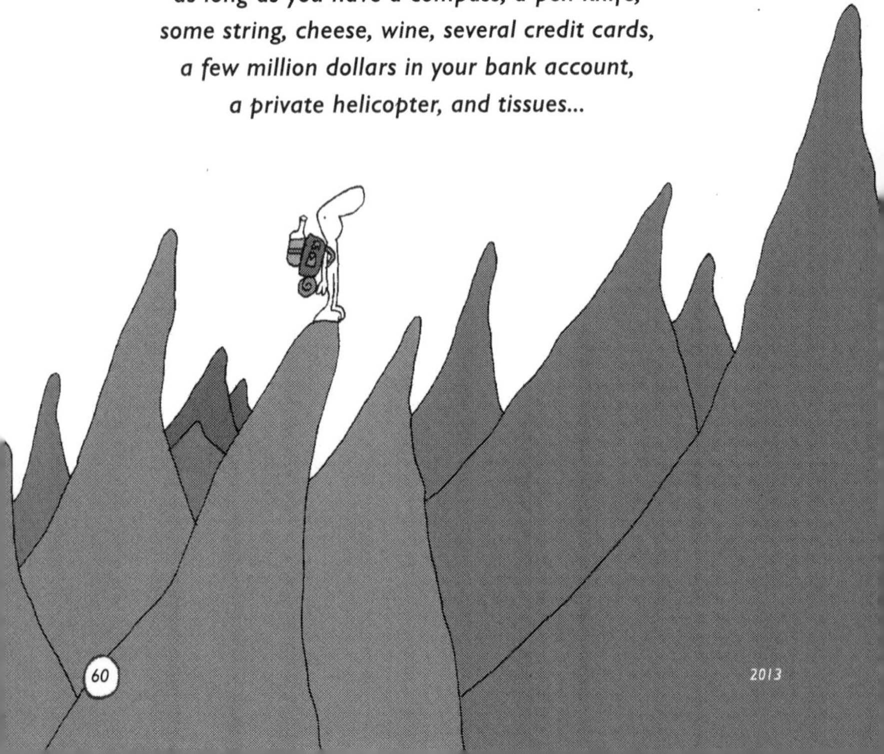

2013

Everyday Meditation #4

Contemplating Washing Up

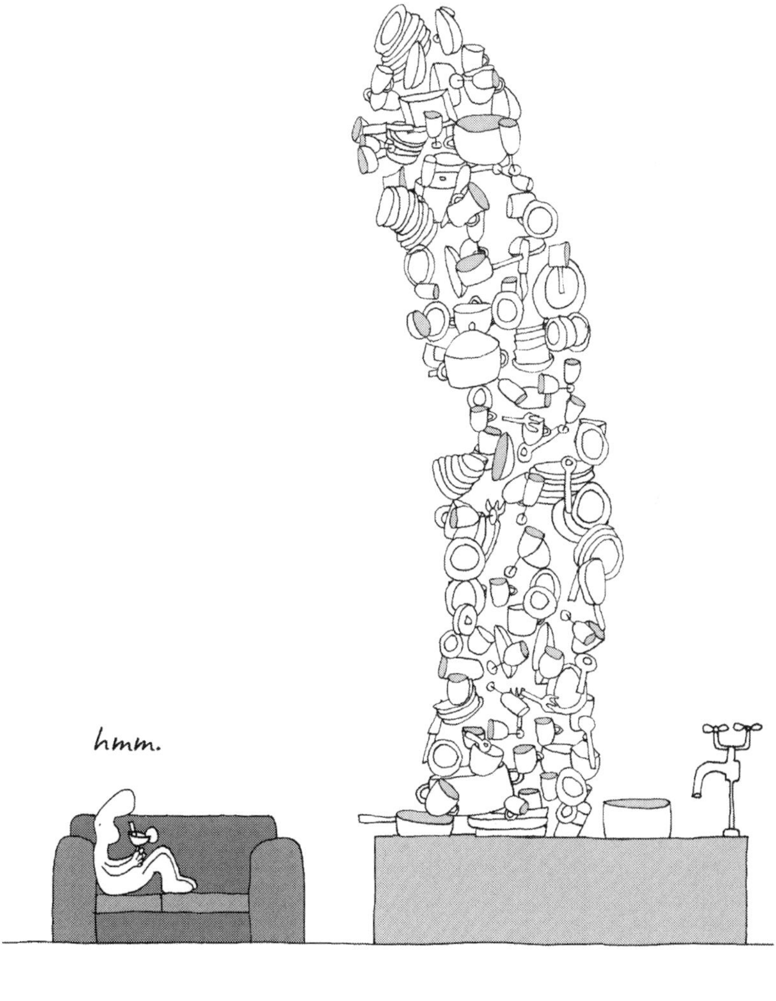
hmm.

2003

Good Places to Put Your Nose

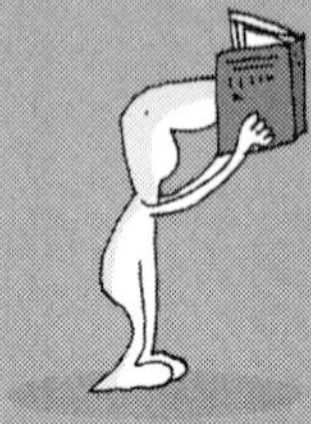

In a book.

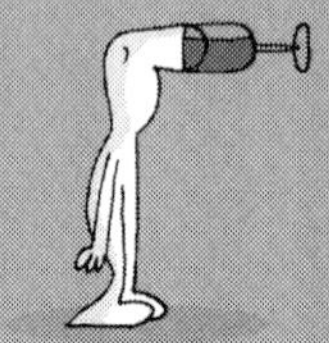

Into a glass of wine.

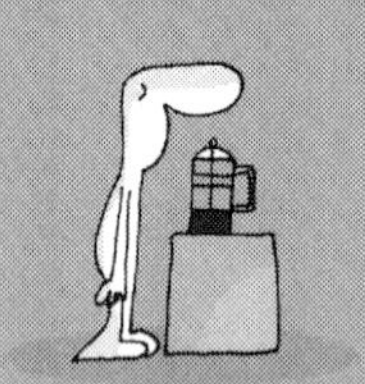

Above a fresh pot of coffee.

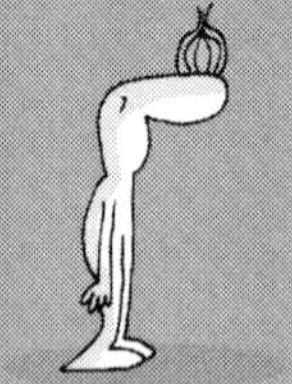

Below garlic.

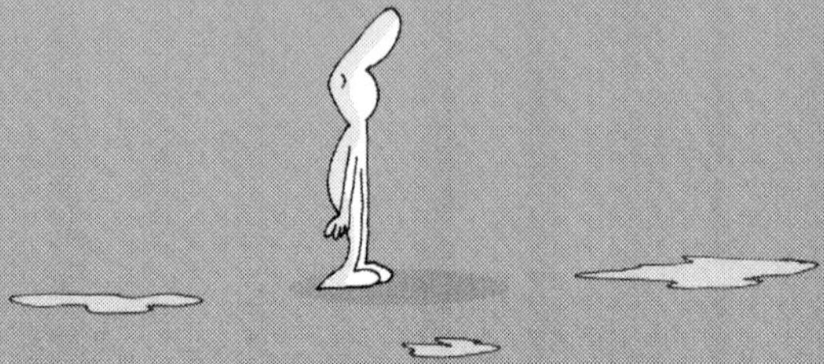

Into the air just as the rain has stopped.

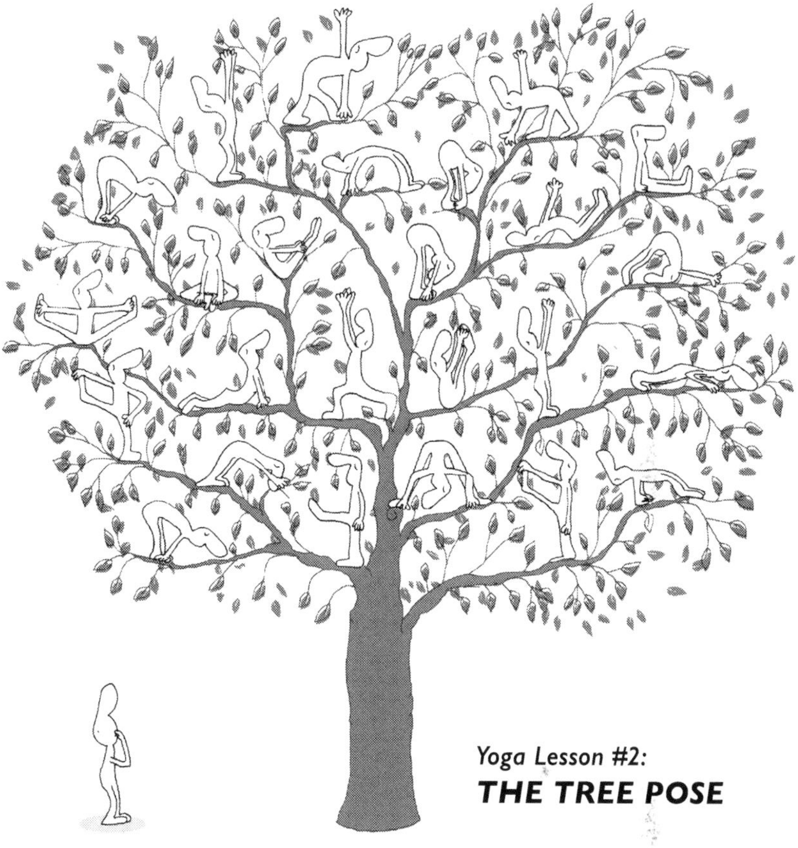

Yoga Lesson #2:
THE TREE POSE

2013

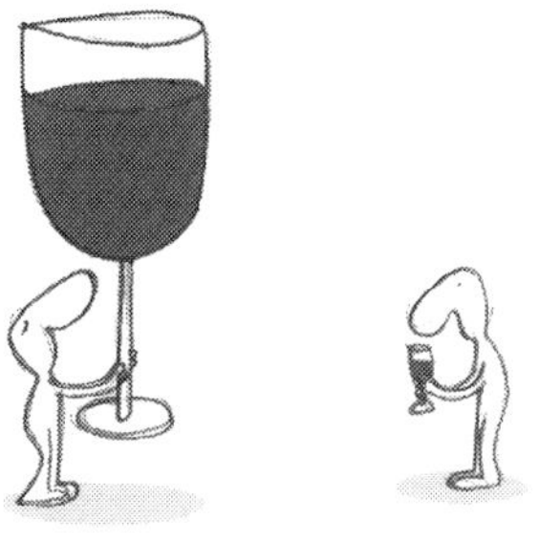

Merlot Merlittle

2013

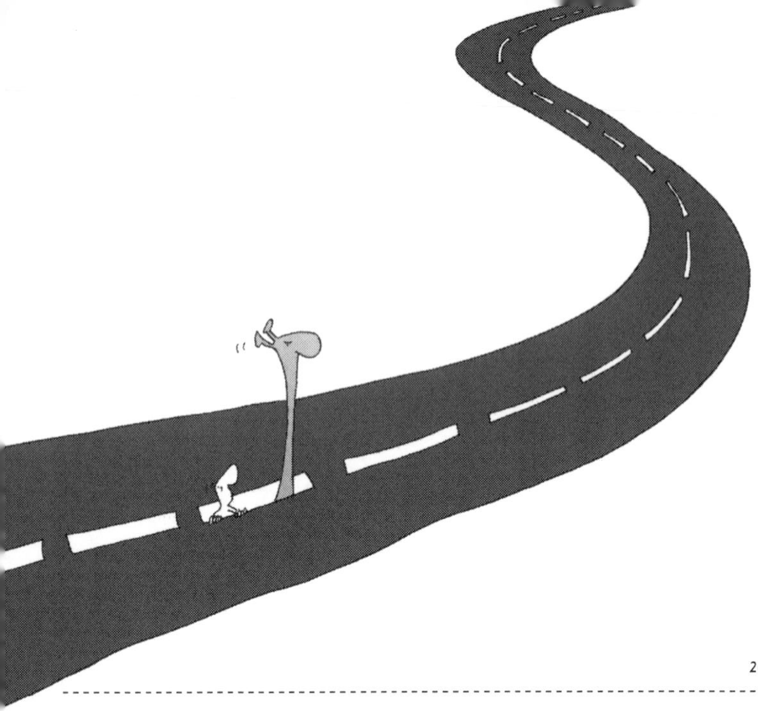

2008

HOW TO LIBERATE TOAST

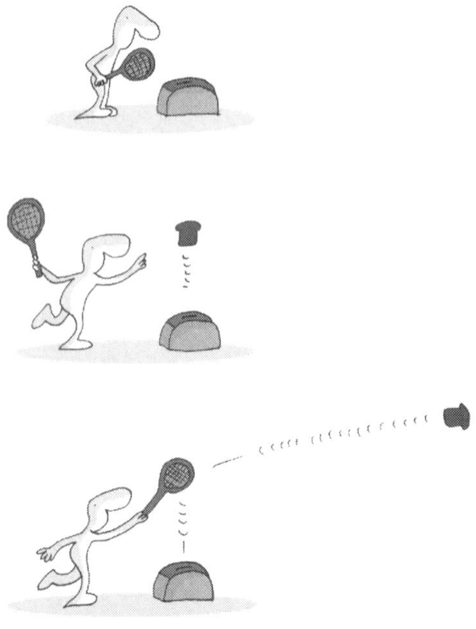

2019

"When I die, I will return to seek
the moments I did not live by the sea"

-Sophia de Mello Breyner

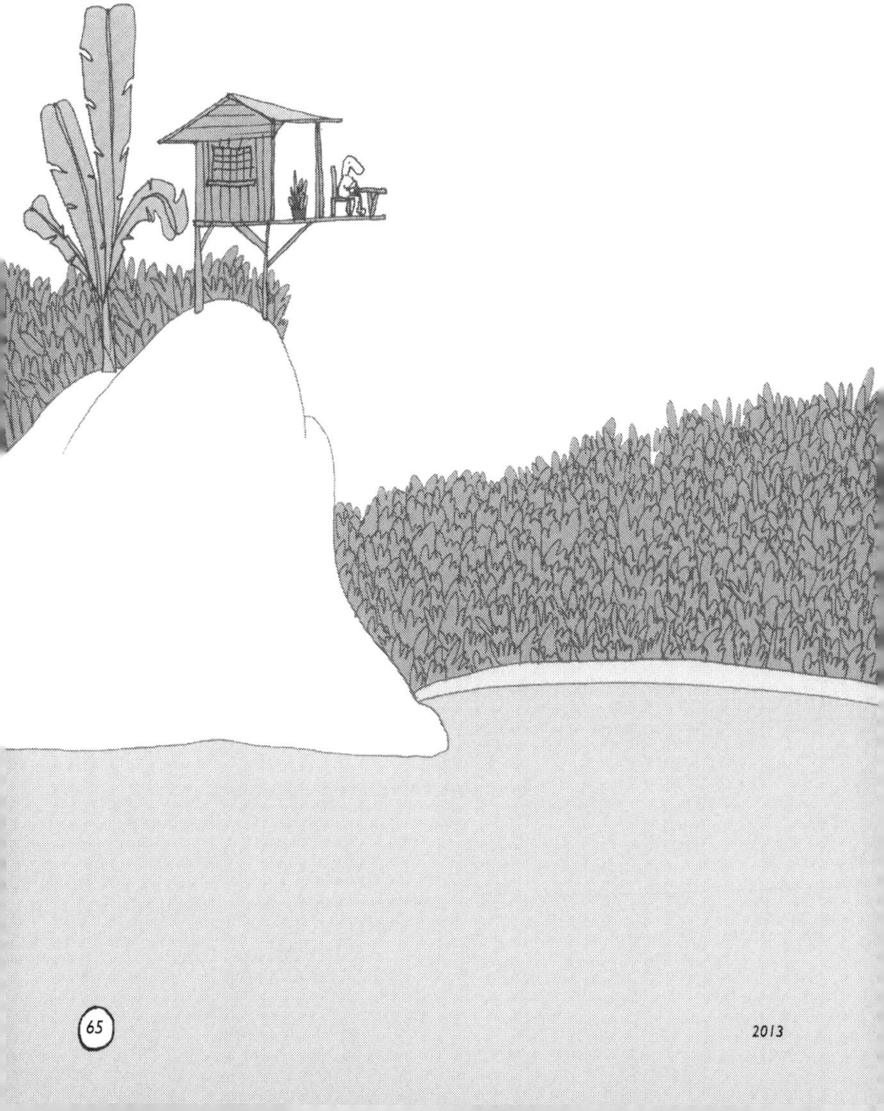

2013

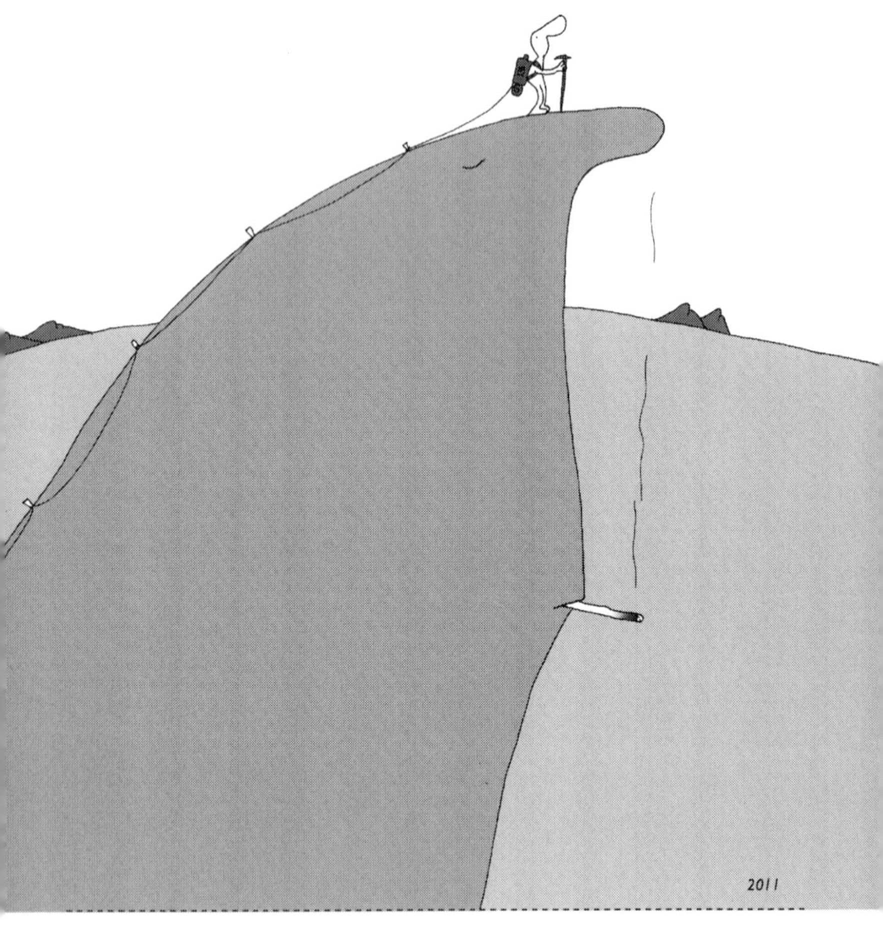
2011

Always take a husband with you
(you never know when you may
come across some dirty dishes...)

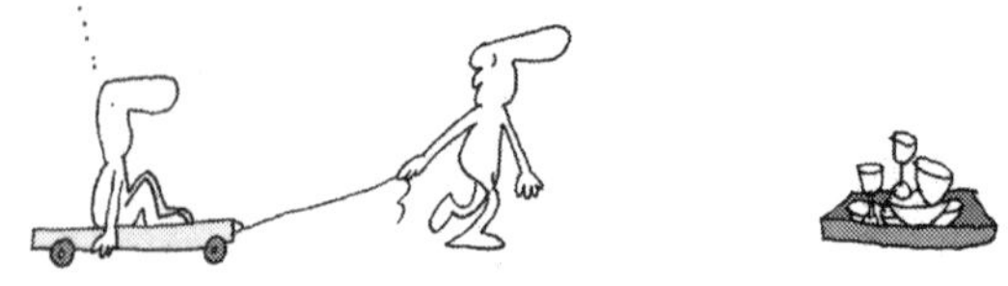
Oh great.

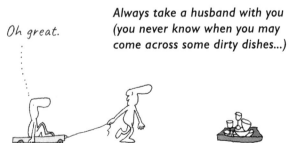

How to Deal with Life's Hurdles I

① Assess.

② Invert.

③ Dismantle.

④ Push some into ground.
Arrange rest into a pile.

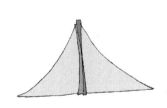

⑤ Voilà.

2003

Hey,
If we're **all** late,
then **no-one** will be late...

2014

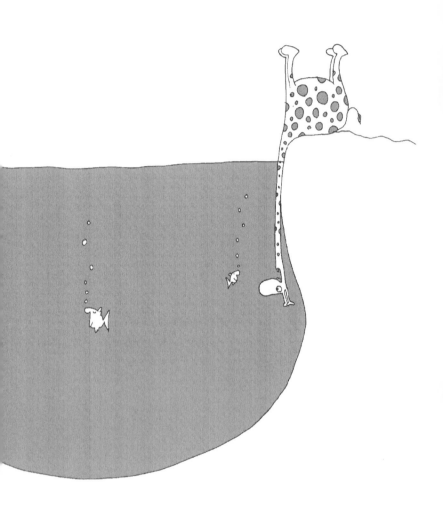

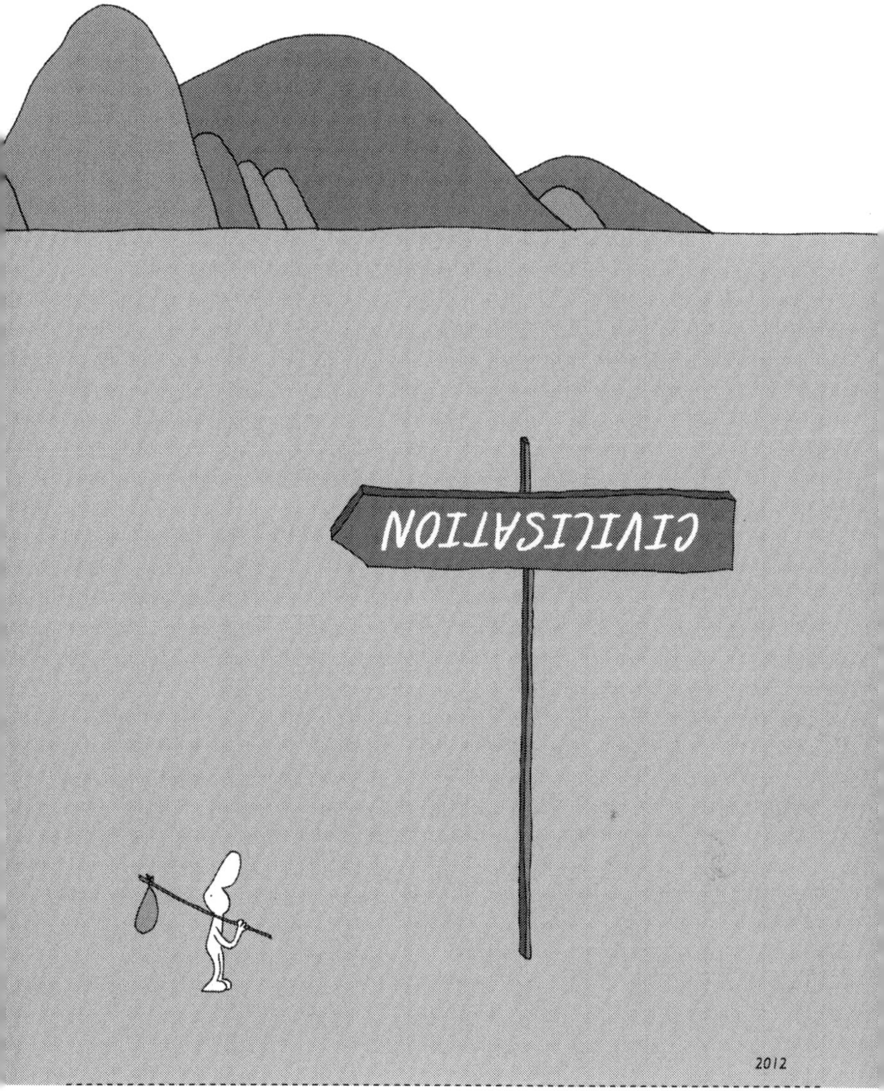
CIVILISATION

2012

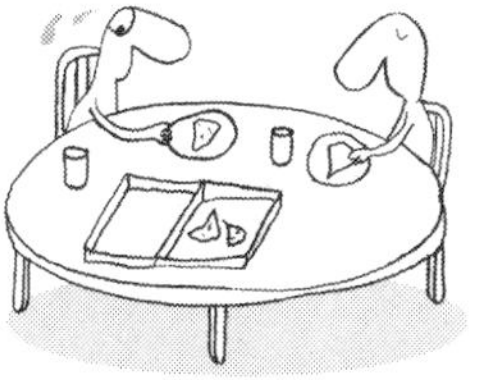

Def. PIZZAFINIPHOBIA

The fear of there not being enough pizza to go round

2014

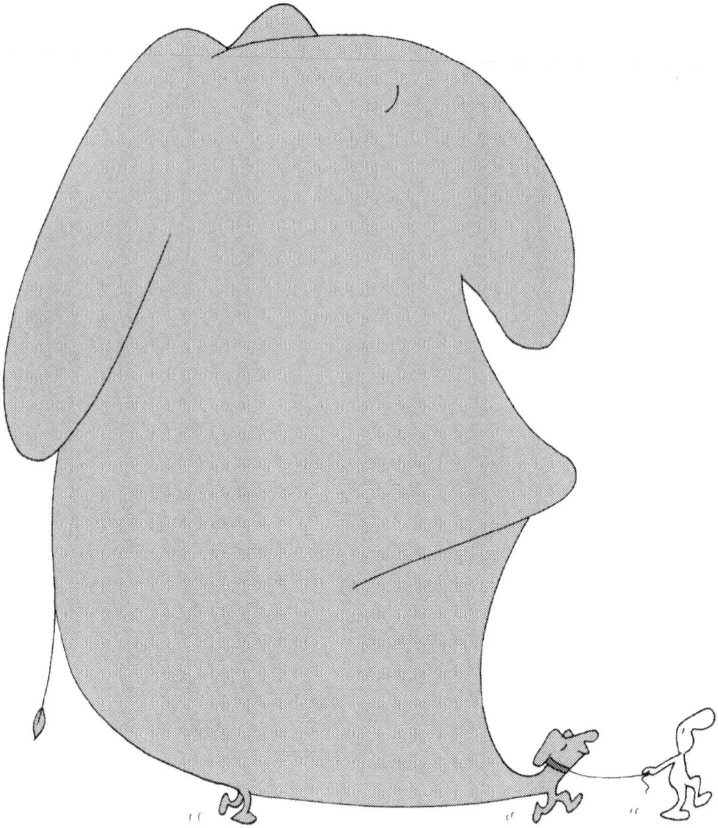

Just taking dogface out for a quick walk

2009

How to *Deal with Technology*

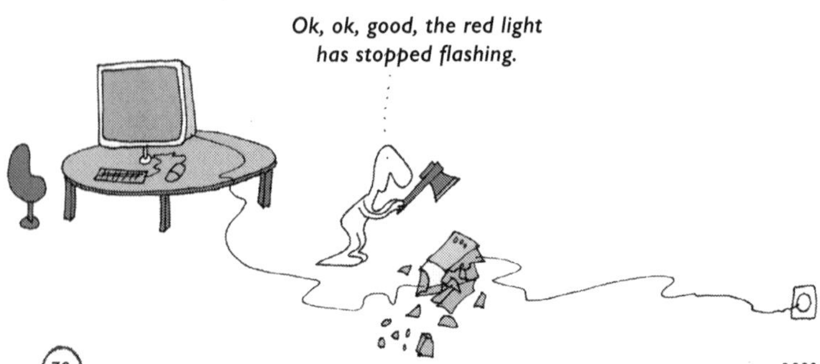
Ok, ok, good, the red light
has stopped flashing.

2009

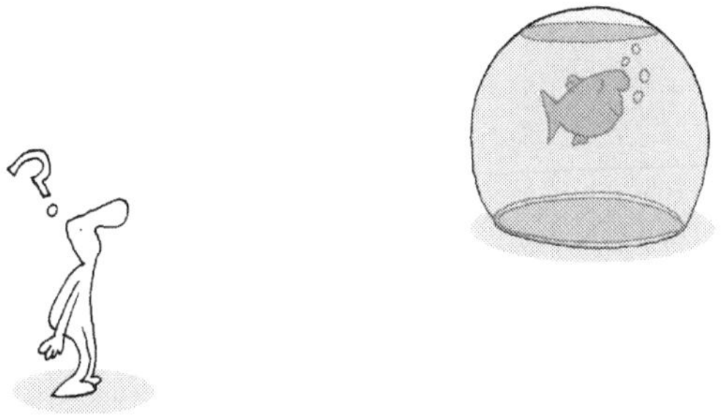

2009

How to *Survive a Day at the Office*

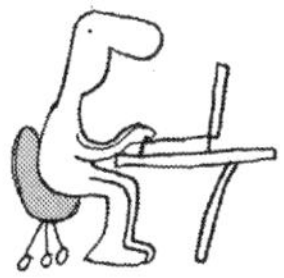

9am: Power up computer.

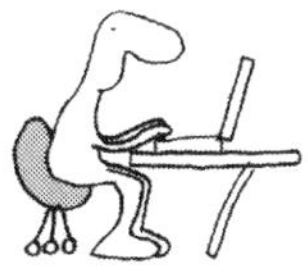

10am: Muck about on Facebook.

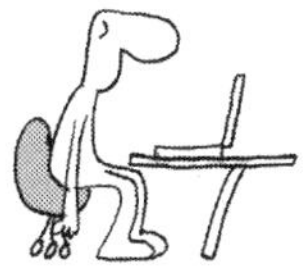

11am: Catch up on sleep.

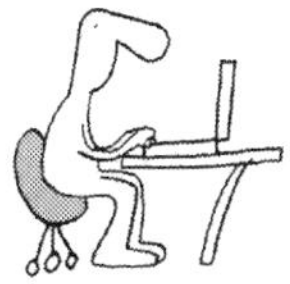

Noon: Organise upcoming holiday.

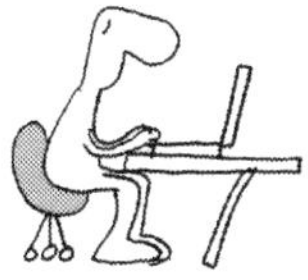

1pm: Digest lunch.

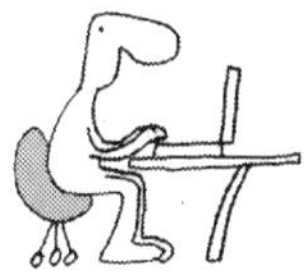

1pm: Think about dinner.

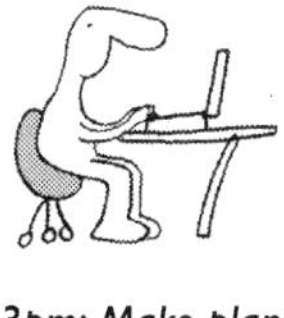

3pm: Make plans for the weekend.

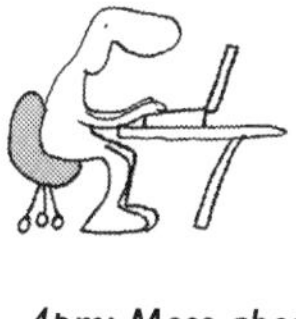

4pm: Mess about online.

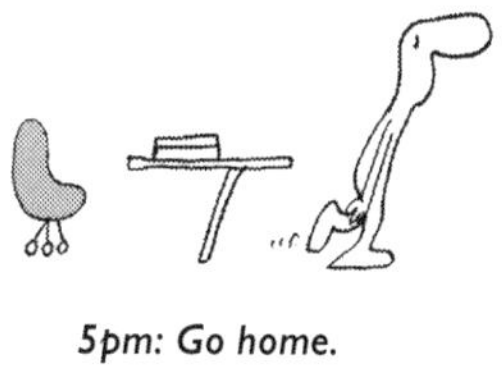

5pm: Go home.

2003

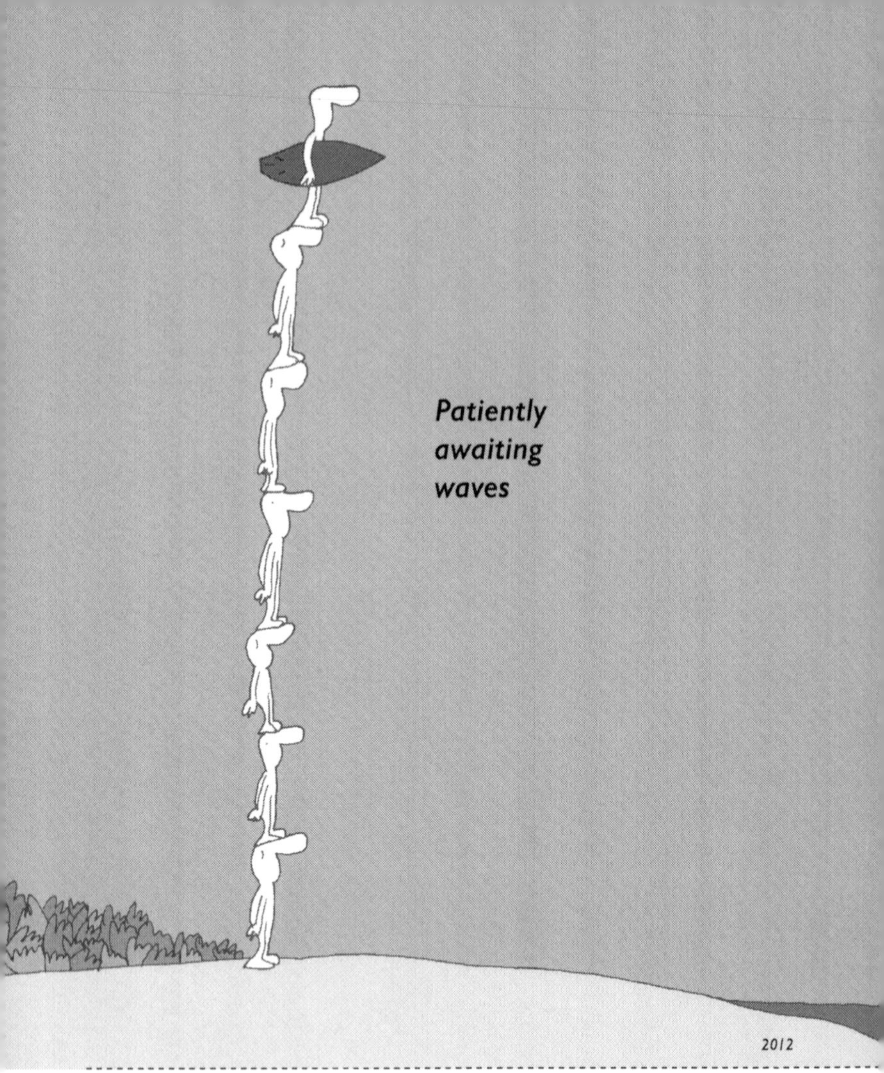
Patiently
awaiting
waves
2012

What happens when you fall asleep at your desk

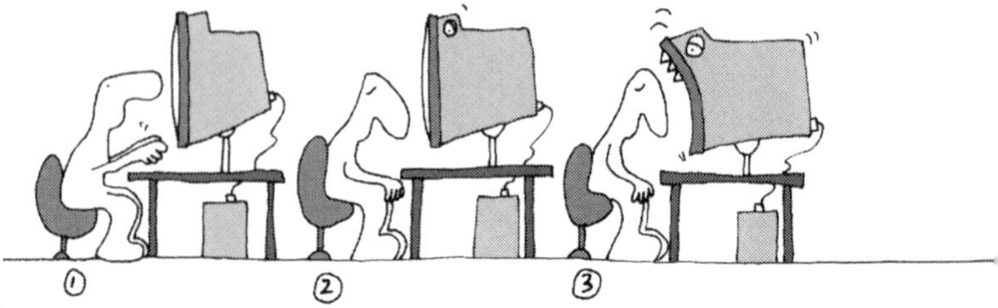
1
2
3

Important smilestones in life

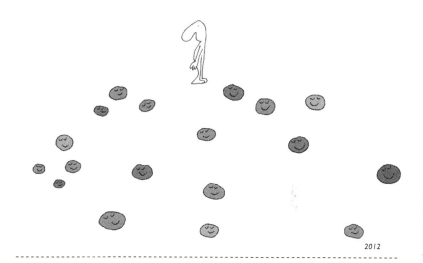

2012

How to *Laminate a Fart*

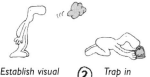

(1) Establish visual contact.

(2) Trap in glass.

(3) Gently insert into laminating machine.

(4) Store for later use.

2012

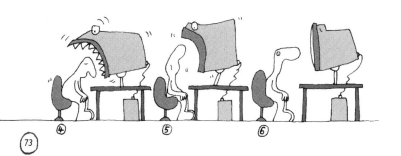

④ ⑤ ⑥

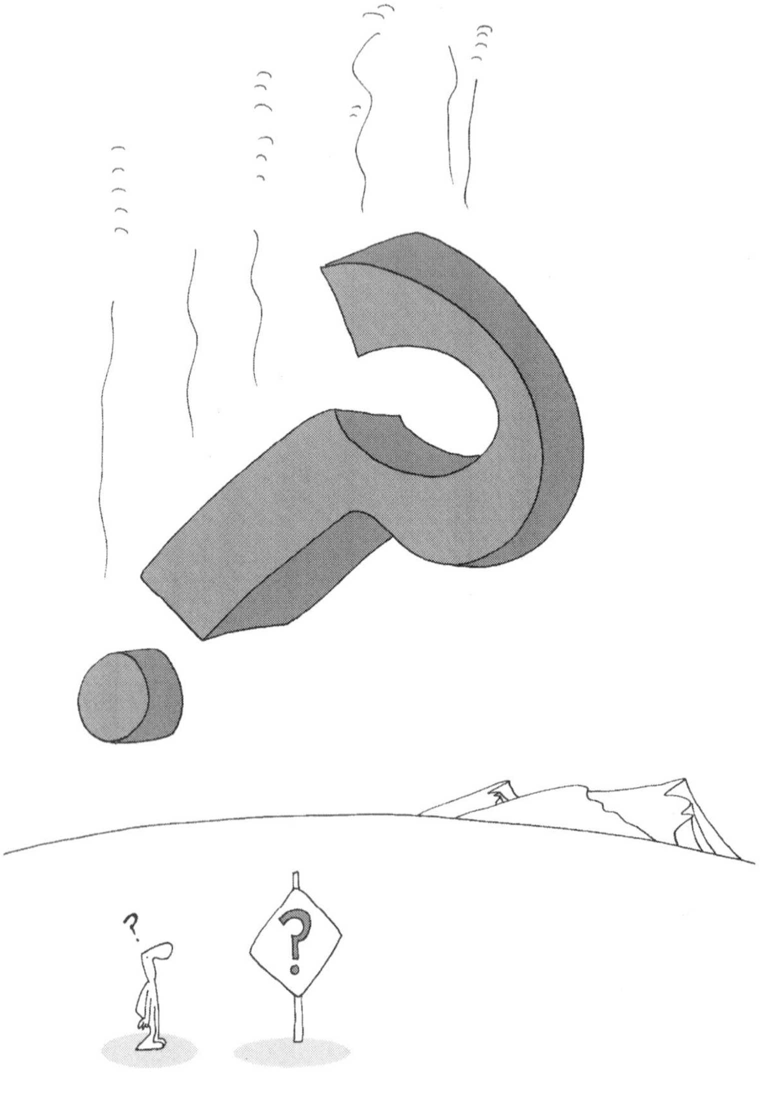
?
?

2008

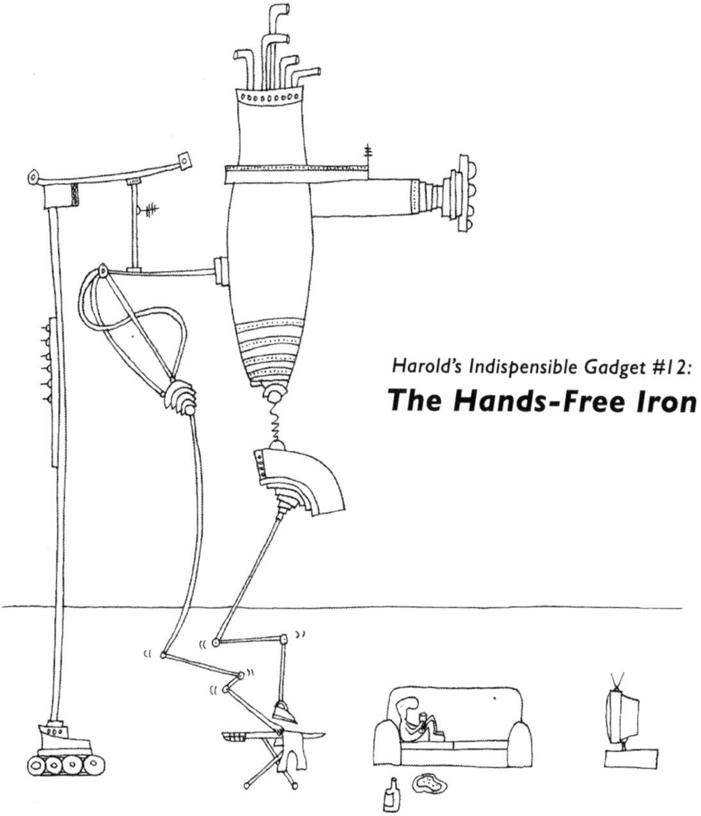

Harold's Indispensible Gadget #12:

The Hands-Free Iron

2006

Just taking a couple of my potatoes out for a quick walk.
It's important to get some fresh air every now and then...

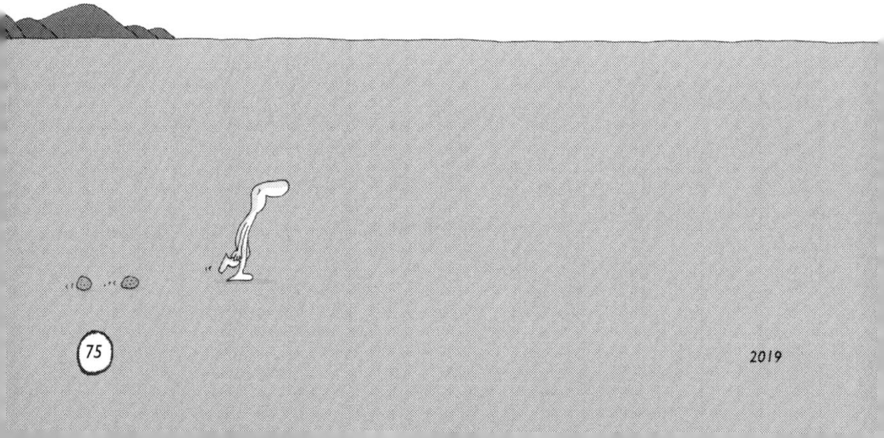

2019

HOW TO BE EPIC

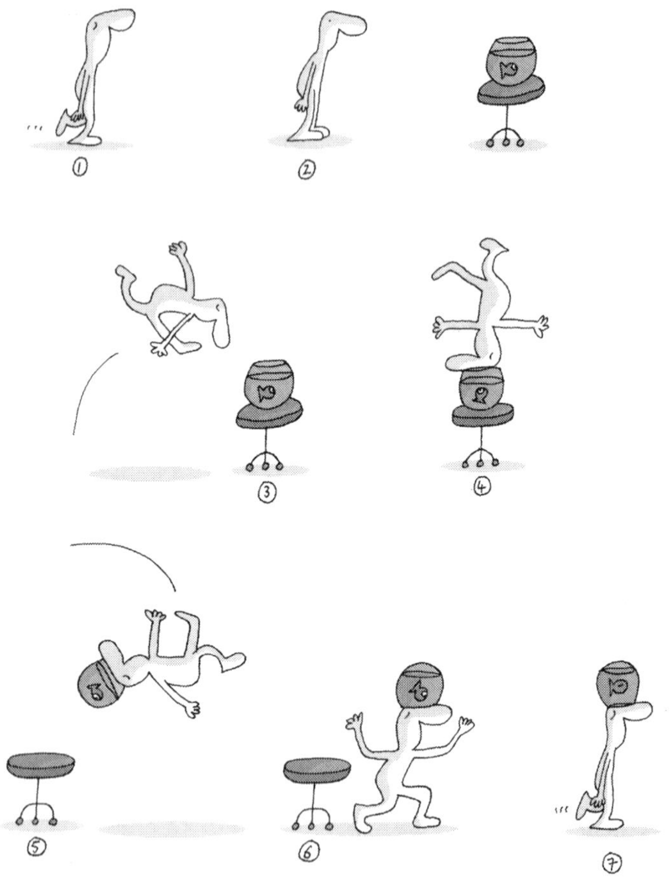

1
2
3
4
5
6
7

2018

How to Deal with a Bad Mood

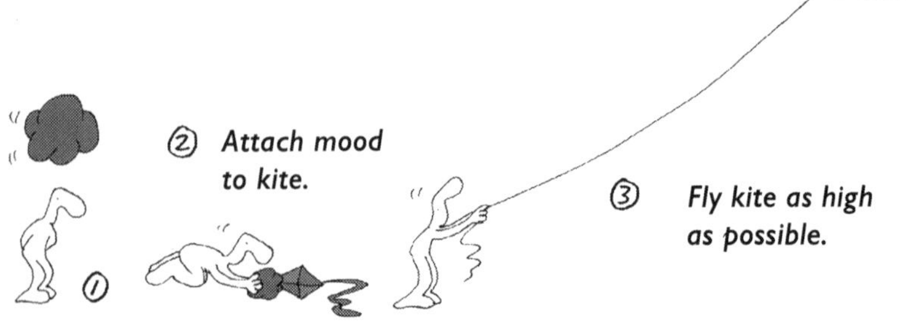

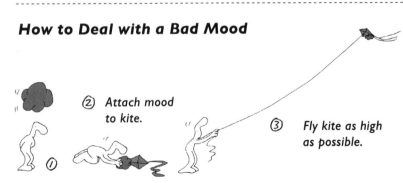

1
2 Attach mood to kite.
3 Fly kite as high as possible.

JUST UNVEILED: **The latest computer with *built-in nose functionality*, capable of sniffing out chocolate anywhere within 200m.**

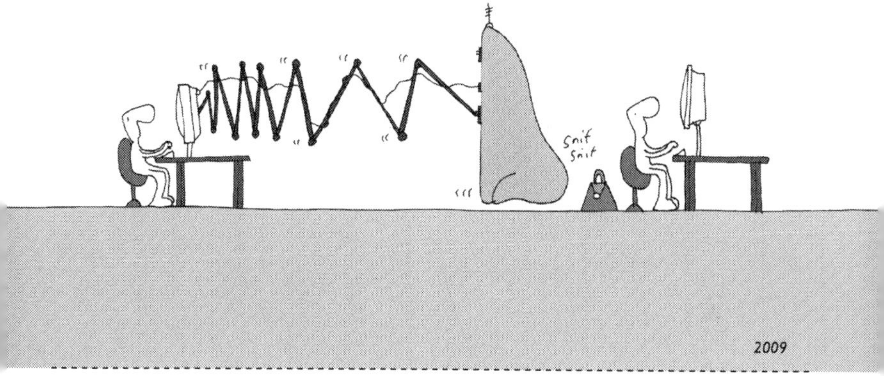
Snif
Snif

2009

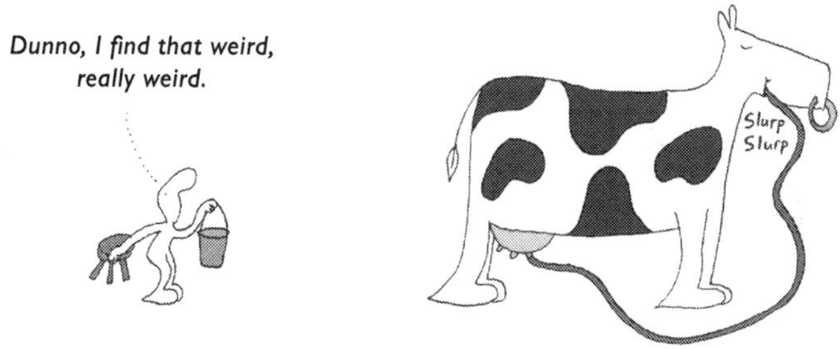
Dunno, I find that weird, really weird.
Slurp
Slurp

2008

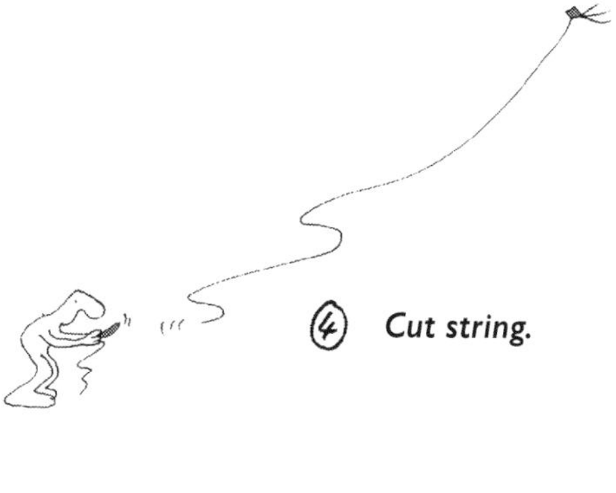
(4) Cut string.

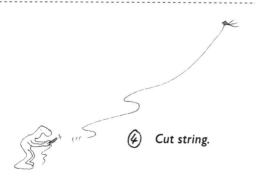

2003 *2003*

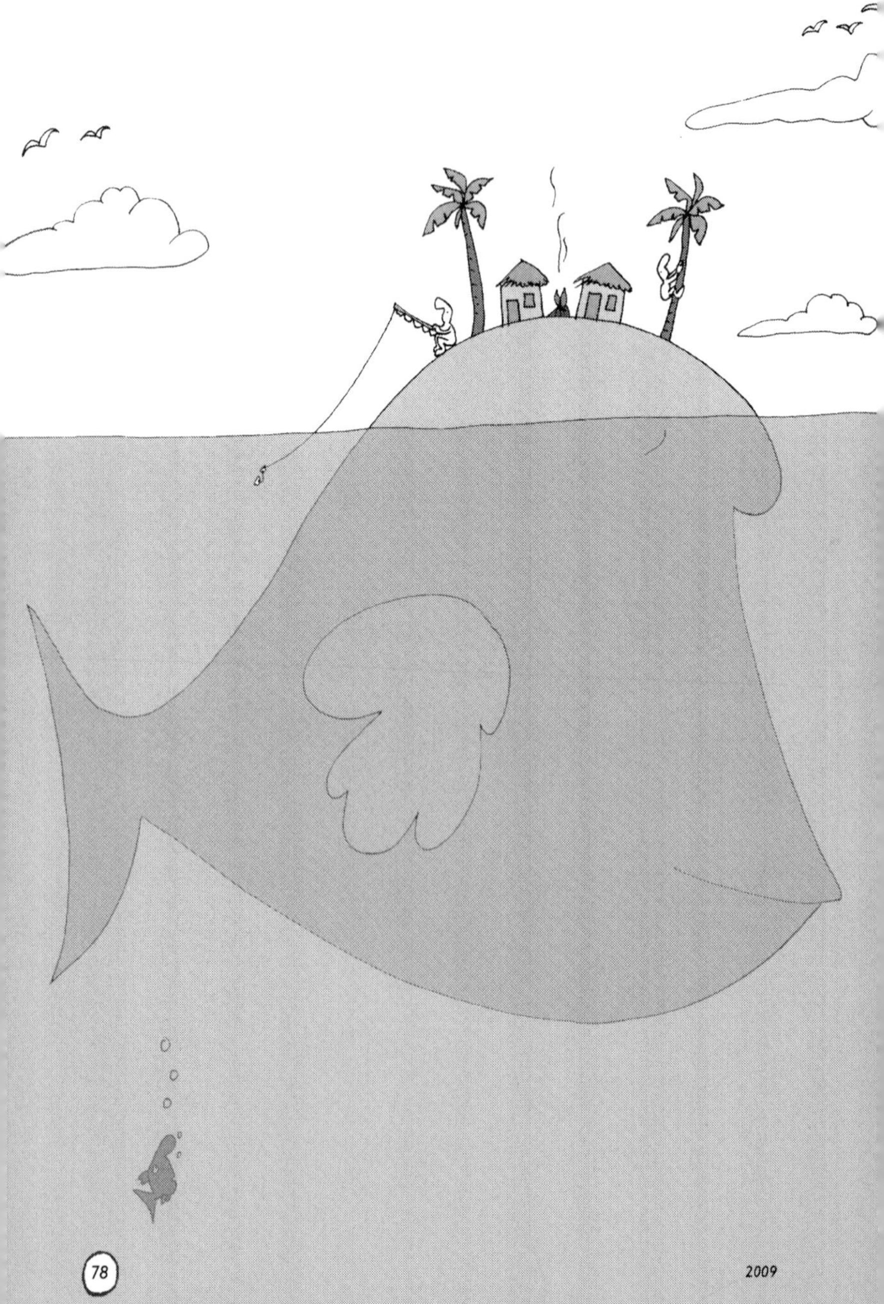

2009

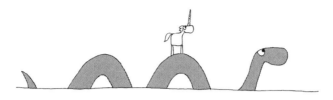

An anything-is-possible kind of day

2012

I think I'll go for a run...

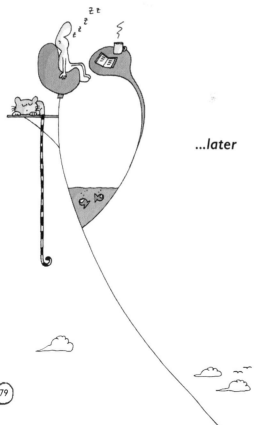

...later

2018

The Great Debatickle

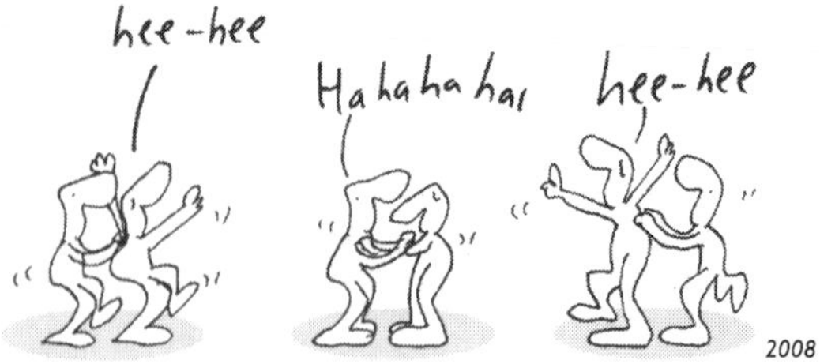
hee-hee
Hahahahaha
hee-hee
2008

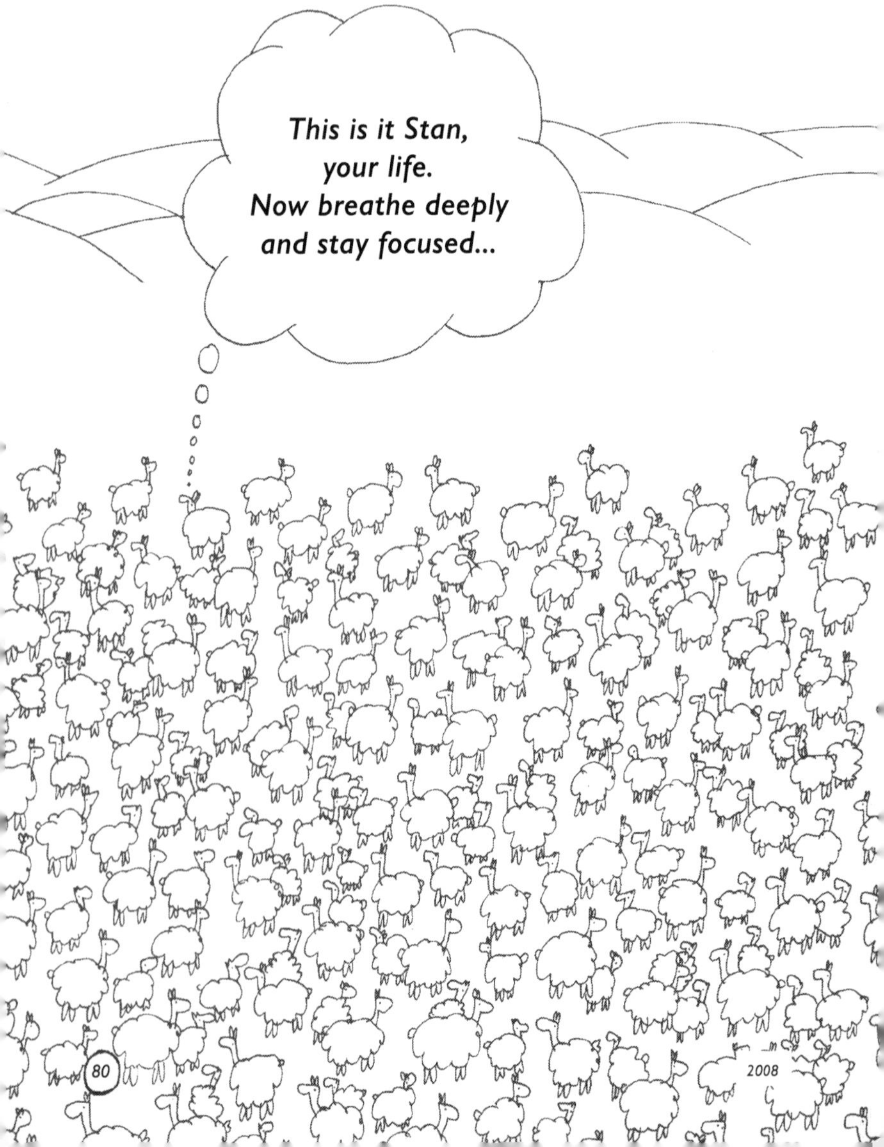
This is it Stan,
your life.
Now breathe deeply
and stay focused...
2008

As we get older...

...EVEN THOUGH WE ACQUIRE DEEP & NOBLE WISDOM, WE STILL KEEP ASKING THE IMPORTANT QUESTIONS:

WHAT IS THE MEANING OF LIFE?

DOES OUR UNIVERSE REALLY EXIST?

WHY DID I COME INTO THIS ROOM AGAIN?

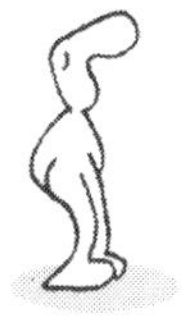

How to know when you have had enough sushi

① Sit at the conveyor belt.

② Eat some...

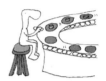

③ ...then eat some more...

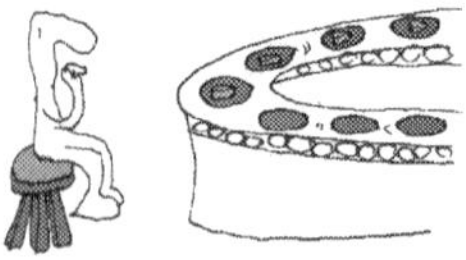

④ ...and some more...

⑤ ...and some more...

⑥ ...and some more...

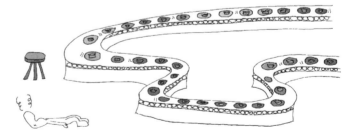

⑦ You have had enough sushi.

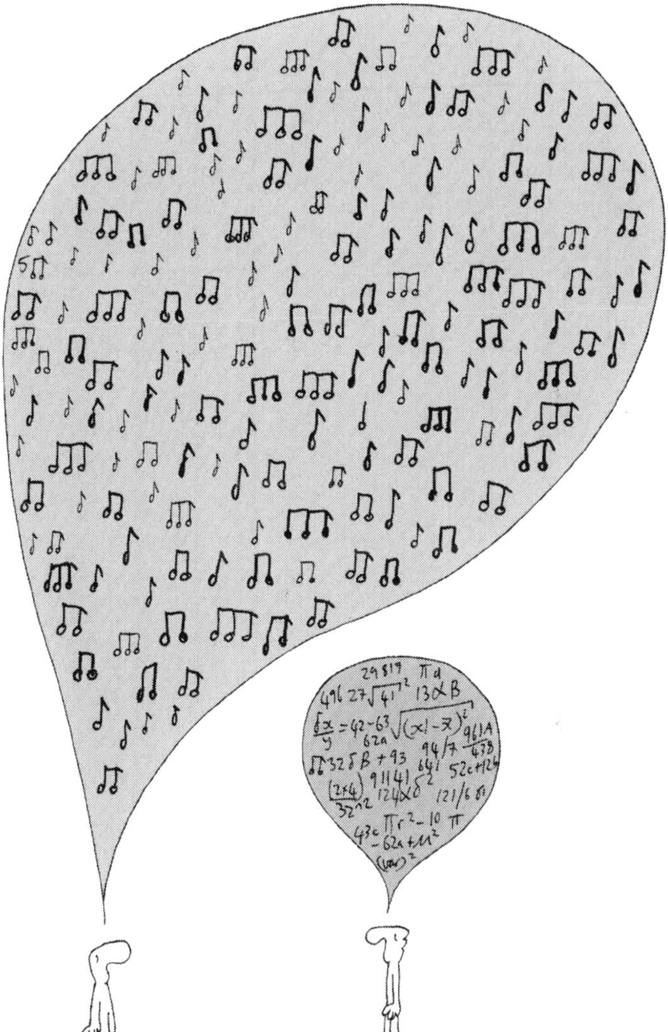

Yet they got on famously

THE DECISION TREE

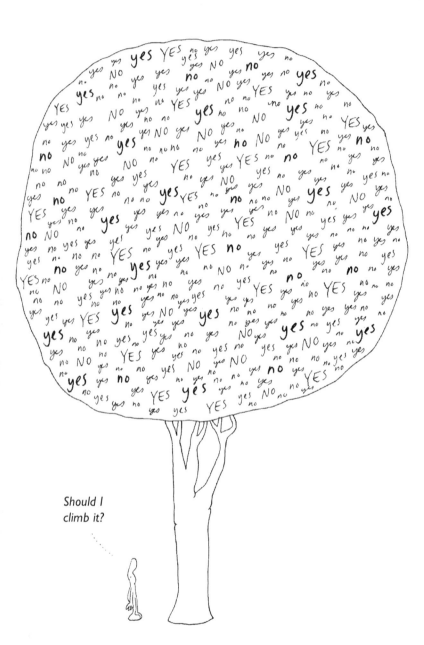

Should I climb it?

Nice people
have holes in their socks

Born to sail,
forced to work

Less is More

e.g. why do you need a twelve-armed head-scratcher & back-massager...

...when a six-armed one does a perfectly good job...

2018

Go where the wind takes you...

2013

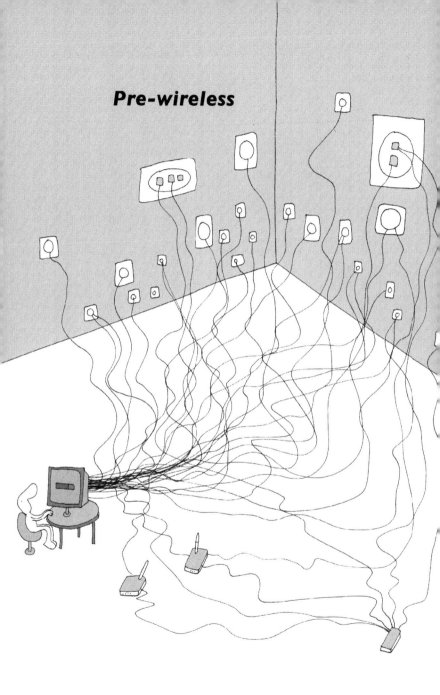

Pre-wireless

HOW TO GET THROUGH A MONDAY

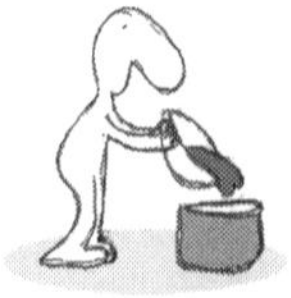

1. Fill a bucket with chocolate mousse.

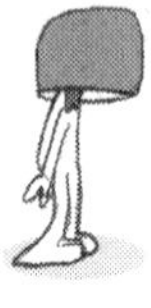

2. Place bucket over head.

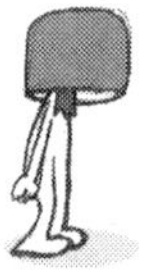

3. Wait till Tuesday.

2013

THE BELOVE DEGG

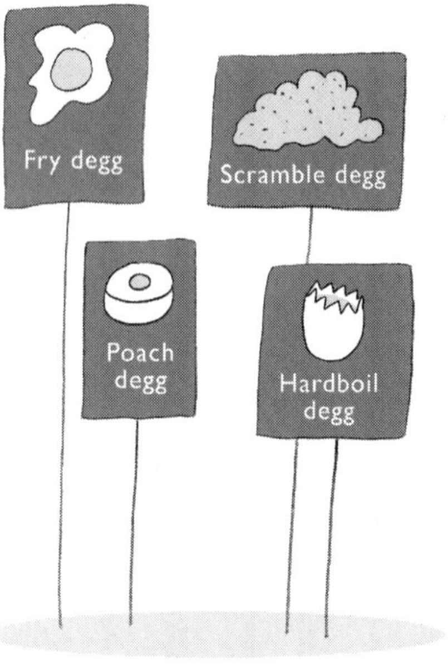
Fry degg
Scramble degg
Poach degg
Hardboil degg

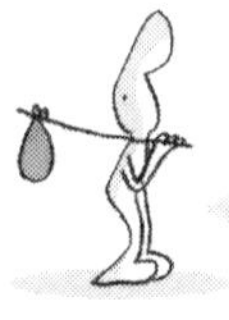

2007

A fine way to start the day...

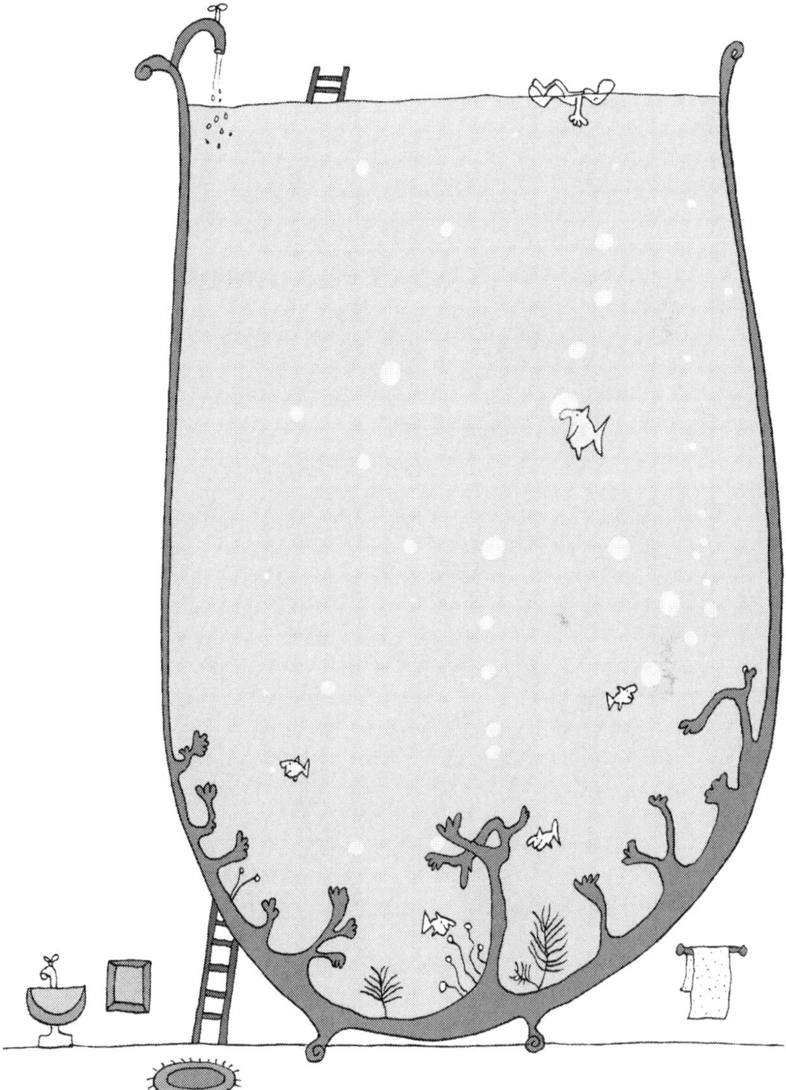

2007

Life is fun!

(and if anyone tells you otherwise, hit them over the head with a pillowslip full of marshmallows)

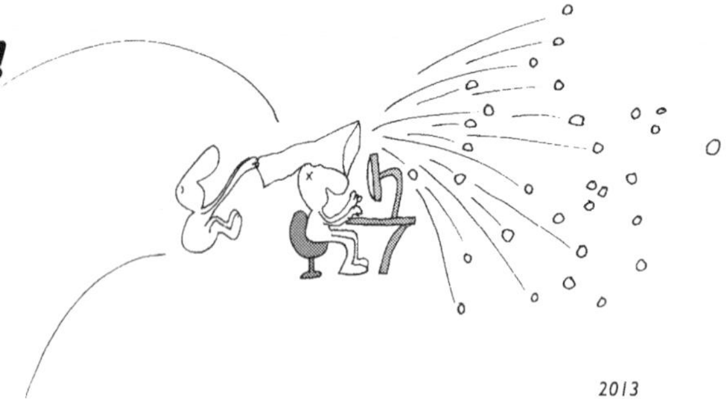

2013

Laws of Nature #6

How the Internet really Works

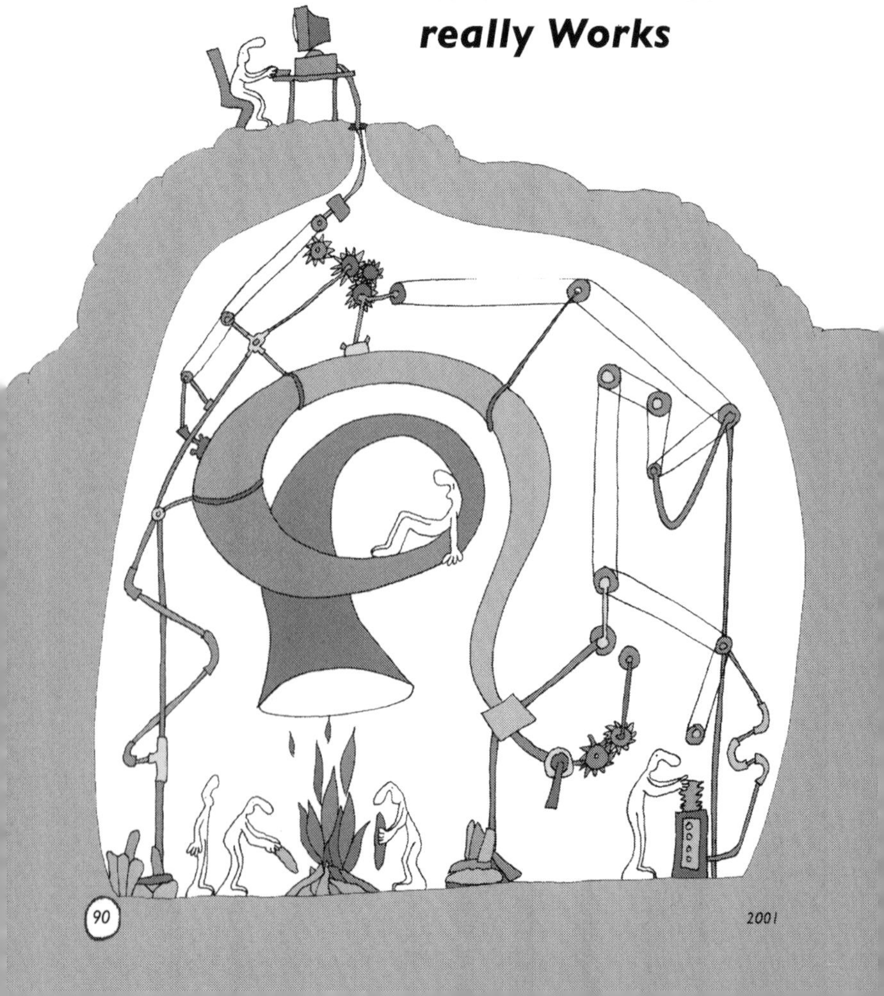

2001

Why walruses should stand by rocks

Scenario 1.

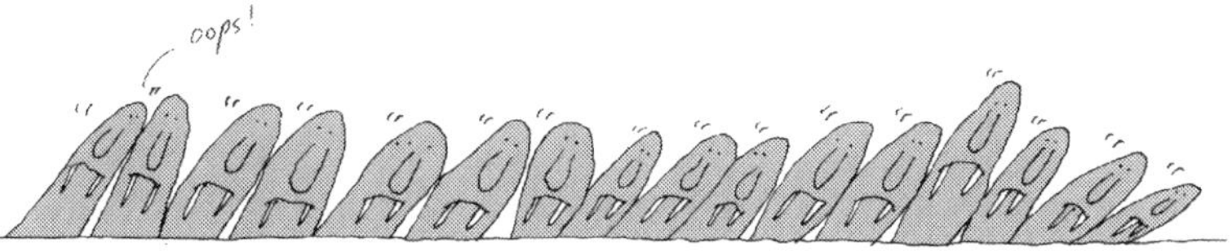
oops!

Scenario 2..

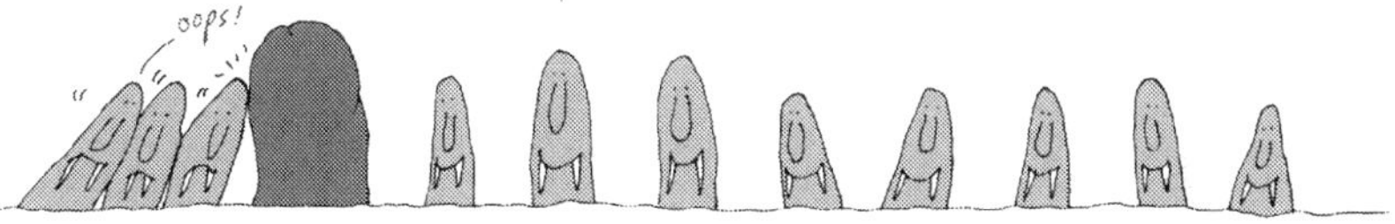
oops!

2003

Fun fondue do

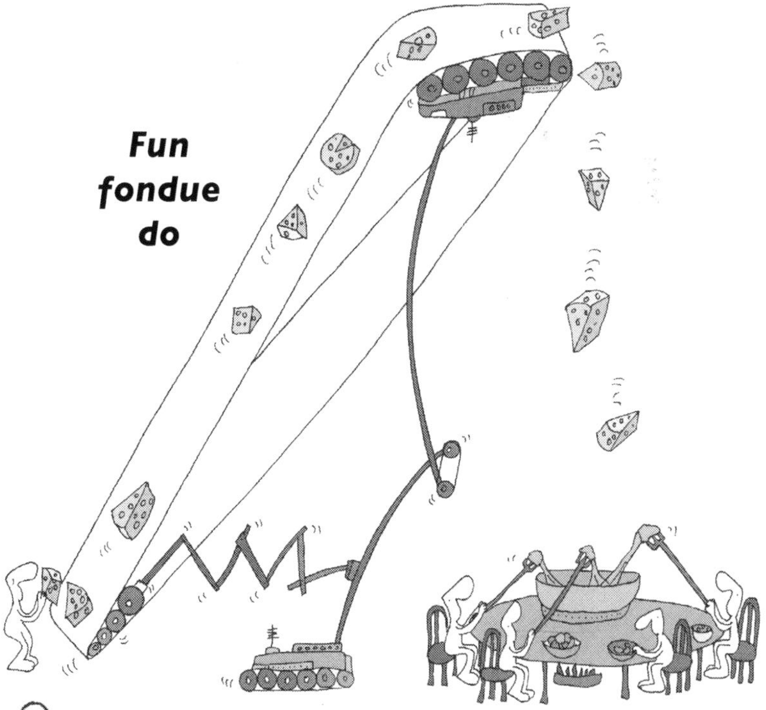

2007

Sleep-working

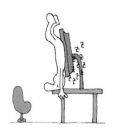

It's never too late...

*Very Big Adventure

2019

Riding the
Great Wooden Ossifier

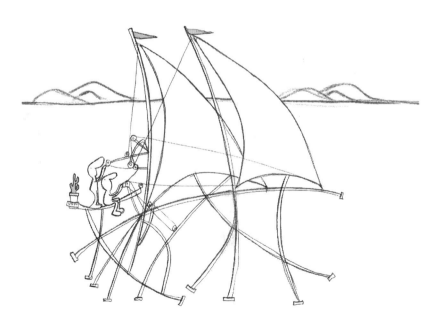

1999

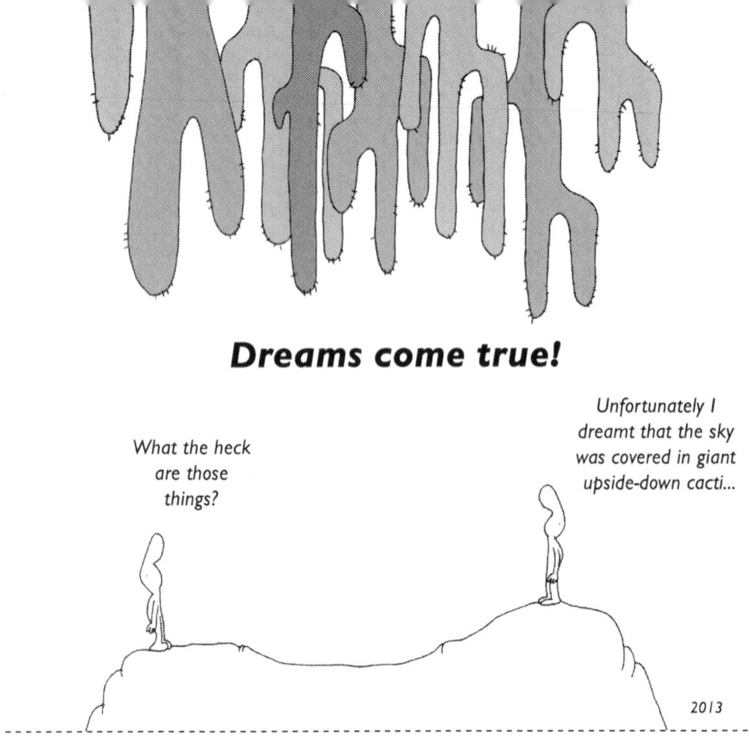
Dreams come true!
What the heck are those things?
Unfortunately I dreamt that the sky was covered in giant upside-down cacti...
2013

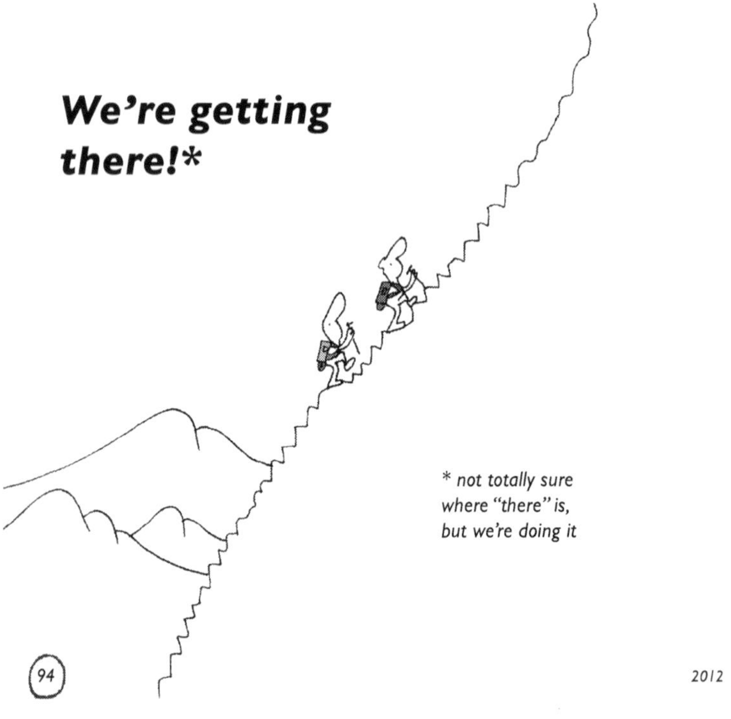
We're getting there!*
* not totally sure where "there" is, but we're doing it
2012

How to Pursue your Dreams

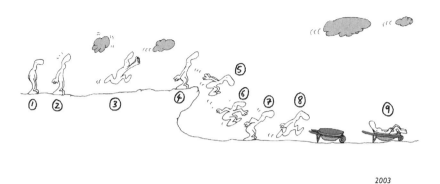

2003

Latin Basics: *Lesson I*

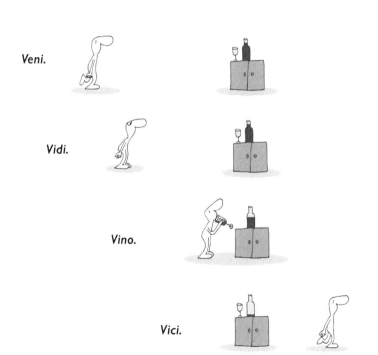

Veni.

Vidi.

Vino.

Vici.

Dare to dream

2008

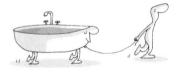

I never go anywhere without taking a bath...

2018

Ode to My Man

Oh my dear man,
You are my rock.
A hairy rock
that requires deodorant.

2003

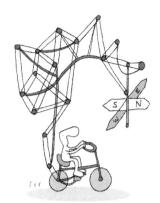

Old-school GPS

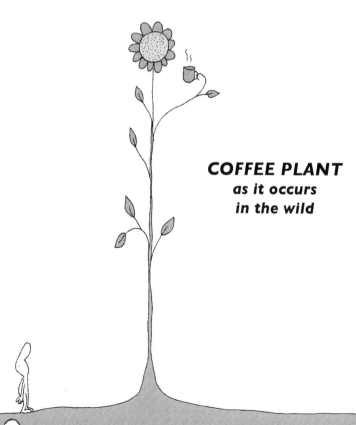

COFFEE PLANT
*as it occurs
in the wild*

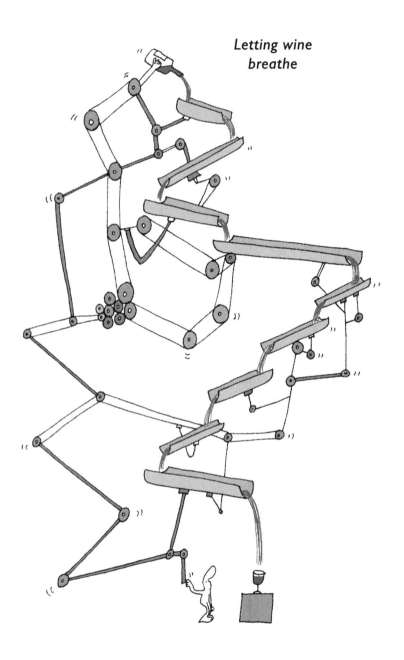

Letting wine breathe

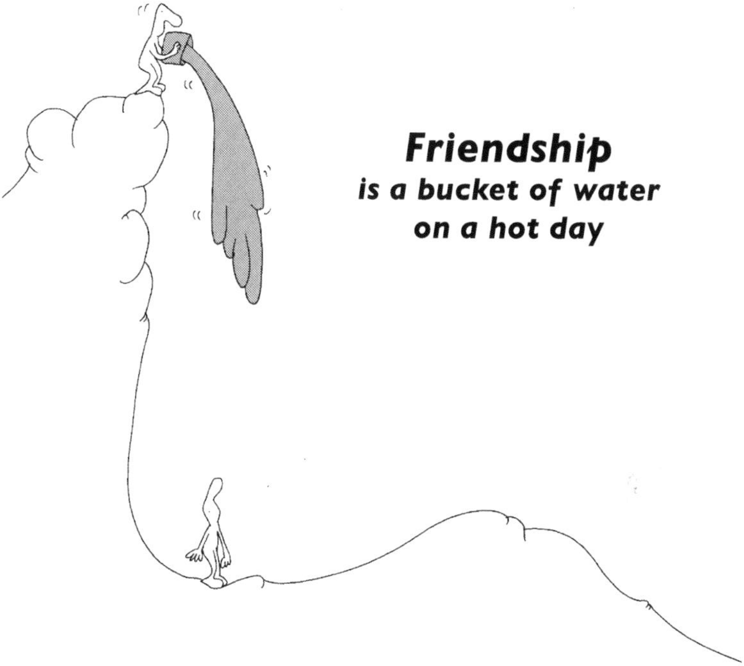

Friendship
is a bucket of water on a hot day

2007

How to *Win Arguments*

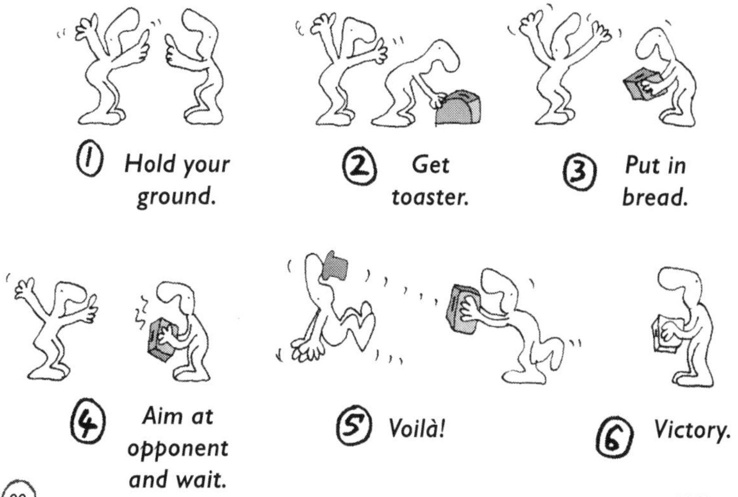

① Hold your ground.
② Get toaster.
③ Put in bread.
④ Aim at opponent and wait.
⑤ Voilà!
⑥ Victory.

2007

USES OF THE HUMBLE BUCKET

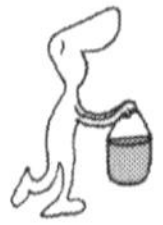

1. Carrying water.

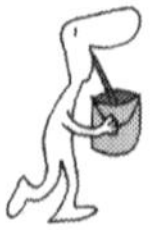

2. Carrying wine.

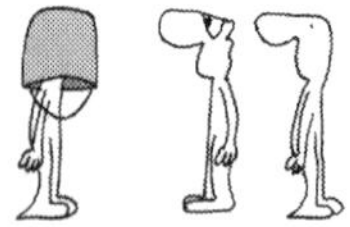

3. Dealing with relatives.

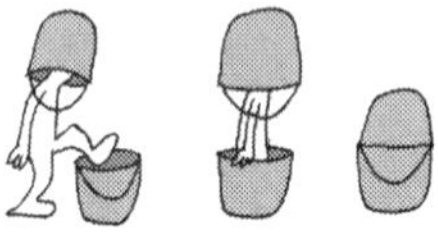

4. Becoming invisible.

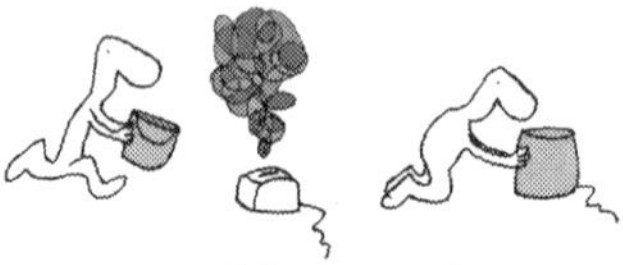

5. Putting out fires.

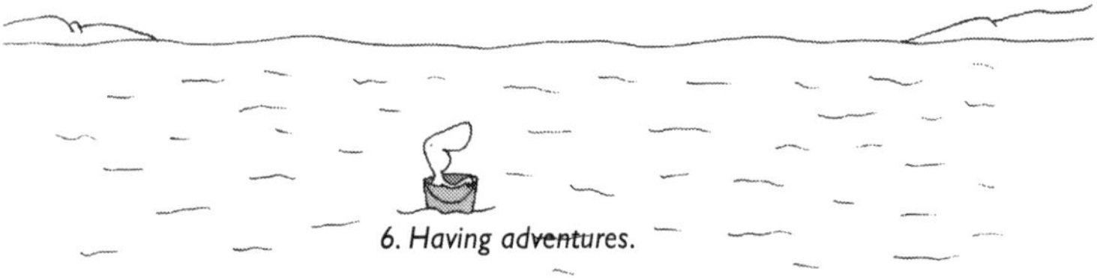

6. Having adventures.

2013

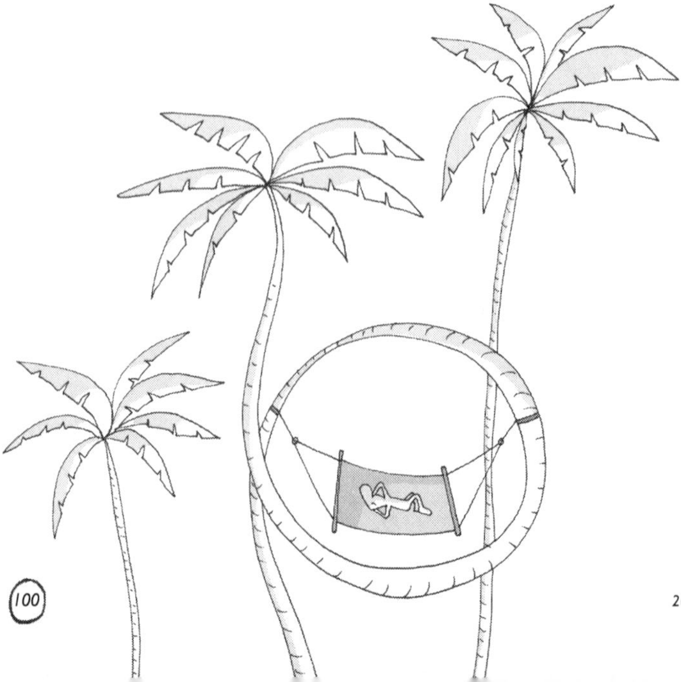

2019

Harold's Handy Gadget #14
THE TELEPATHIC DRINK SERVER
(serves you the perfect drink, at just the right moment)

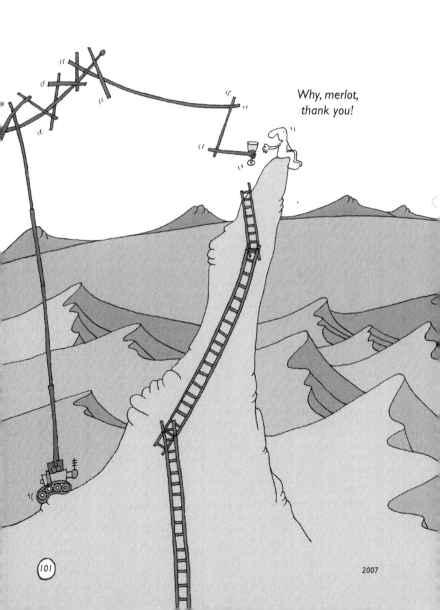

2007

Regular
snail.

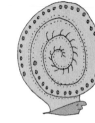

Designer
snail.

2009

2008

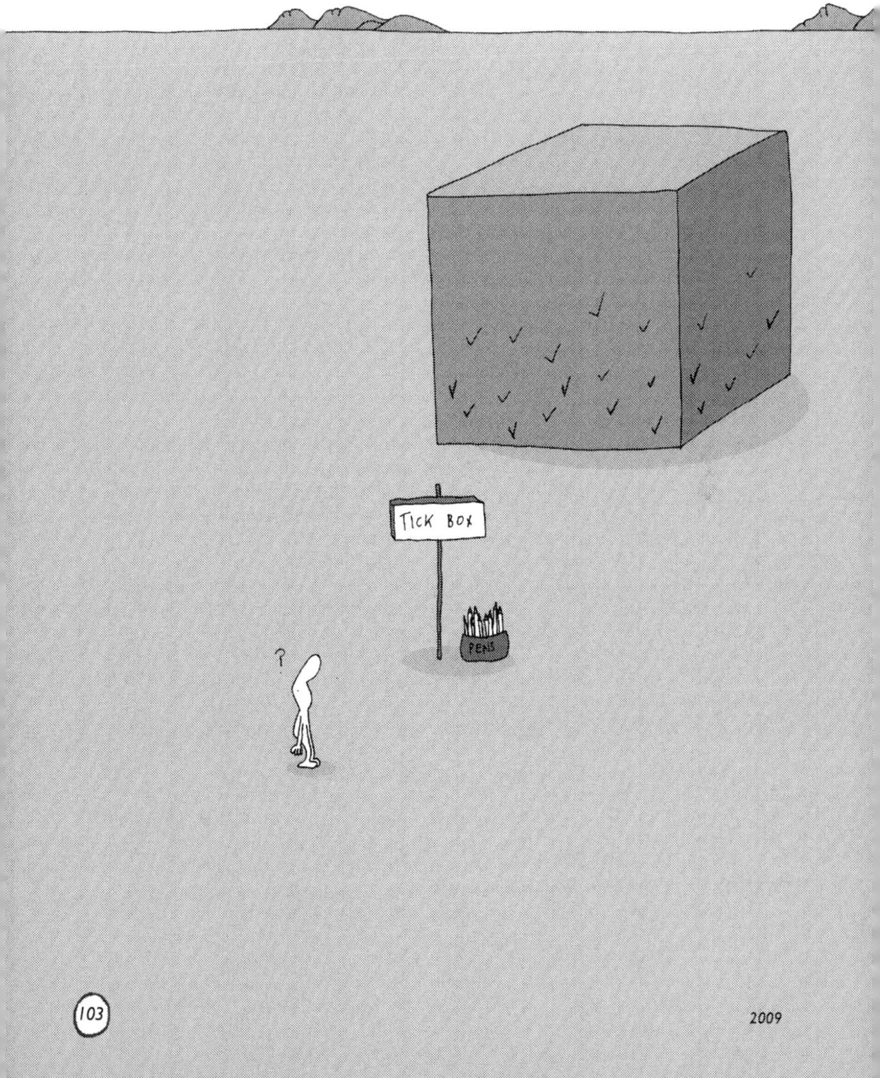
TICK BOX
PENS
?

2009

How to Get Rich

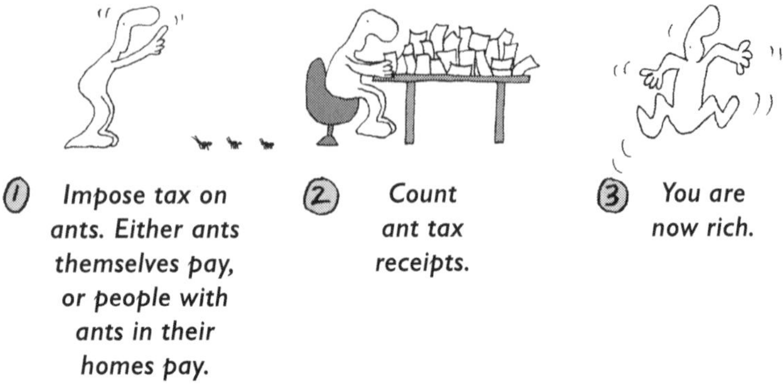
1 Impose tax on ants. Either ants themselves pay, or people with ants in their homes pay.
2 Count ant tax receipts.
3 You are now rich.

2003

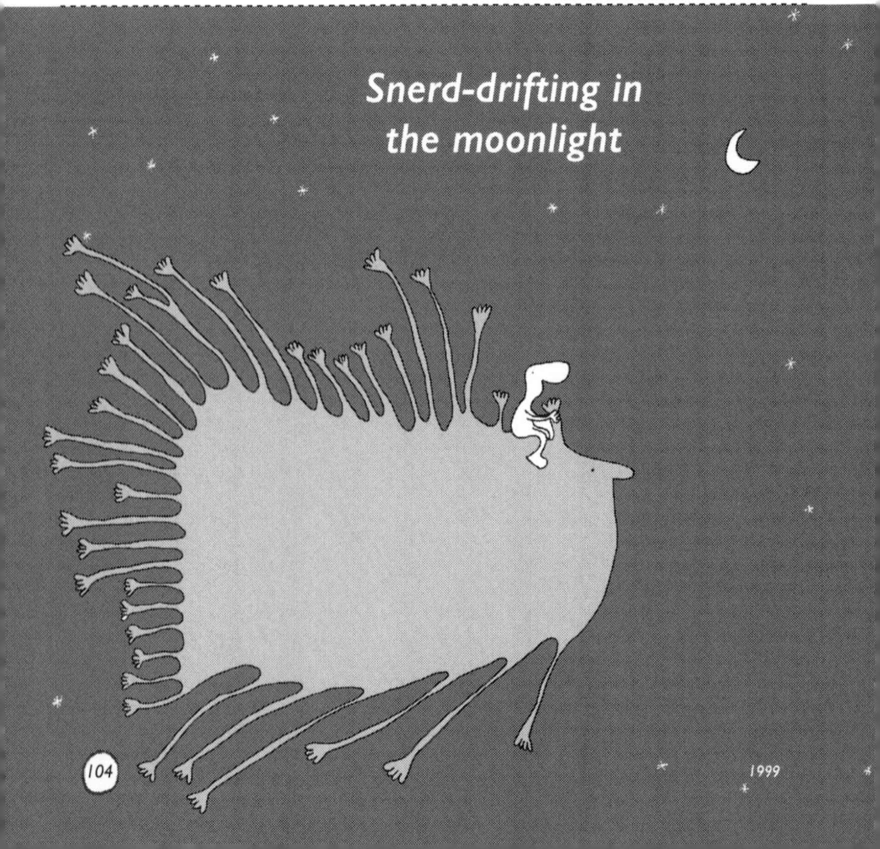
Snerd-drifting in the moonlight
1999

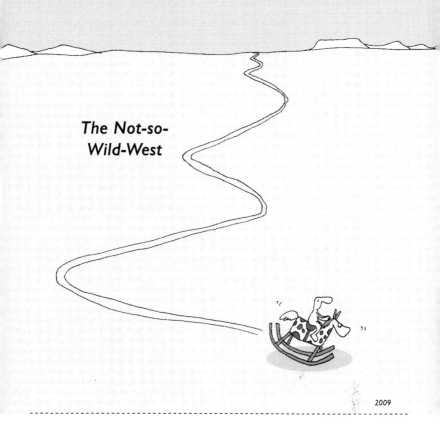

The Not-so-Wild-West

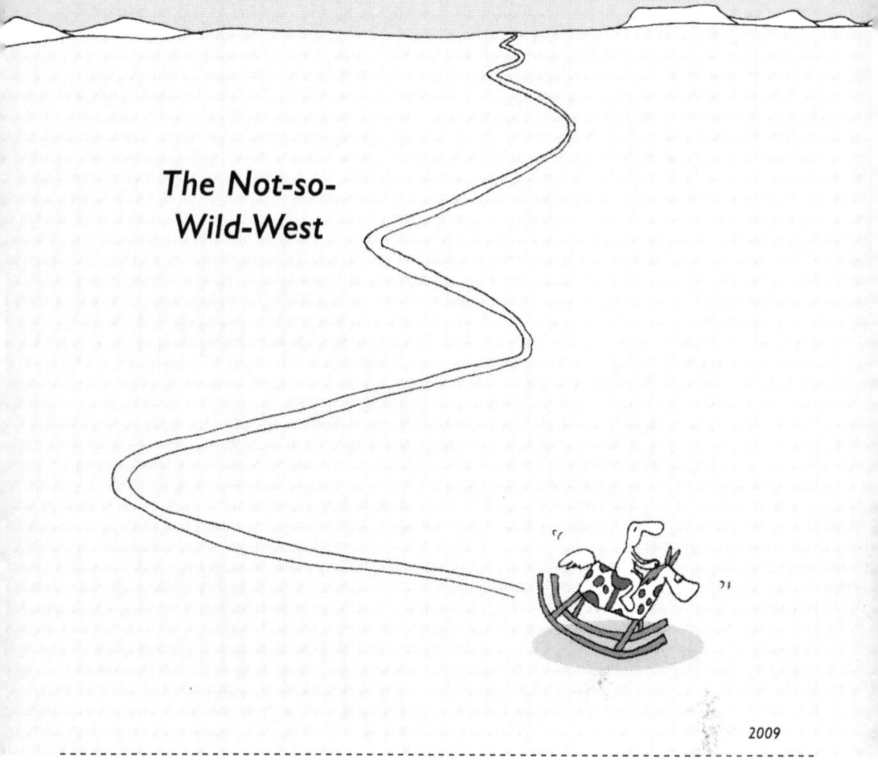

2009

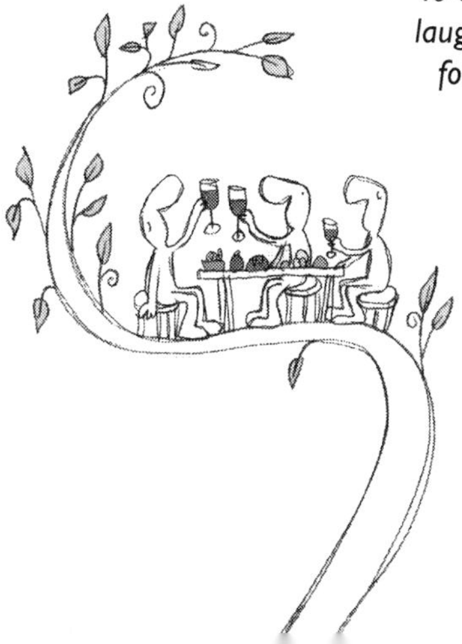

To eat and drink and laugh for a while, and forget everything...

2014

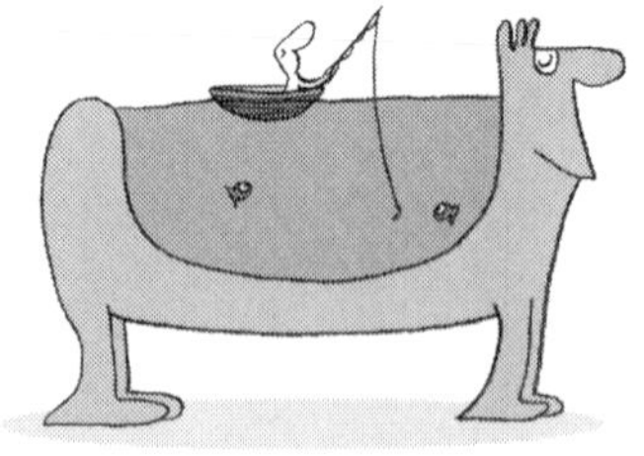

2014

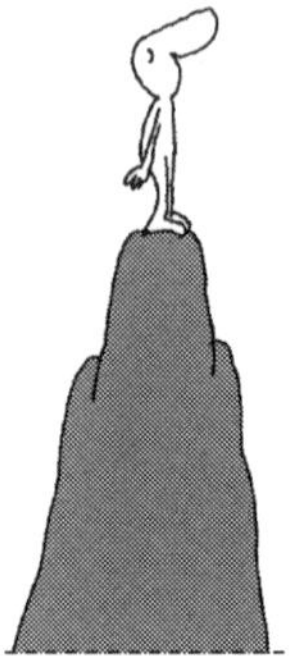

We are all mere specks
on a **huuuuge** planet...

...so let's not take
ourselves too seriously.

2008

CYCLING FOR
BEER AFICIONADOS

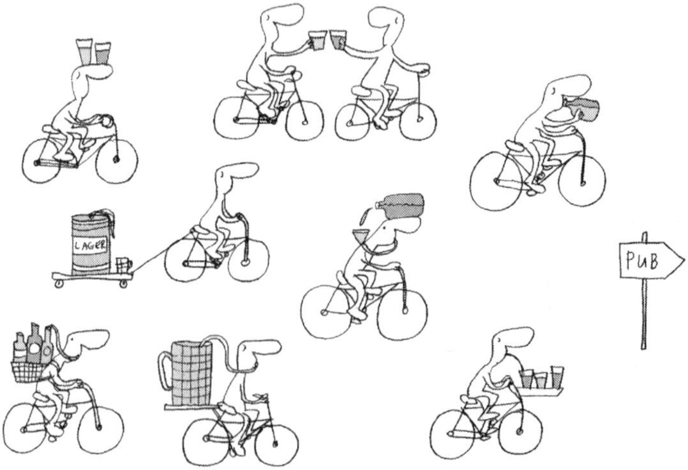
LAGER
PUB

2014

Lovely guy,
lousy pirate

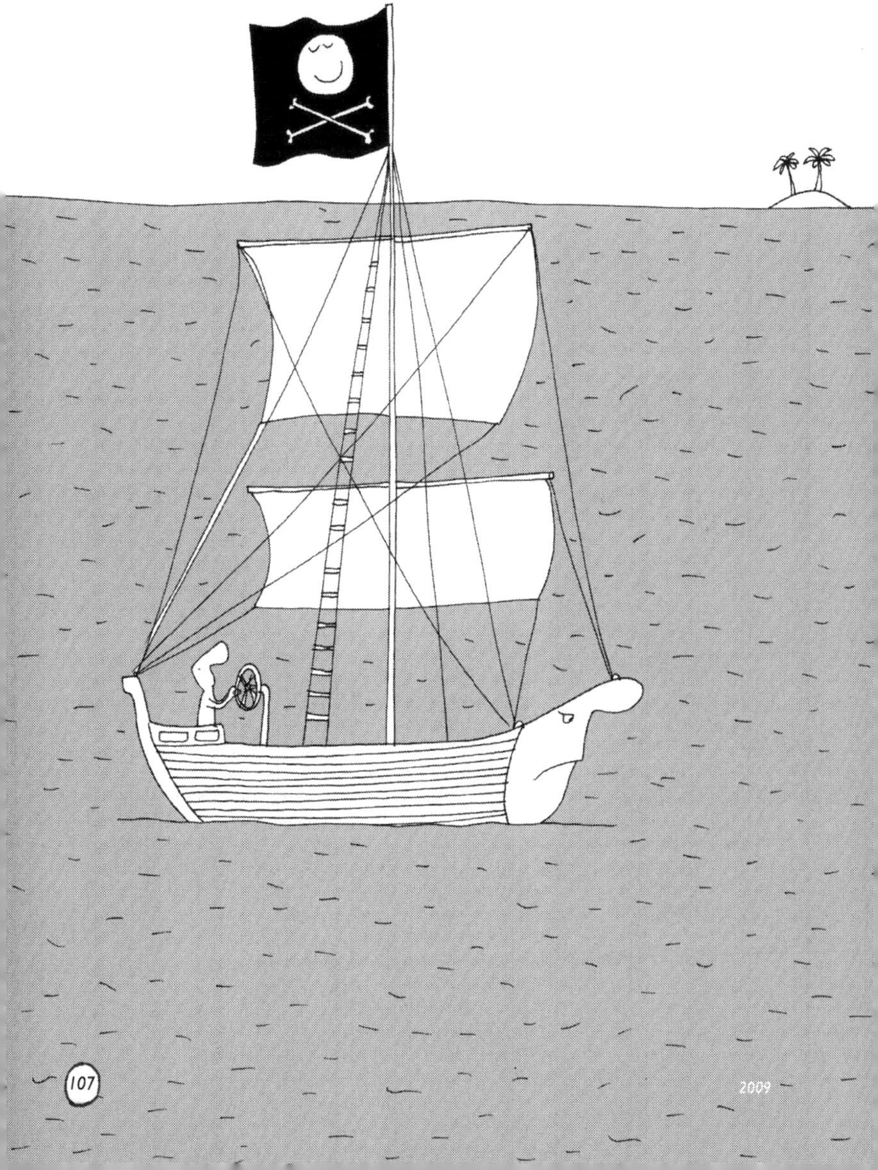
2009

THE JOY OF STICKY NOTES

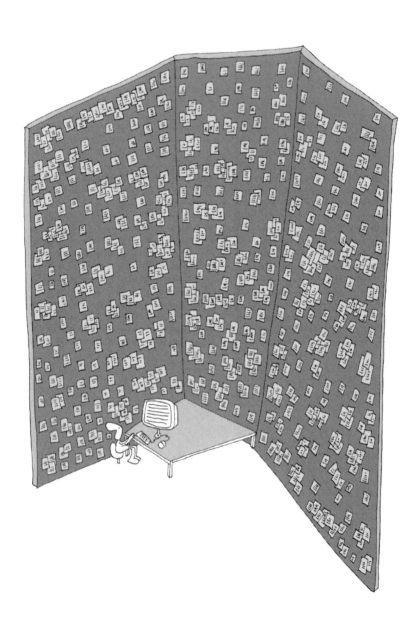

May the Little Helicopter of Happiness follow you wherever you go, even if it gets a bit annoying...

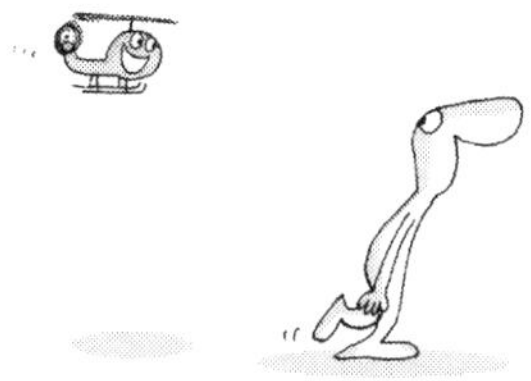

2019

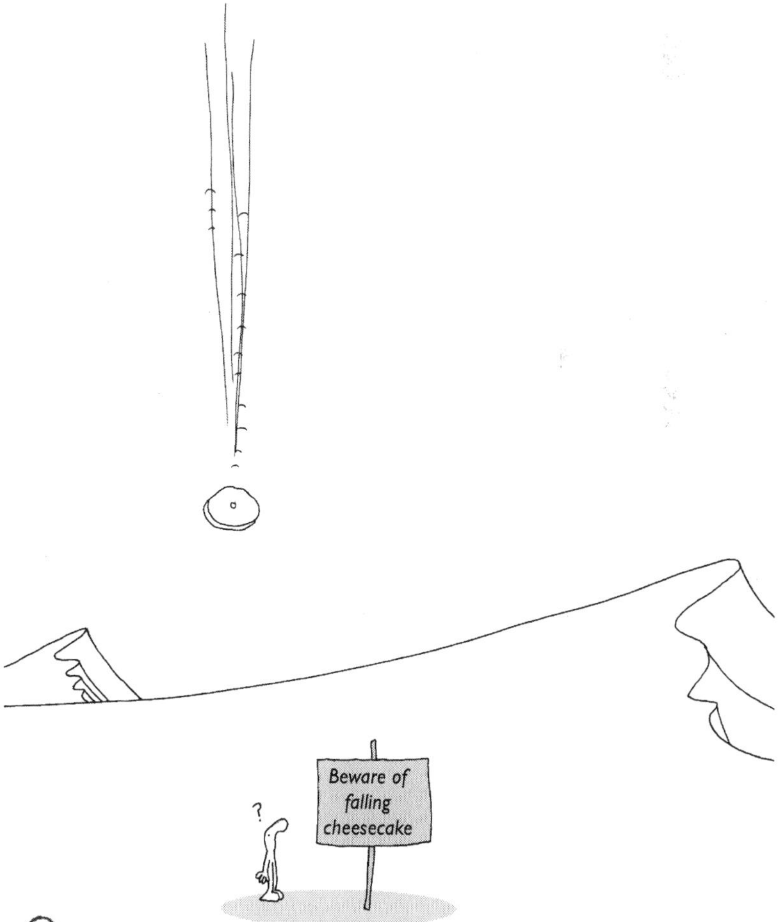
?
Beware of falling cheesecake

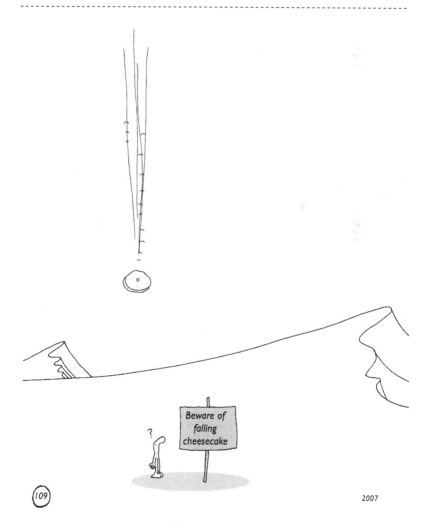

2007

Def. **NOVINOPHOBIA**
The fear of running out of wine.

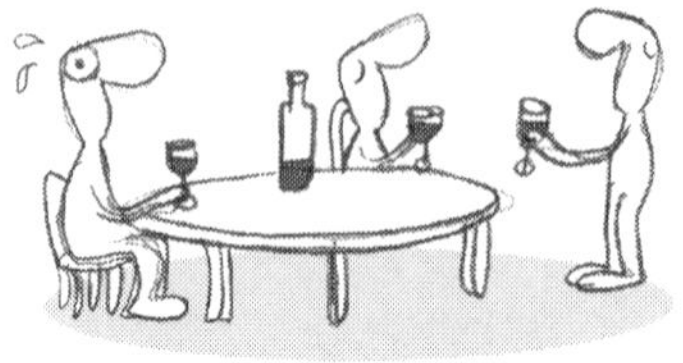

2014

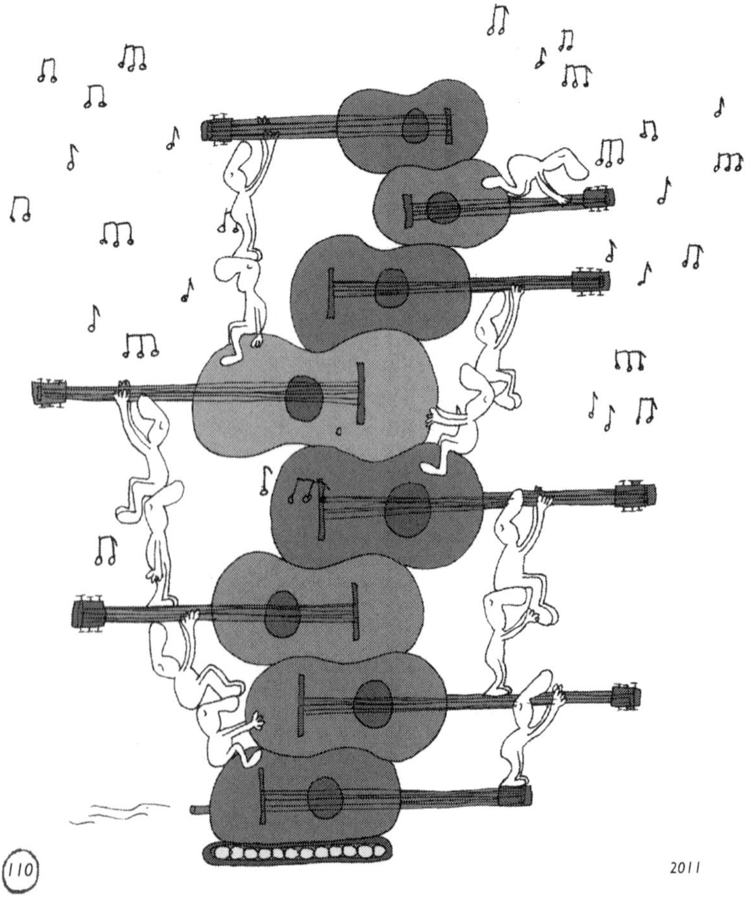

2011

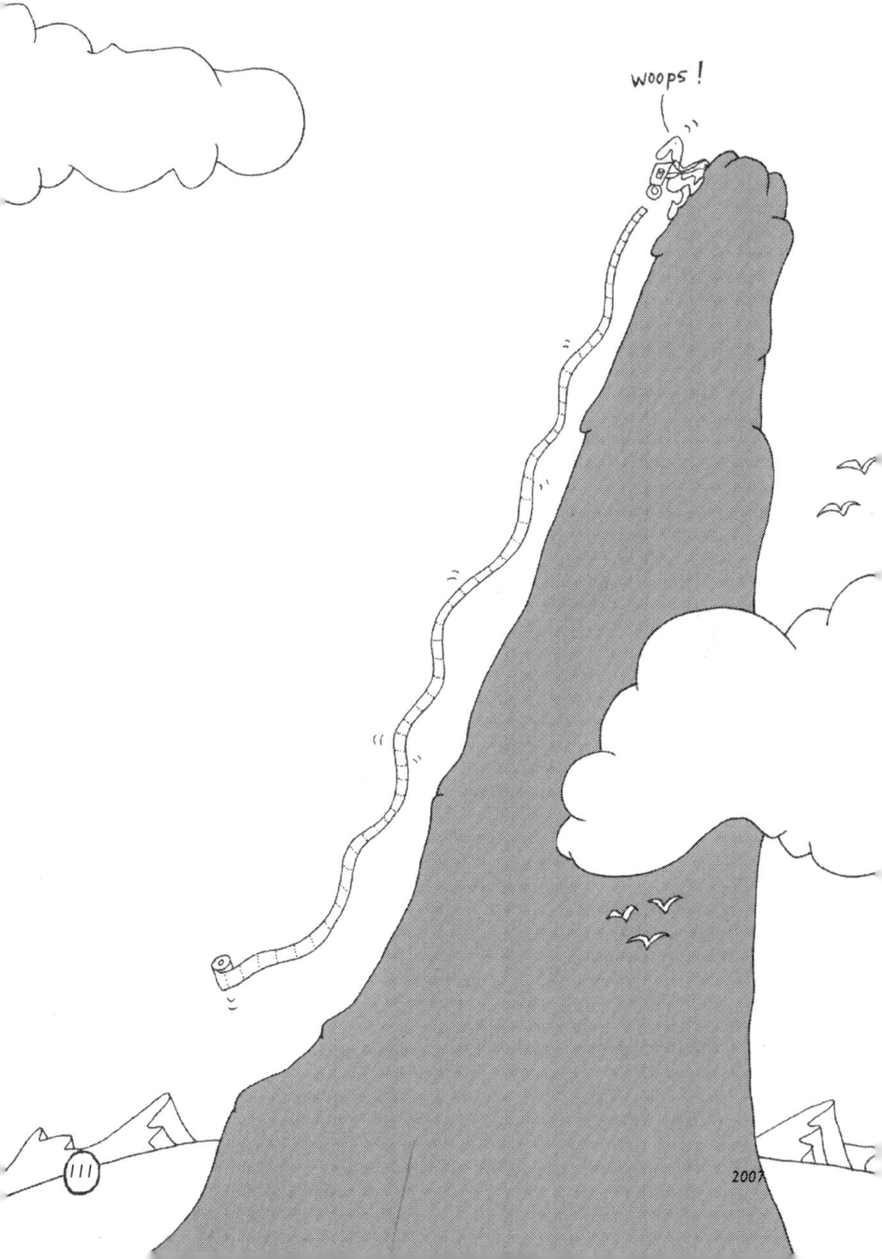
woops !
2007

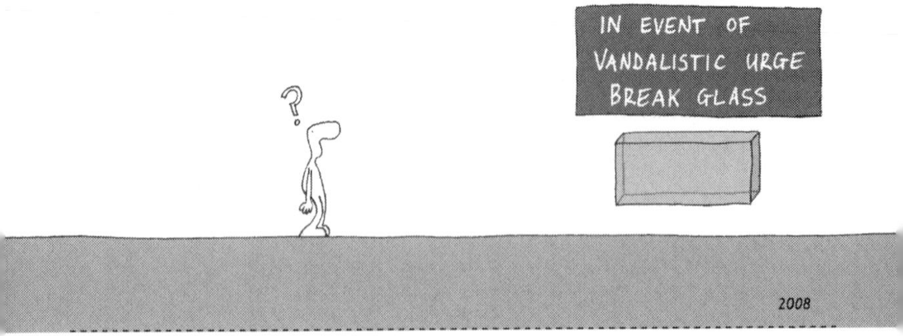
IN EVENT OF
VANDALISTIC URGE
BREAK GLASS

2008

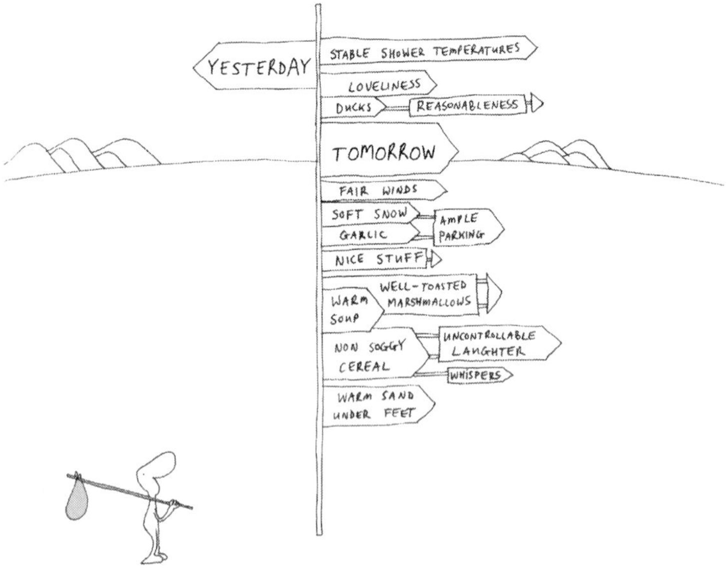
YESTERDAY
STABLE SHOWER TEMPERATURES
LOVELINESS
DUCKS
REASONABLENESS
TOMORROW
FAIR WINDS
SOFT SNOW
GARLIC
AMPLE PARKING
NICE STUFF
WARM SOUP
WELL-TOASTED MARSHMALLOWS
NON SOGGY CEREAL
UNCONTROLLABLE LAUGHTER
WHISPERS
WARM SAND UNDER FEET

2013

The wonderful
Seesaw-head

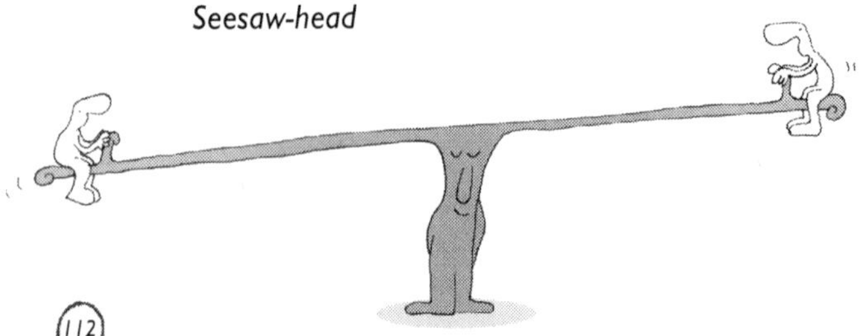

2004

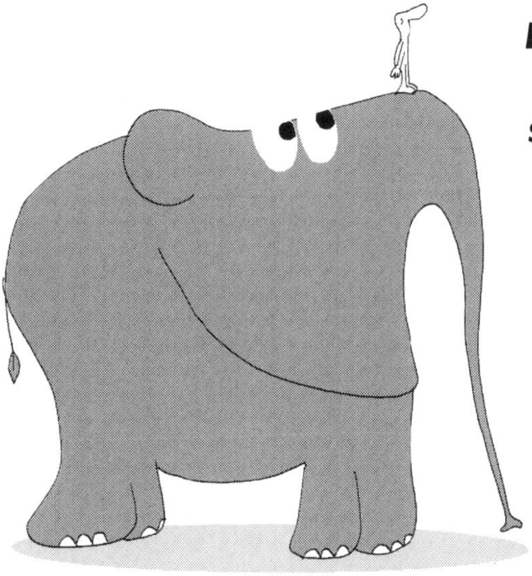

Life is good atop a smilephant

2012

"More grows in the garden than the gardener knows he has sown"

Spanish Proverb

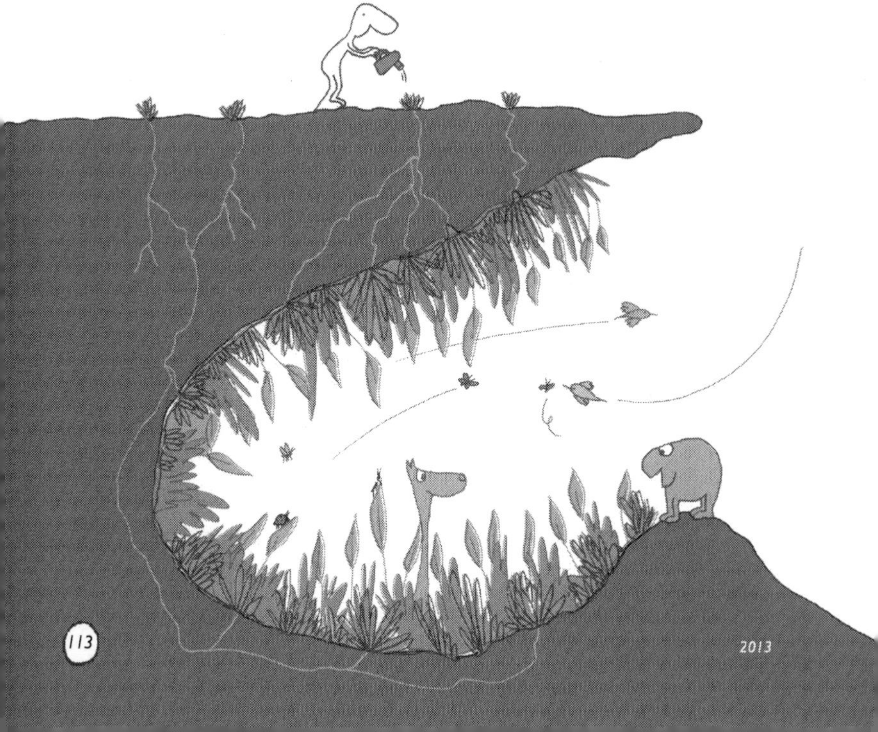

2013

"Do not be satisfied with stories that came before you...

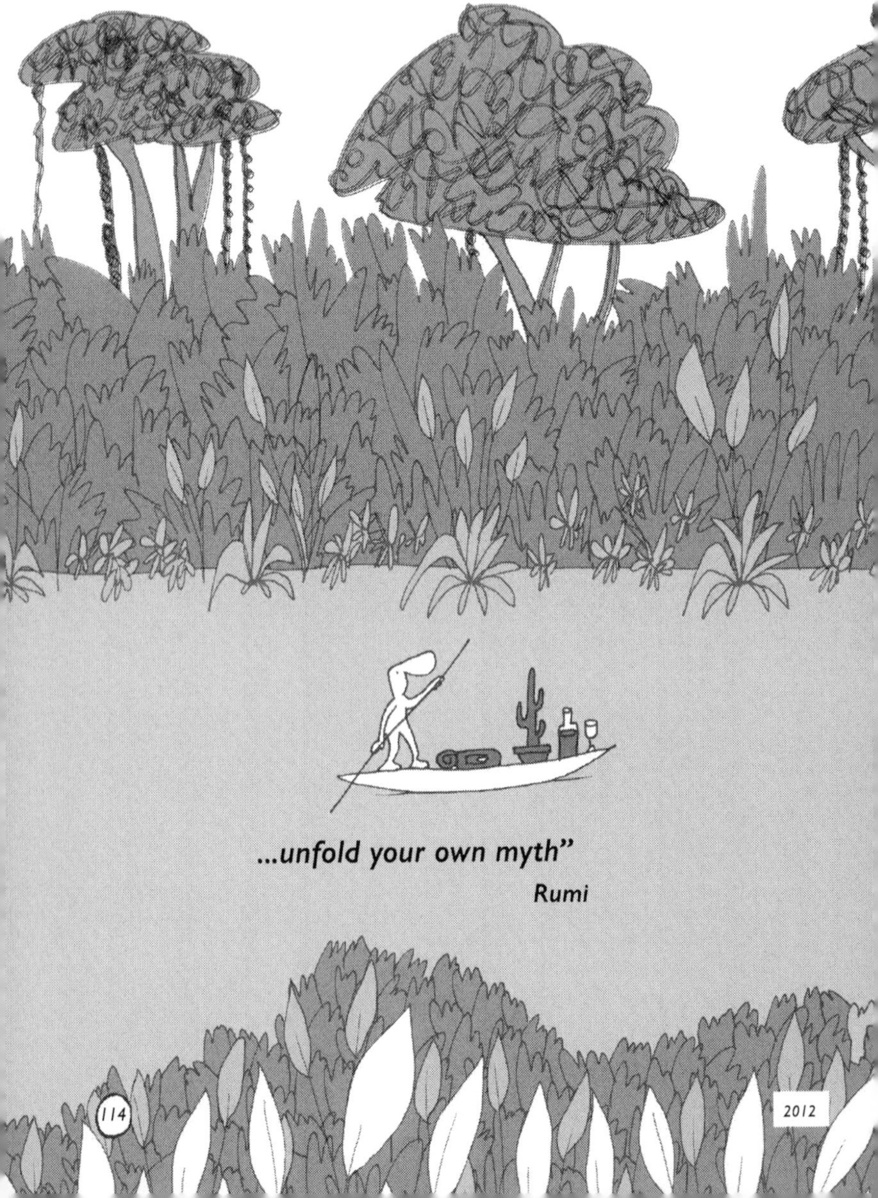

...unfold your own myth"

Rumi

How to Deal with Stress

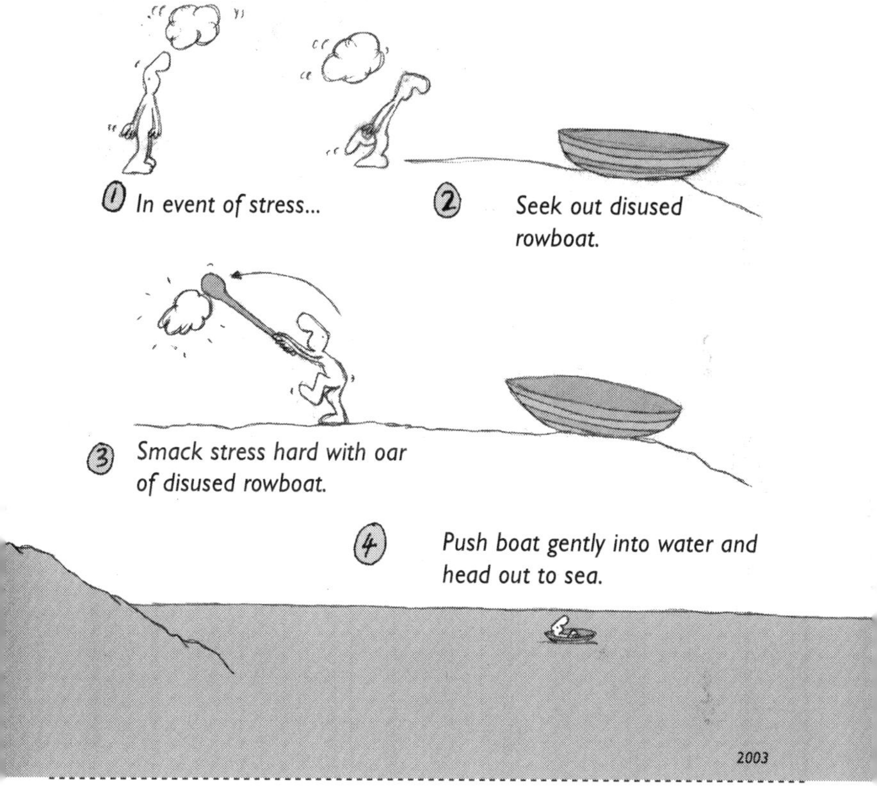

1 In event of stress...
2 Seek out disused rowboat.
3 Smack stress hard with oar of disused rowboat.
4 Push boat gently into water and head out to sea.
2003

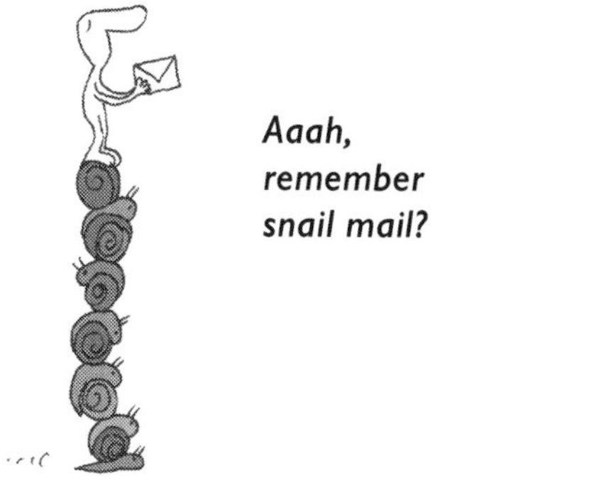

Aaah, remember snail mail?

2012

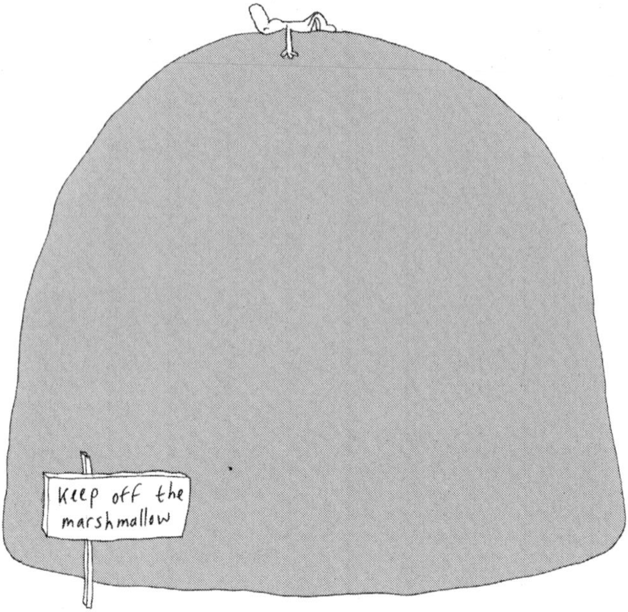
Keep off the marshmallow

2012

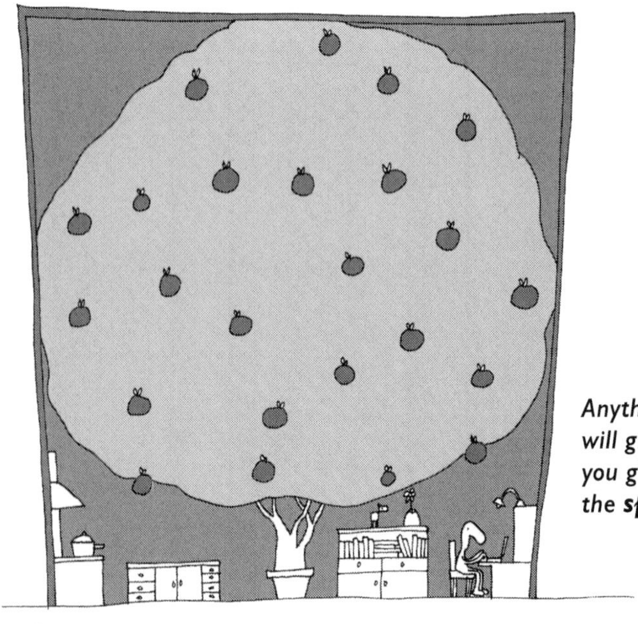

Anything will grow if you give it the ***space***

2008

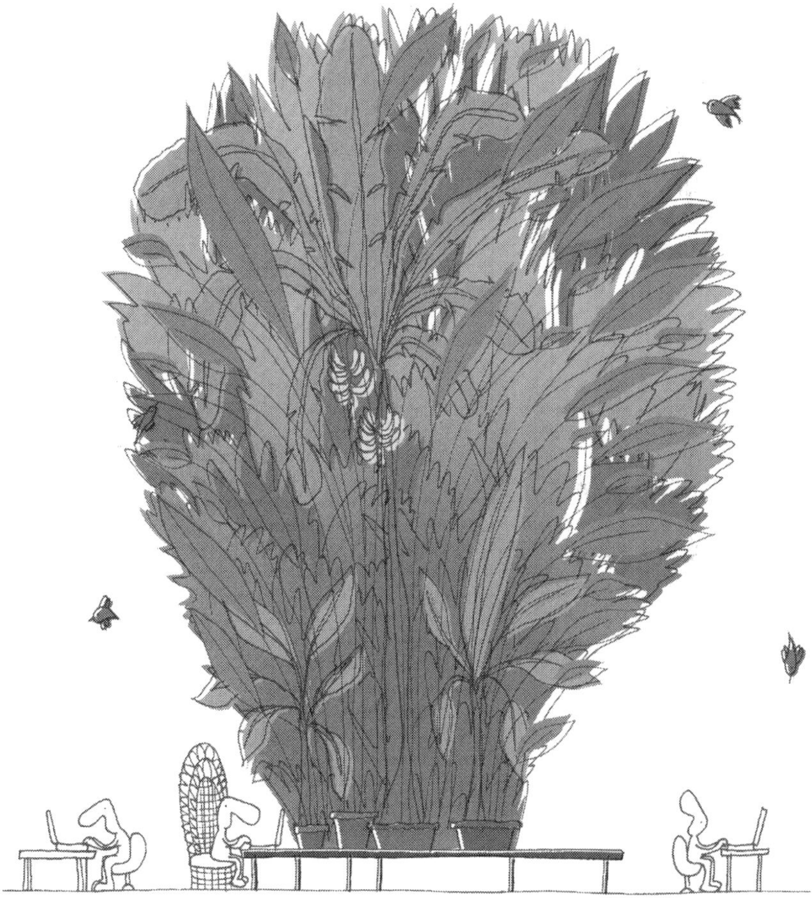

2012

The Evolution of the Computer

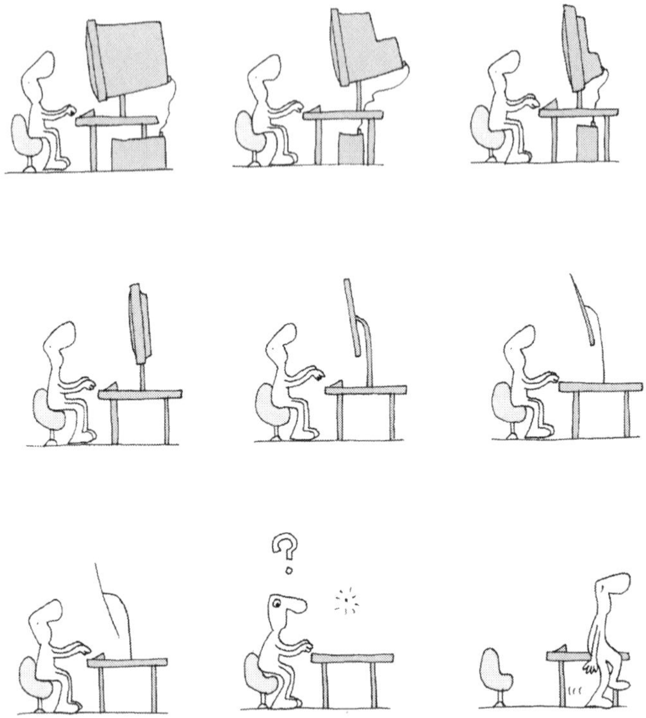

ALSO AN ANIMATION! **www.lastlemon.com/harolds-planet/animations** 2009

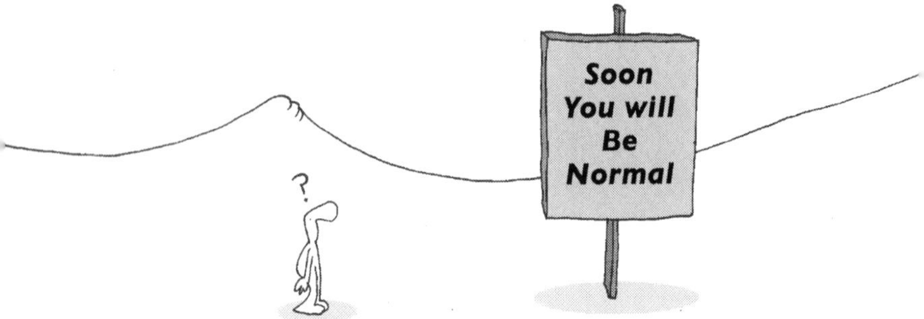
Soon You will Be Normal

2008

The fly who loved me

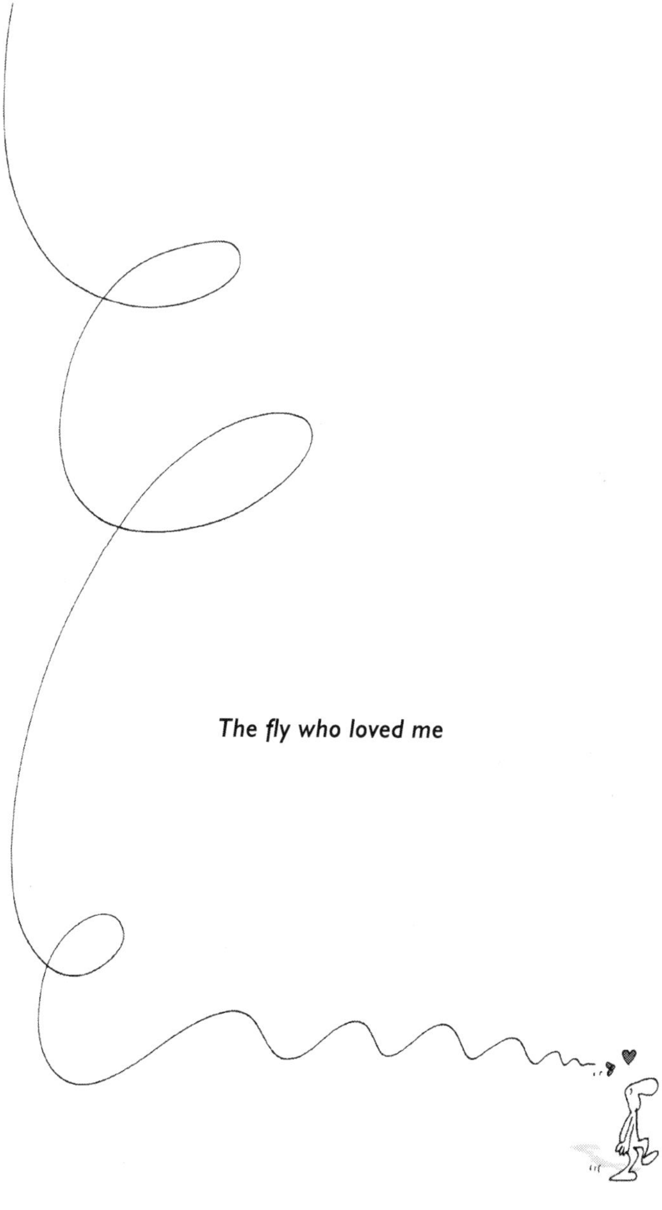

2009

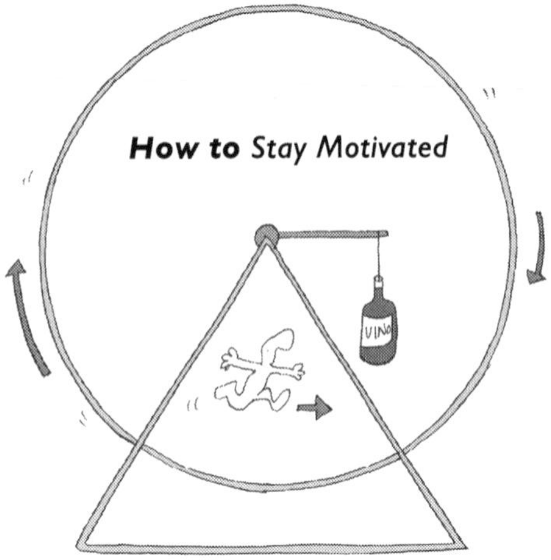
How to Stay Motivated
VINO

2013

TOILET LID ETIQUETTE

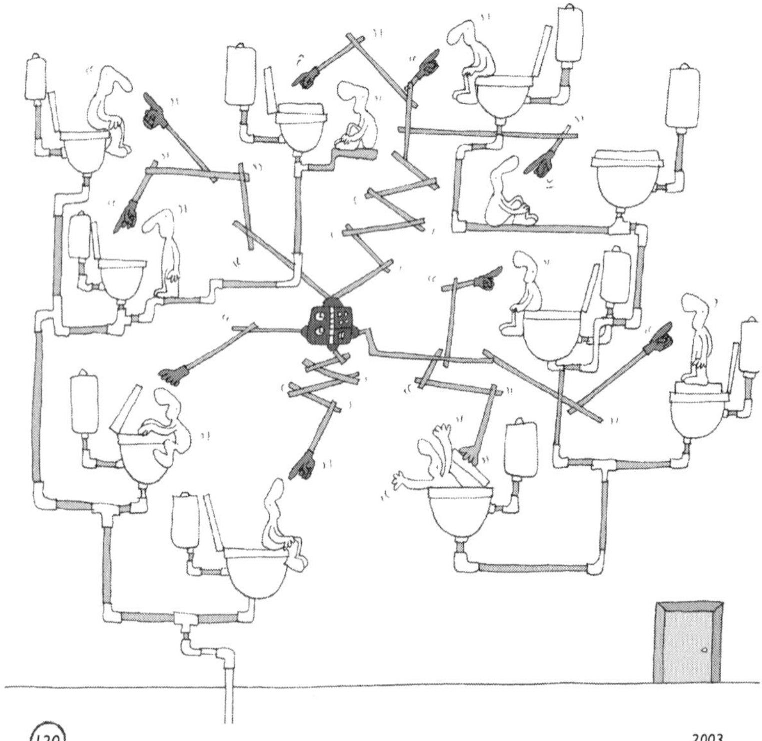

2003

Def. **AARDPHOBIA**

The fear of being followed by an aardvark

2014

What really goes on in a man's shed...

2011

**Fortune
favours
the brave**

2012

How to *Appreciate Wine*

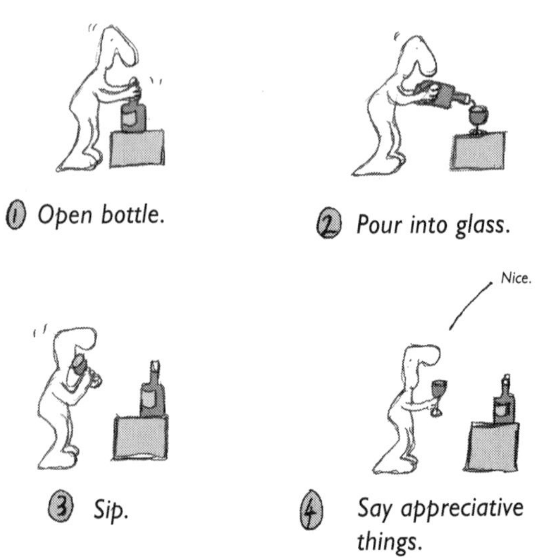

① *Open bottle.*

② *Pour into glass.*

③ *Sip.*

Nice.

④ *Say appreciative
things.*

2003

An origami-ish kind of day

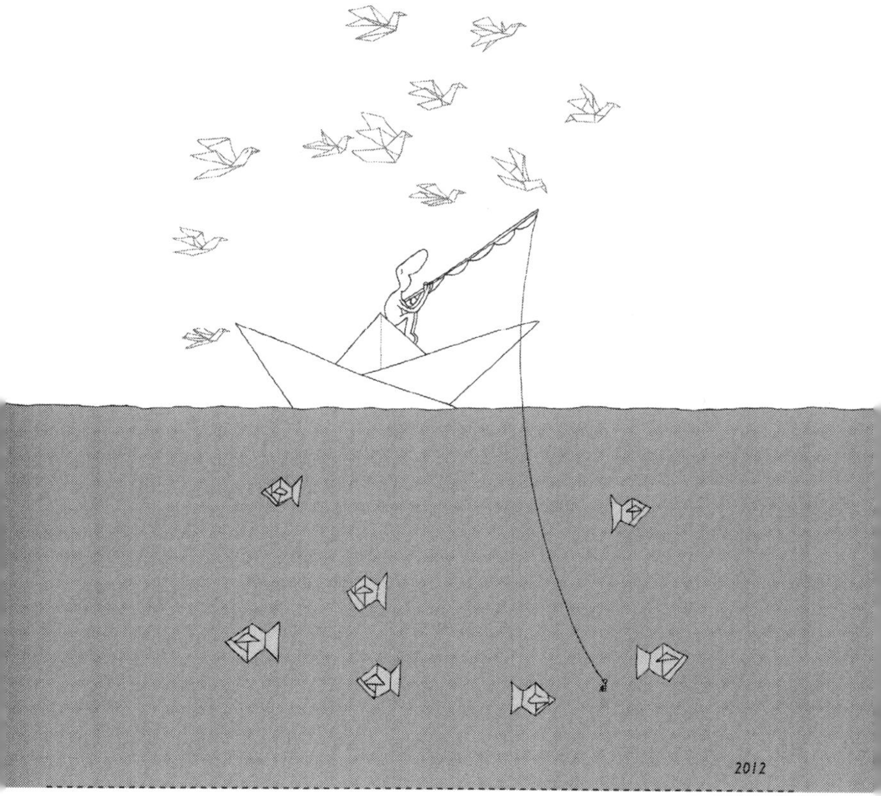
2012

Def. **APOSTROPHOBIA**

The fear of incorrectly positioned apostrophe's

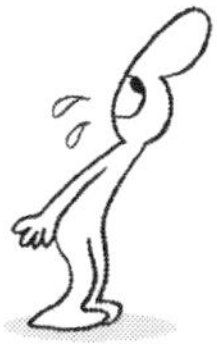

2014

TRAVELING CACTUS SALESMEN

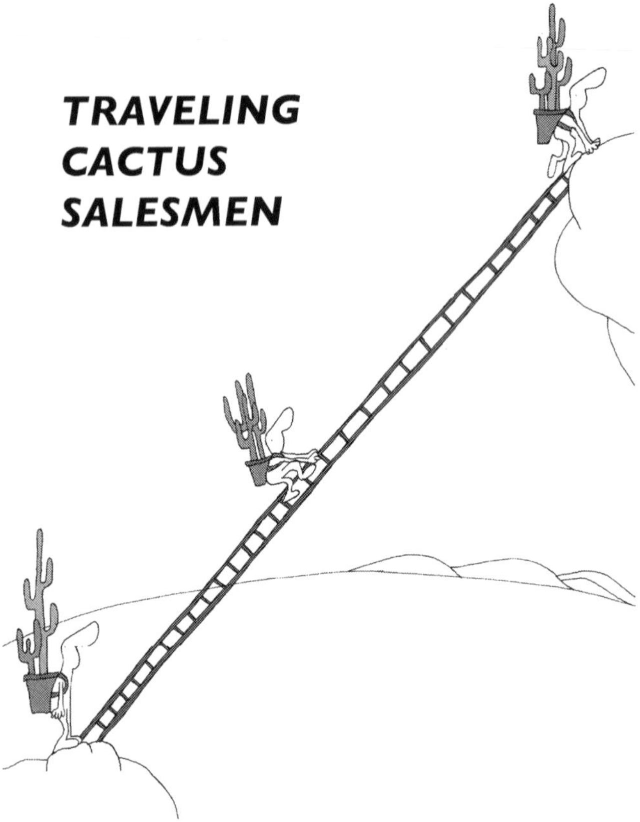

2011

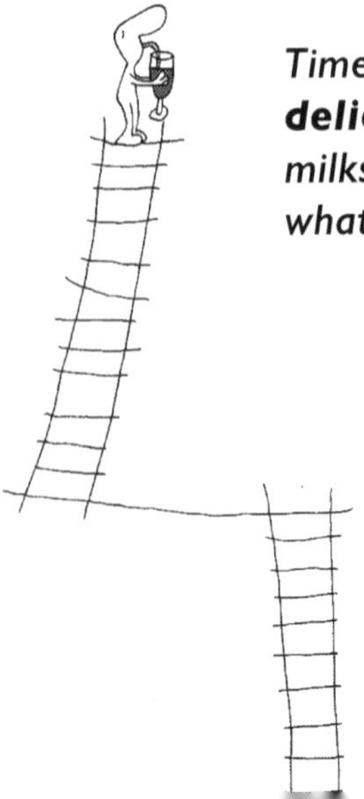

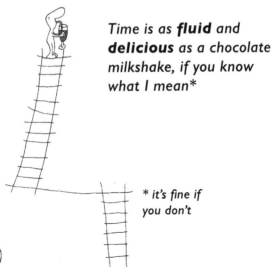

*Time is as **fluid** and **delicious** as a chocolate milkshake, if you know what I mean**

** it's fine if you don't*

2012

If I could float like a duck I'd...

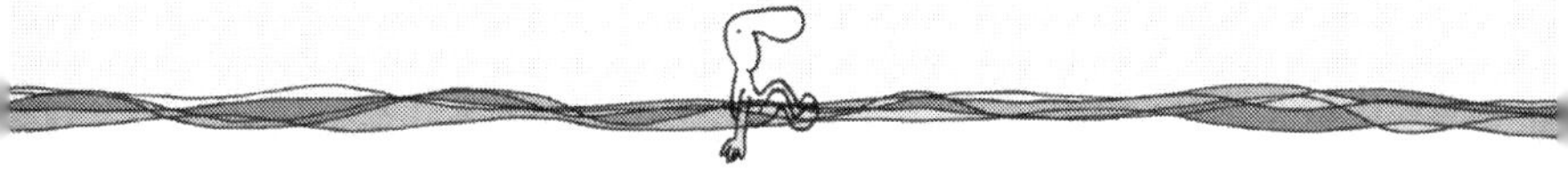

...float like a duck.

2012

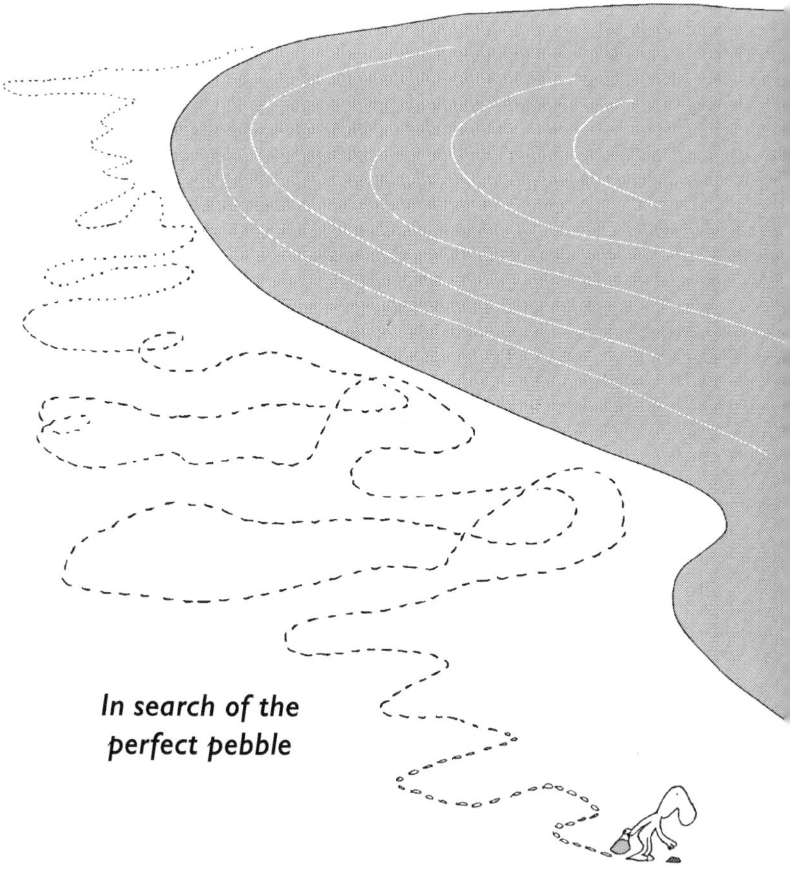

In search of the perfect pebble

2012

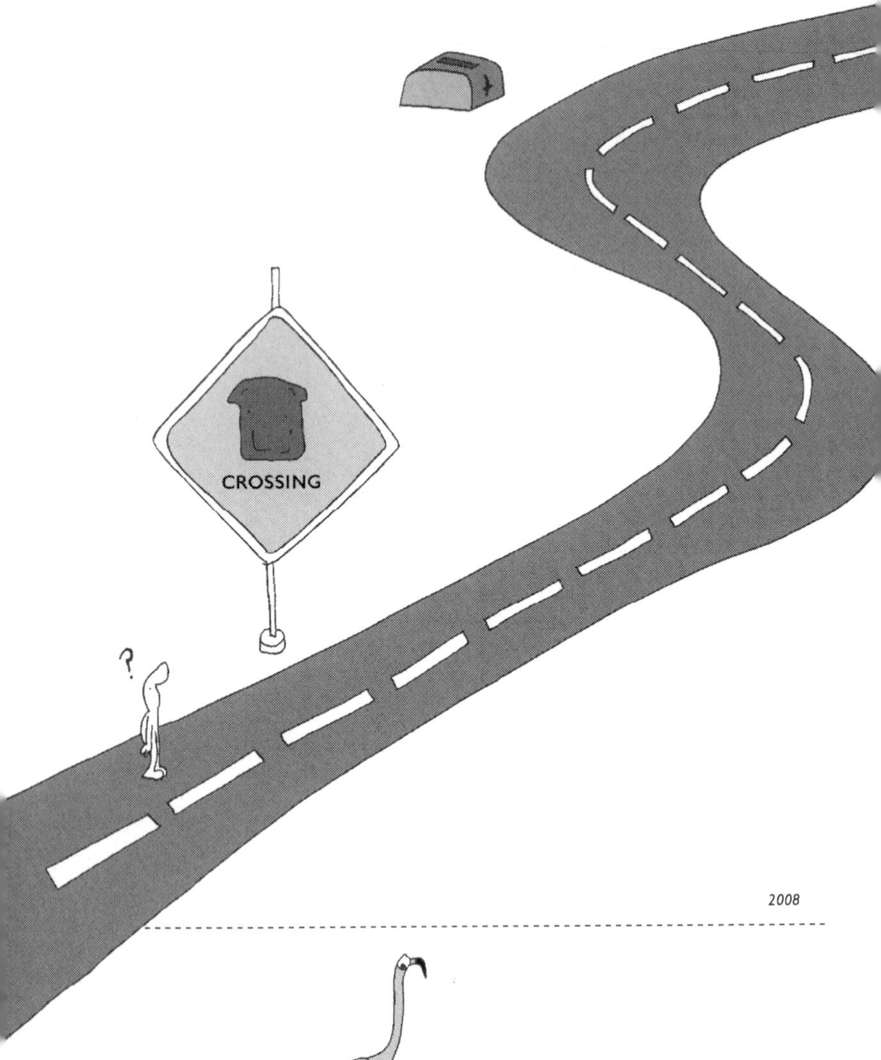
?
CROSSING

2008

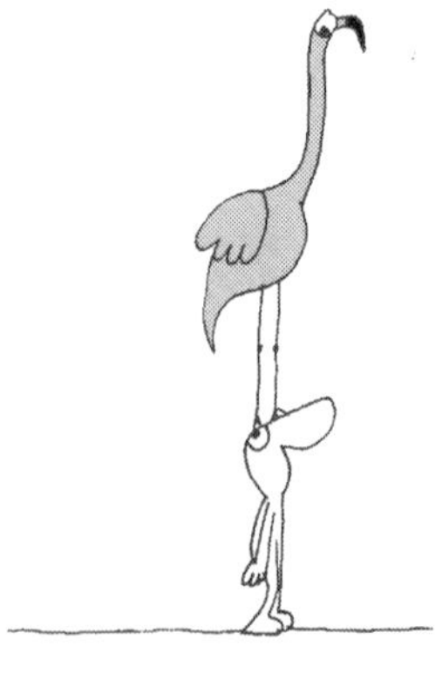

A flamingoish sort of day

2012

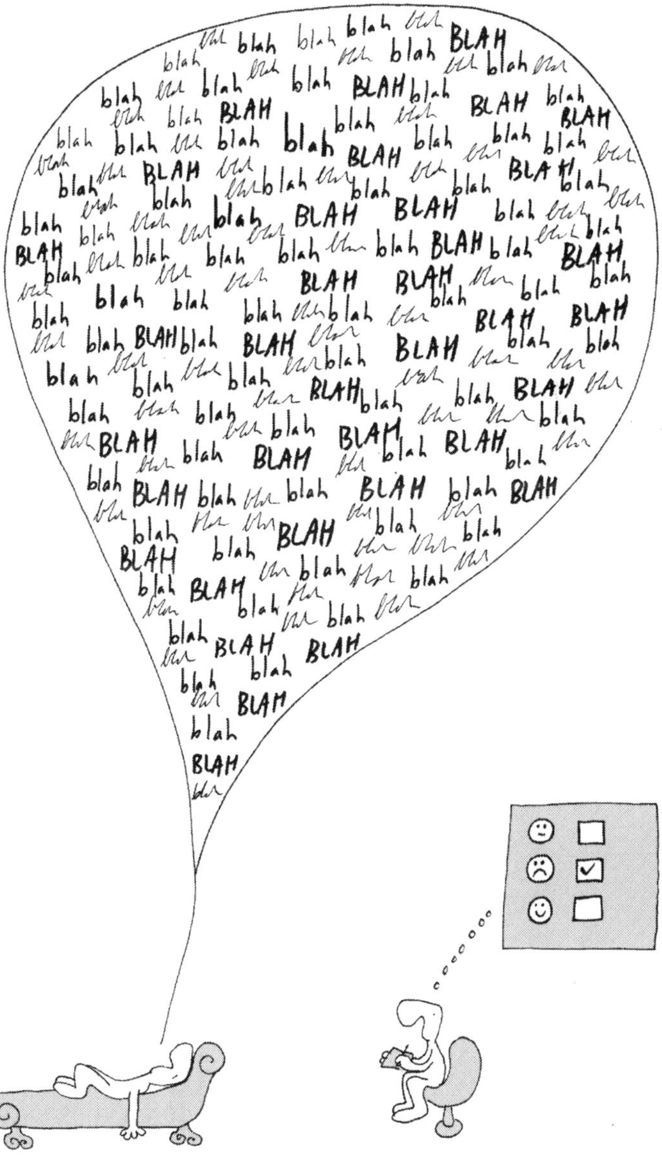
blah blah blah BLAH
blah blah BLAH blah BLAH blah
blah BLAH blah blah BLAH
blah blah blah blah BLAH blah blah
blah BLAH blah blah BLAH blah
blah blah blah BLAH BLAH blah
BLAH blah blah blah blah BLAH blah BLAH
blah BLAH BLAH blah blah
blah blah blah blah BLAH BLAH
blah BLAH blah BLAH blah BLAH blah blah
blah blah blah blah BLAH blah blah BLAH
blah blah blah blah blah
BLAH blah BLAH BLAH blah BLAH blah
blah BLAH blah blah BLAH blah BLAH
blah BLAH blah blah
BLAH blah blah blah
blah BLAH blah blah
blah BLAH BLAH blah
blah BLAH
blah
BLAH

2007

How to Deal with Life

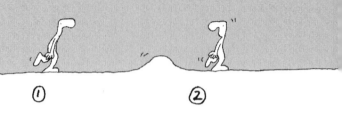

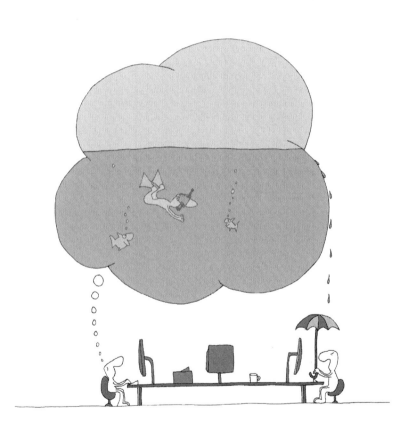

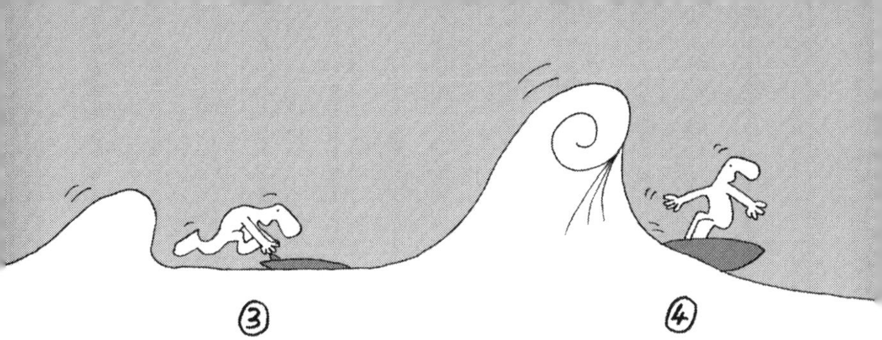
③
④

2003

Harold Headwear #4:
The Suburb Hat

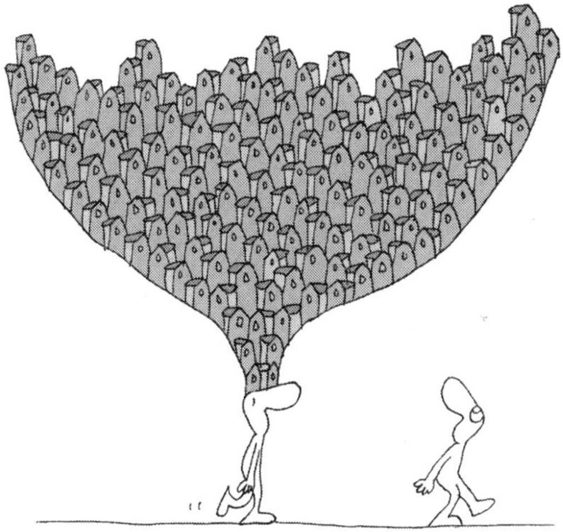

2011

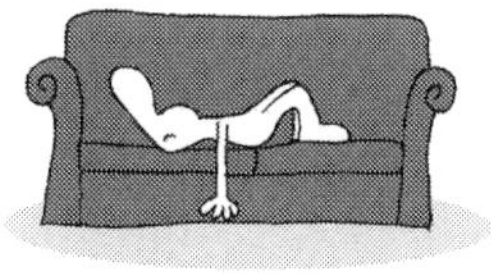

Some Mondays I like to work from home

2011

HOSPITAL
INPATIENTS
OUTPATIENTS
INSIDEOUT PATIENTS

2011

There were three main schools of thought

yes
no
epiglottis

2007

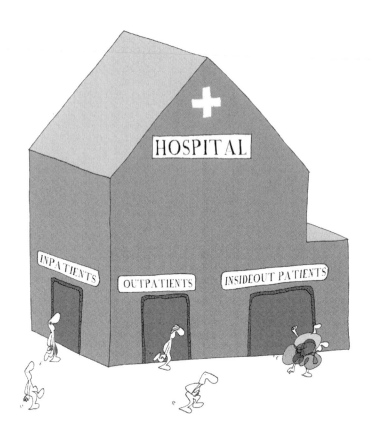

Automated Parenthood

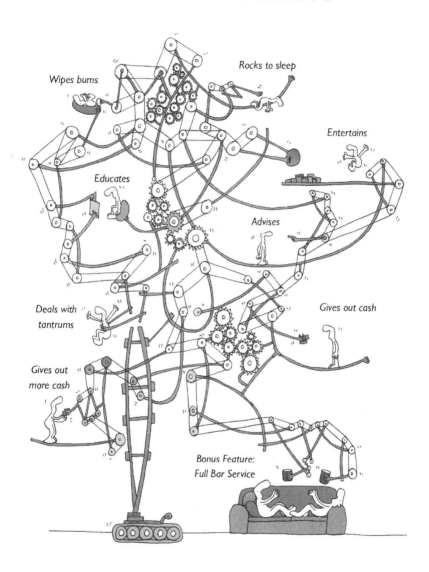

Wipes bums

Rocks to sleep

Entertains

Educates

Advises

Deals with
tantrums

Gives out cash

Gives out
more cash

Bonus Feature:
Full Bar Service

Def. NOPYROPHOBIA & NOMARSHIEPHOBIA

The fear of running out of firewood

The fear of running out of marshmallows

2014

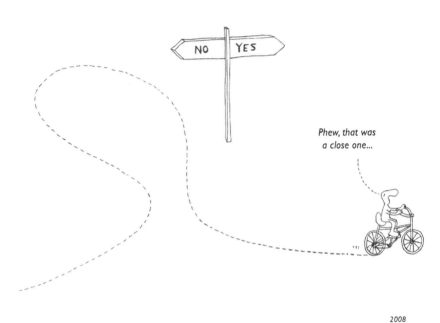

Phew, that was a close one...

2008

Generally I don't like to go anywhere without my ESPC*

* Emotional Support Pickled Cucumber

2018

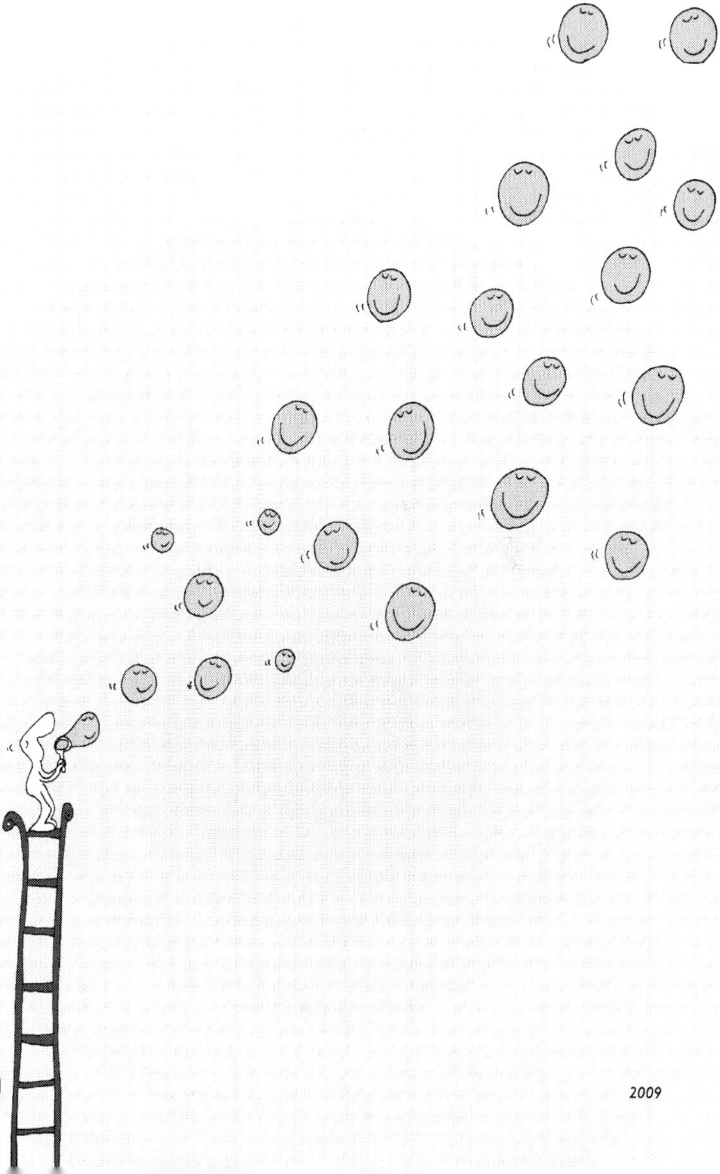

2009

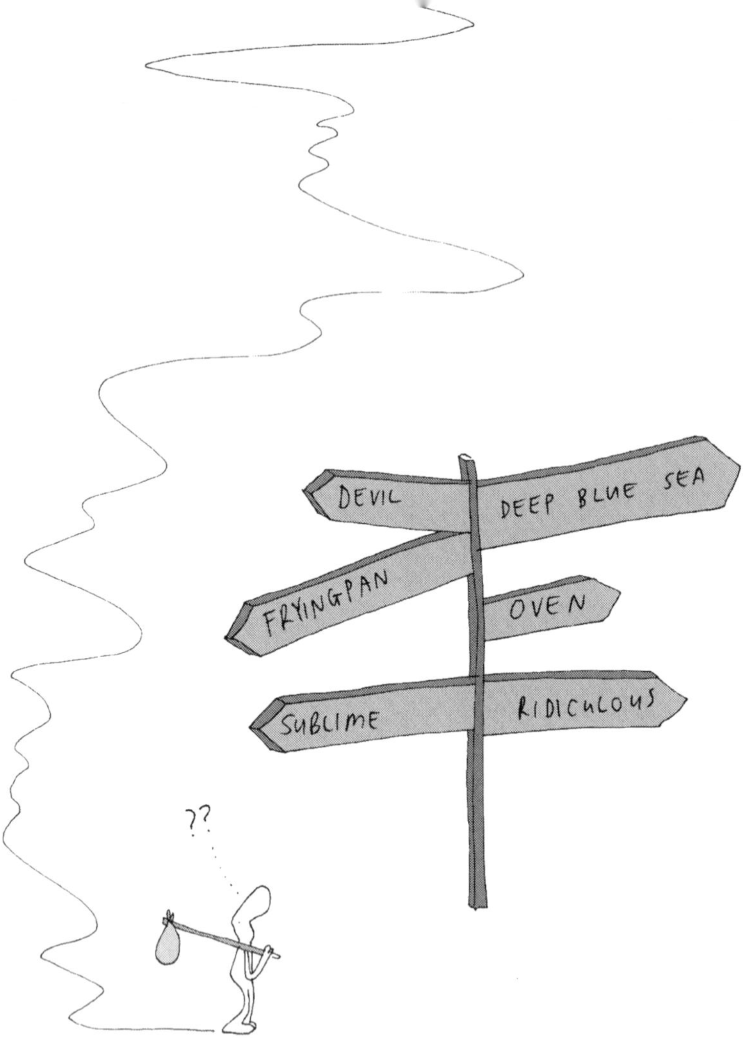
DEVIL
DEEP BLUE SEA
FRYINGPAN
OVEN
SUBLIME
RIDICULOUS
??

2009

Nothing quite as satisfying as going through paperwork

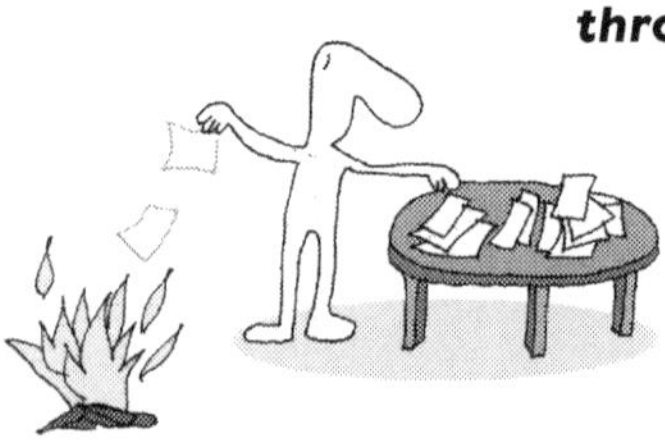

2012

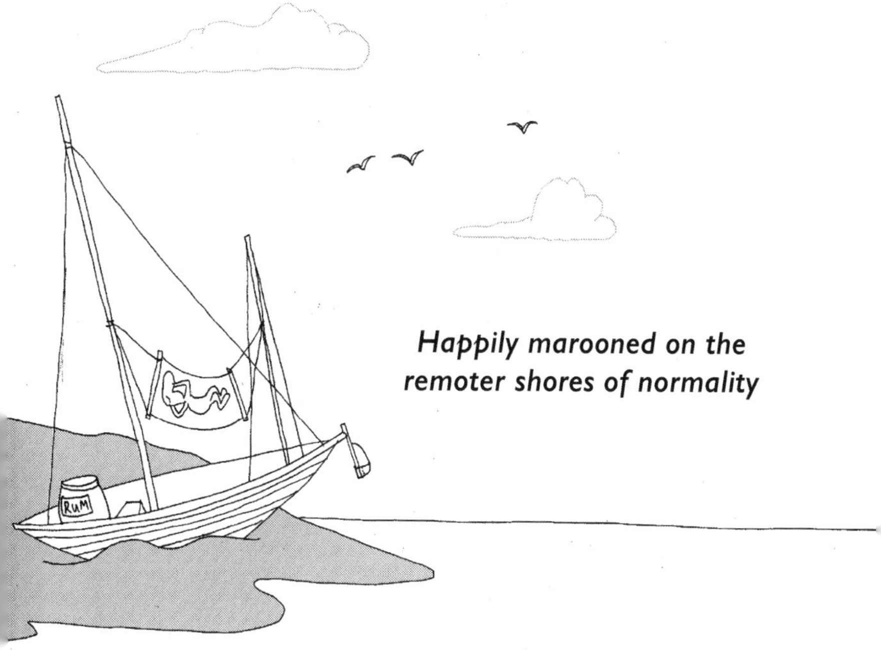
RUM

Happily marooned on the remoter shores of normality

2012

Everyone wants to change the world...

...but no-one wants to change the toilet roll...

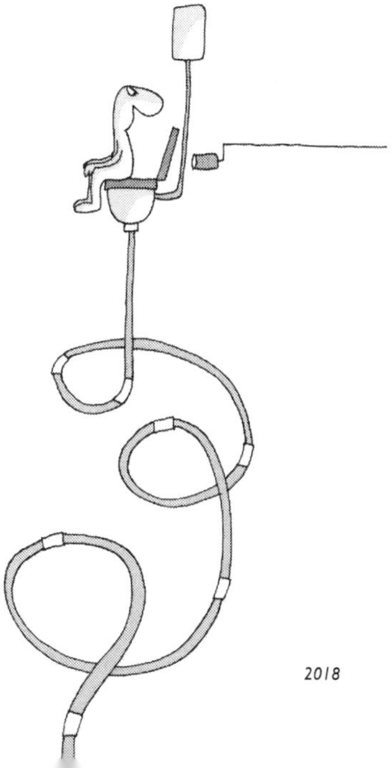

2018

"Wishing to be friends is quick work,
but friendship is a slow ripening fruit."

Aristotle

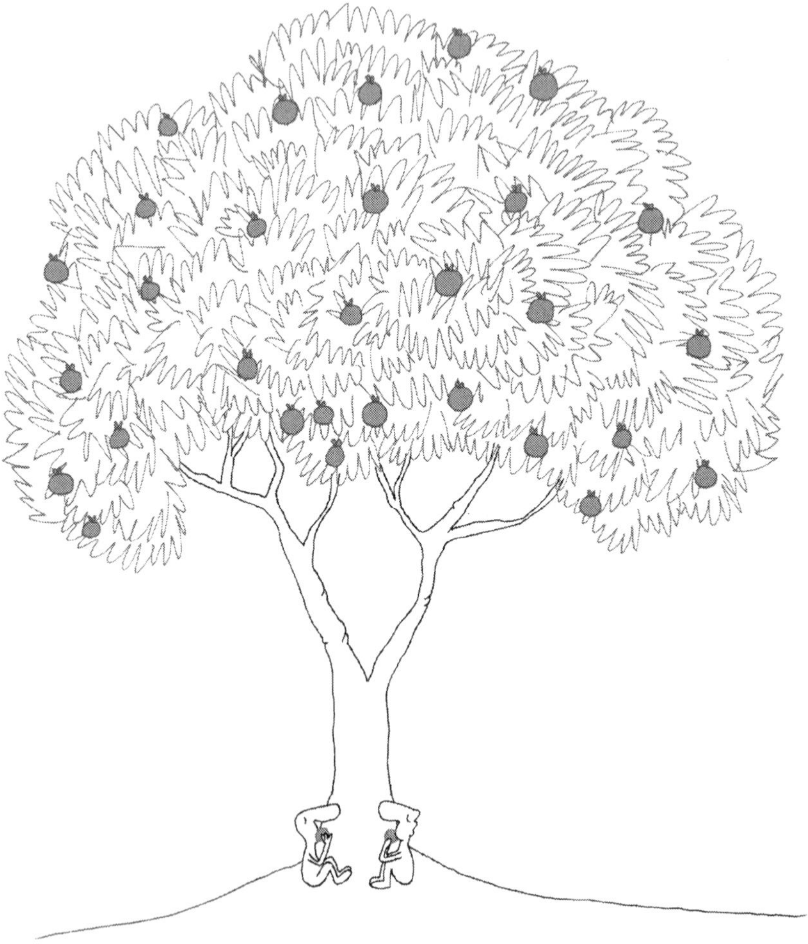

Simple Pleasures #7

THE SMELL OF A NEW BOOK

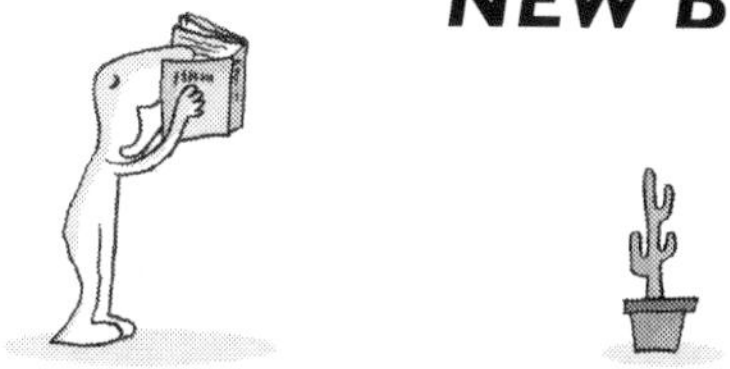

2016

An Elephantish
kind of day

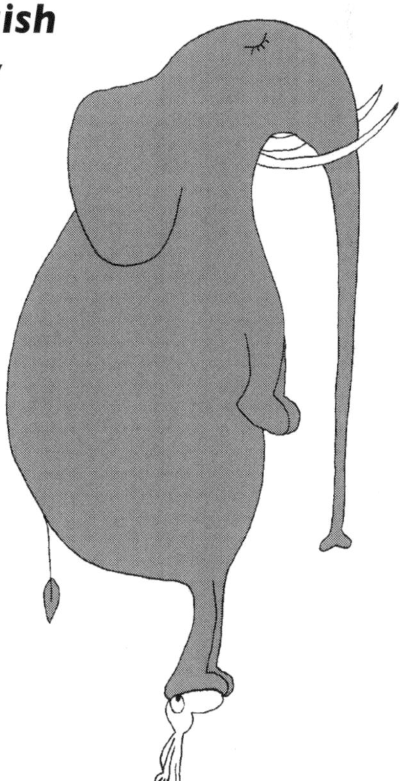

2012

*Just taking my life out
for a quick walk*

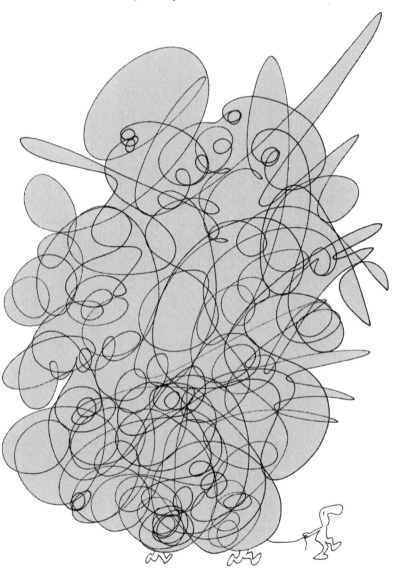

You know what I love?

Not having to do anything or go anywhere...

2013

How to Catch Toast

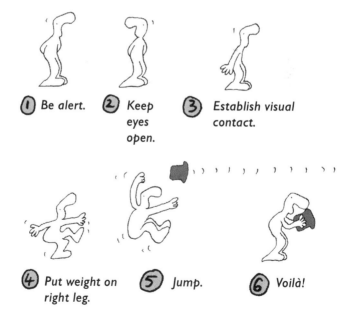

① Be alert. ② Keep eyes open. ③ Establish visual contact.

④ Put weight on right leg. ⑤ Jump. ⑥ Voilà!

2003

Men on rocks,
holding grudges

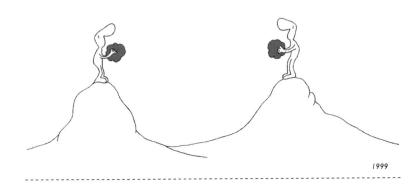

1999

High hopes for the
British Synchronised Peeing Team

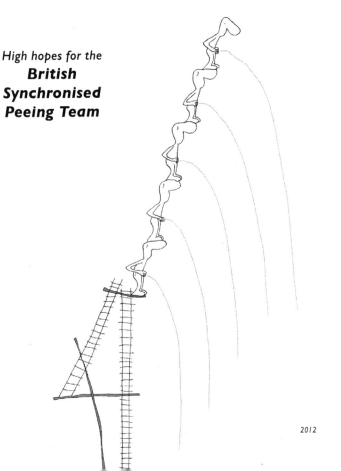

2012

How to Properly Load a Dishwasher

1. Glasses first...
2. then mugs...
3. ...cutlery...
4. ...crockery...
5. ...laundry...
6. ...husband.
7. Voila!

*You can always trust someone who has
brought a book along with them...*

2014

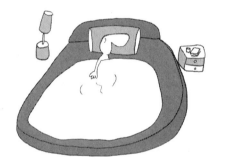

*Aaaah, the
afternoon nap.
Nothing quite
as civilised...*

2014

What Women Think About in the Bath

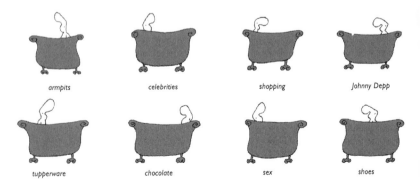

armpits   celebrities   shopping   Johnny Depp

tupperware   chocolate   sex   shoes

2003

Finally, a moment's peace.

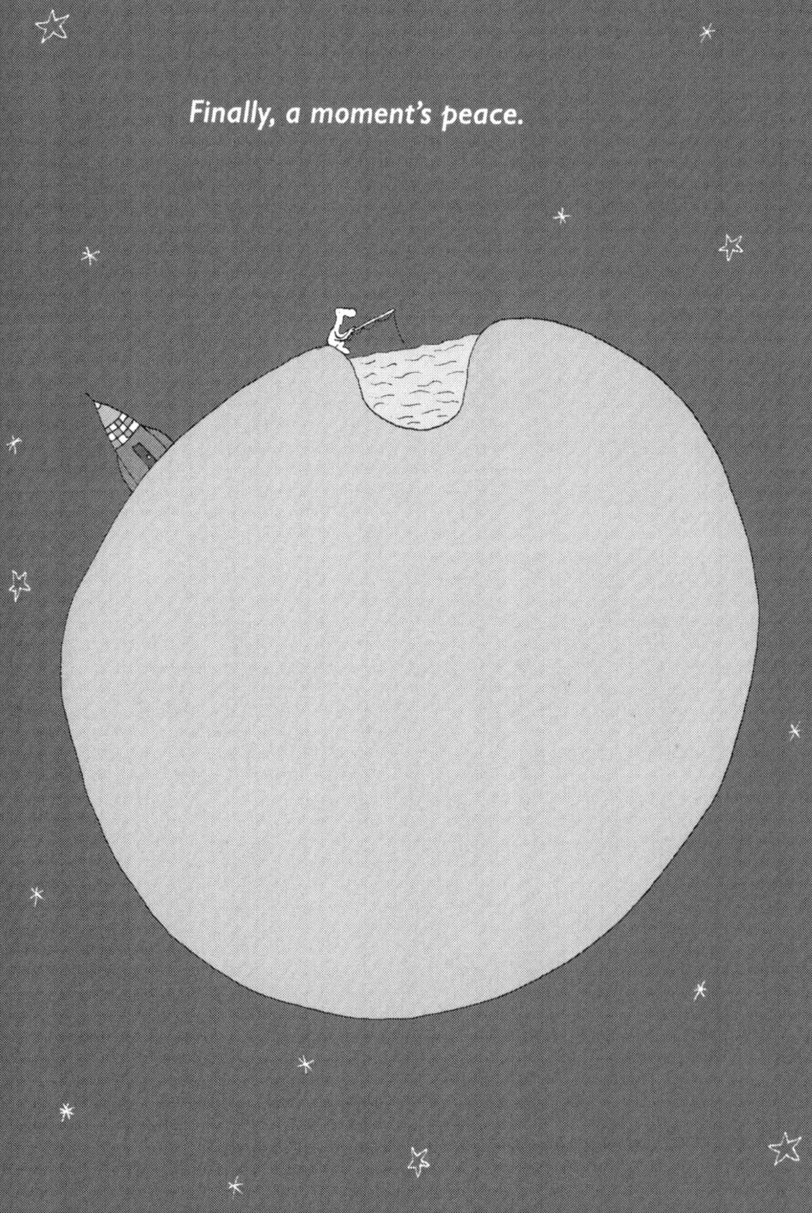

2009

Appreciate the *amazing* things in life...

Like the waves...

...and the spaces between them.

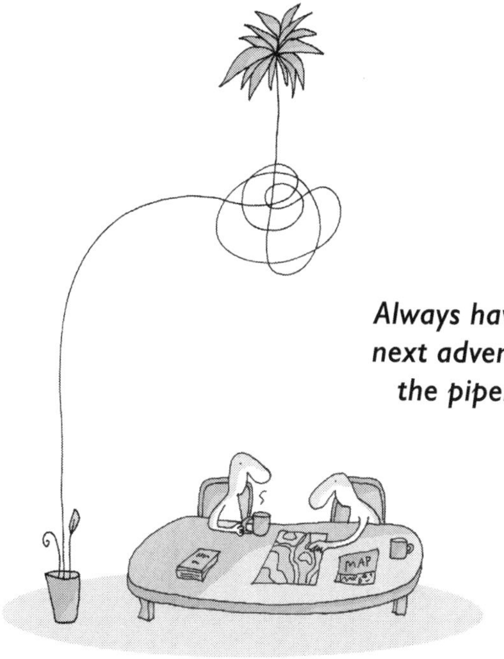
MAP

Always have your next adventure in the pipeline...

2018

Def. **HIPSTERPHOBIA**

Fear of hipsters & hipster accoutrements*

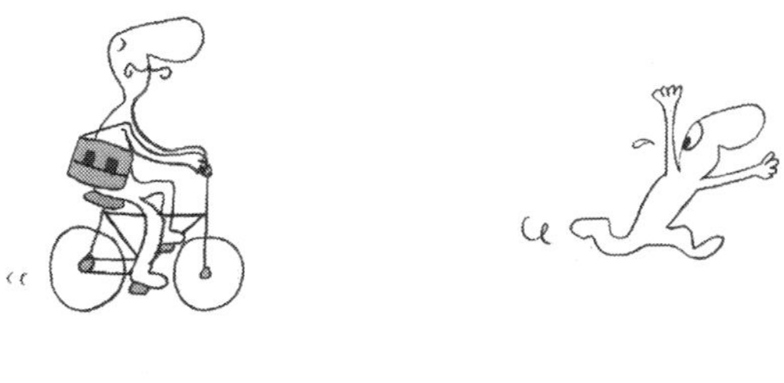

*Incl. messenger bags, bicycles without brakes, precious manscaping et al...

2014

There's nothing quite like
a hot cuppa
on a gloomy day

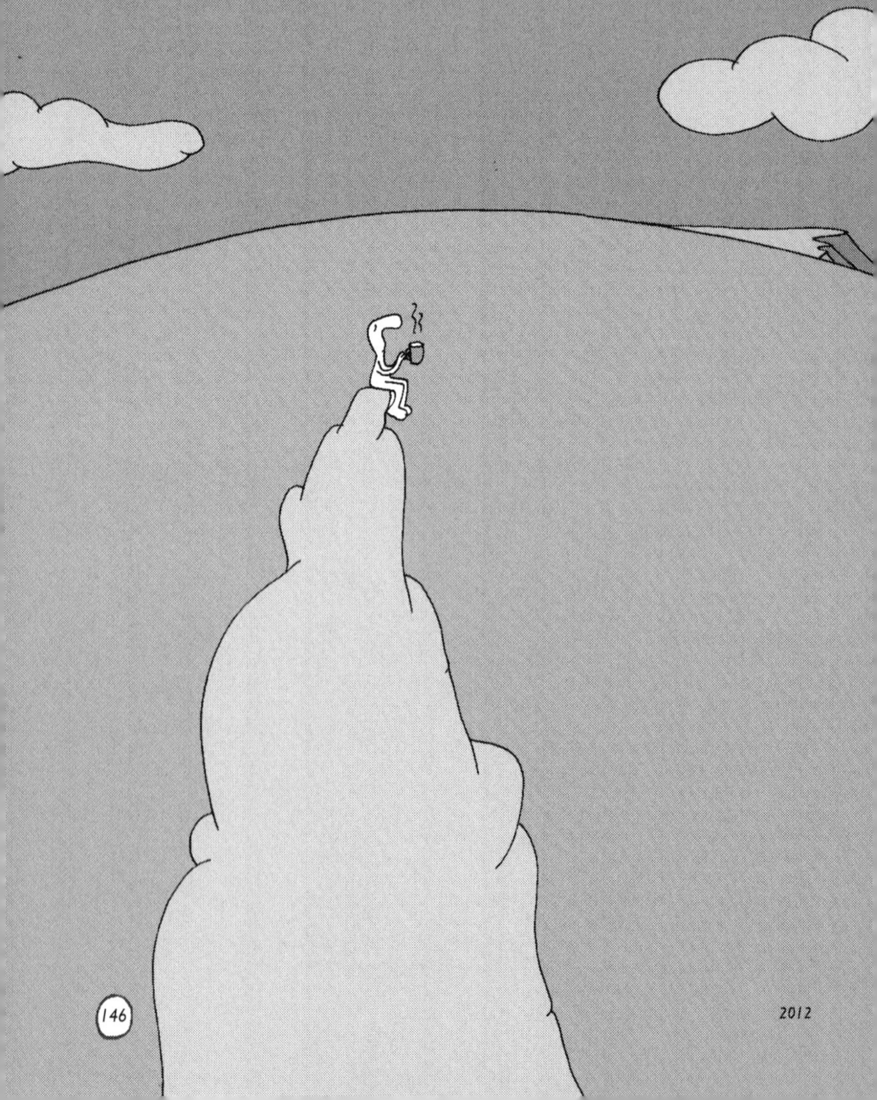

2012

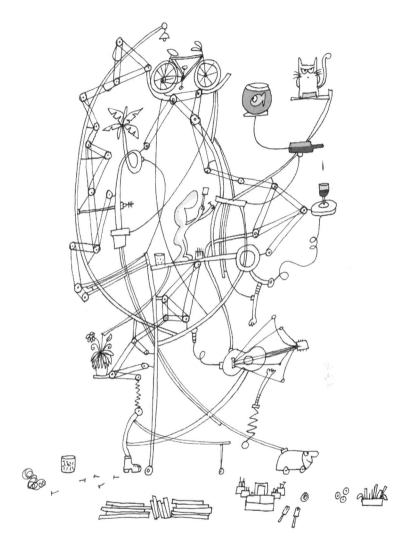

When you don't know quite what you're doing,

ANYTHING IS POSSIBLE

Welcome to
INSANITY

pop: 6.75bn

2011

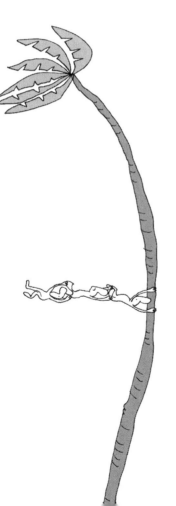

*Some days
are just
crazier
than others*

2012

Where the missing tupperware lids go

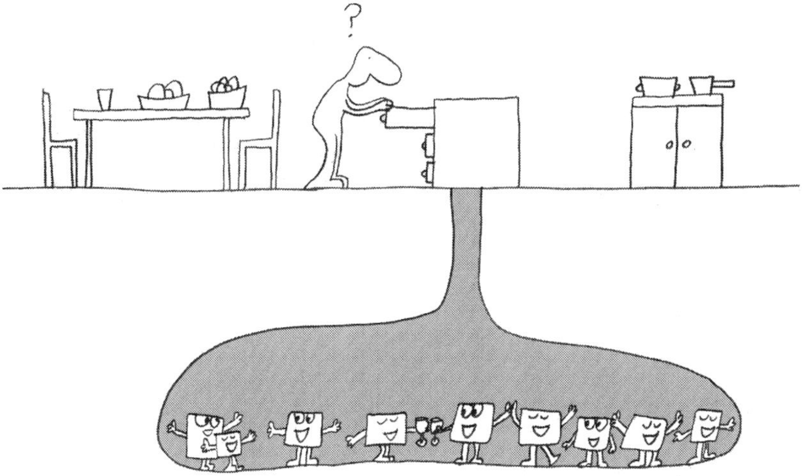
?

2014

Procrastination
is the only way forward

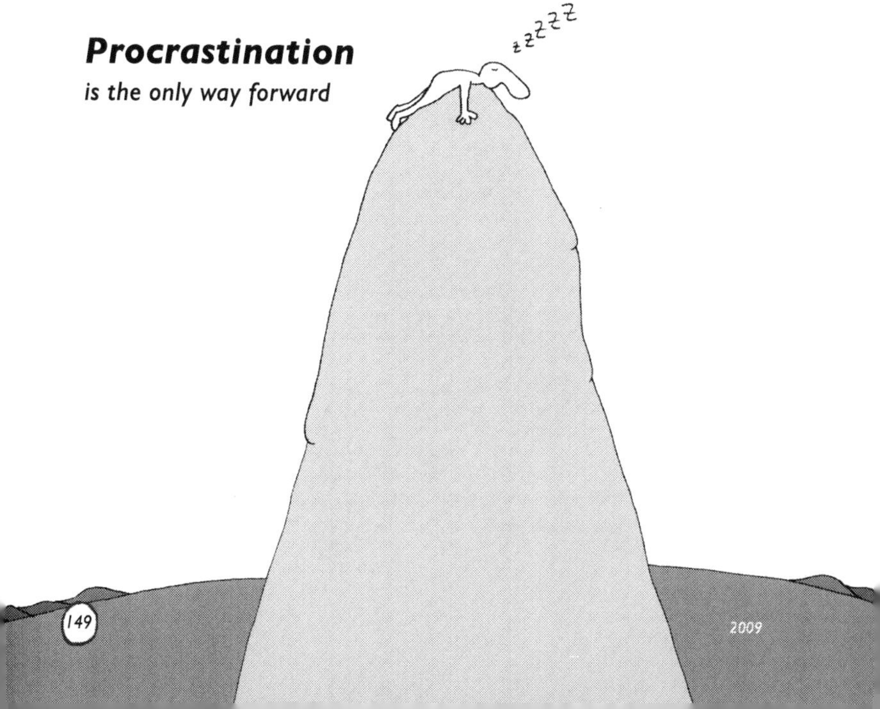
zzZZZ

2009

Pretend to not be nuts.

Everyone is doing it.

2013

Yoga for Book Lovers

2015

WHAT WE LOOK LIKE TO BATS

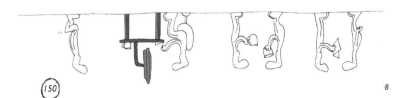

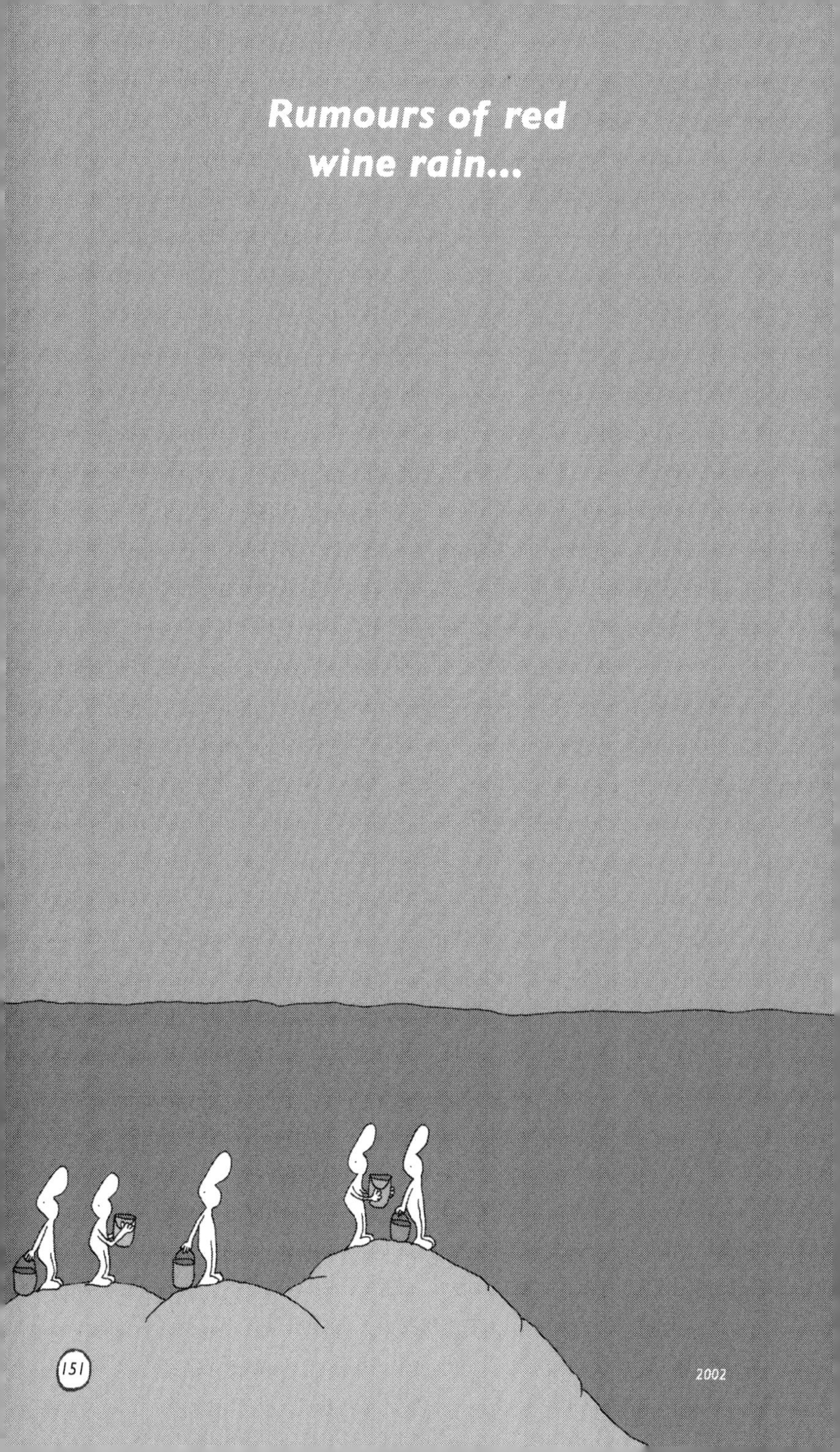
Rumours of red wine rain...
2002

Man vs Computer:
Possible Scenario

1990

2000

2002

2004

2006

2008

2010

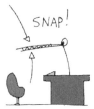

SNAP!

The Legendary Bogroll Aeronautics Team

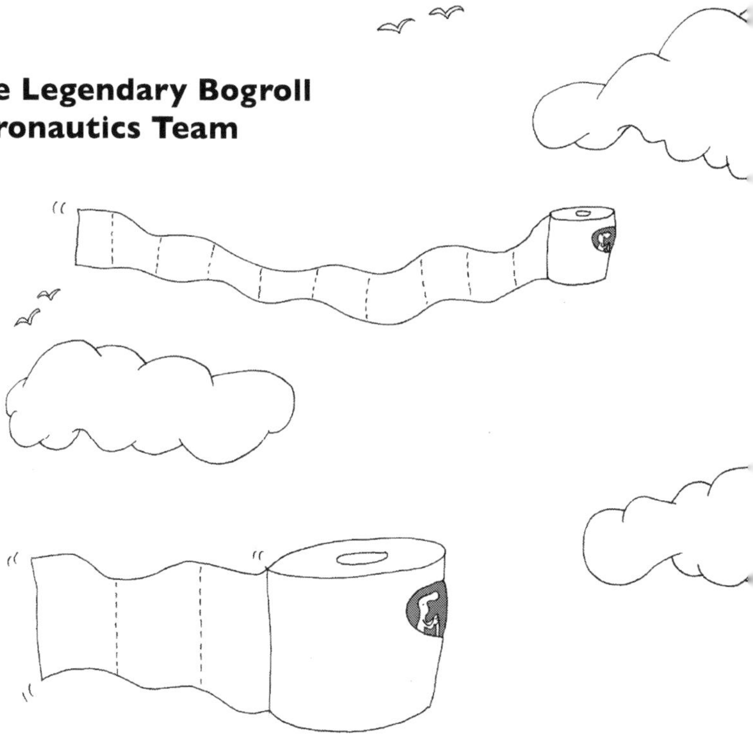

2008

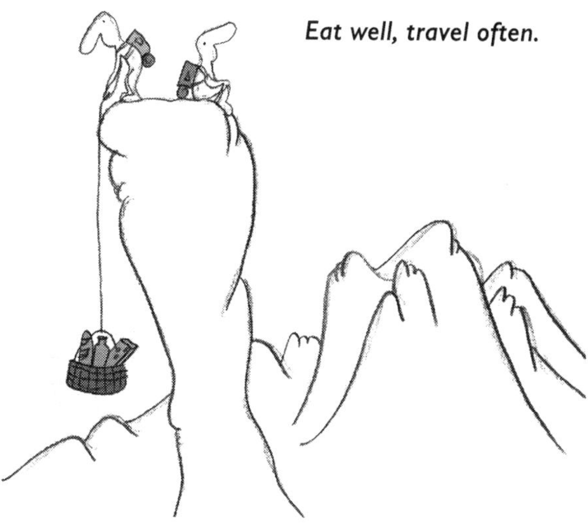

Eat well, travel often.

2013

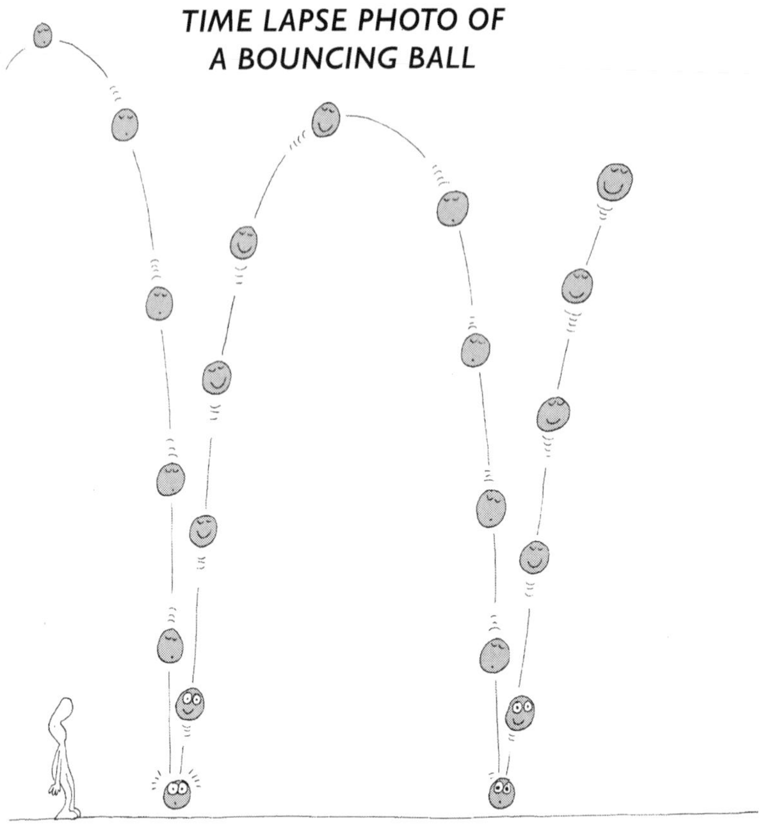
TIME LAPSE PHOTO OF
A BOUNCING BALL

2008

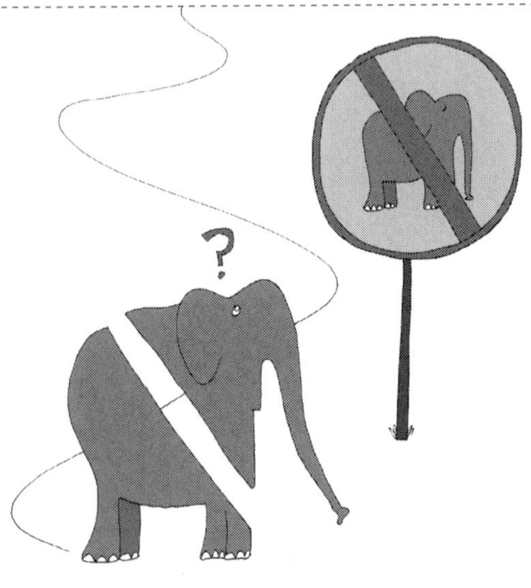
?

2010

Existential crisis nipped in the bud

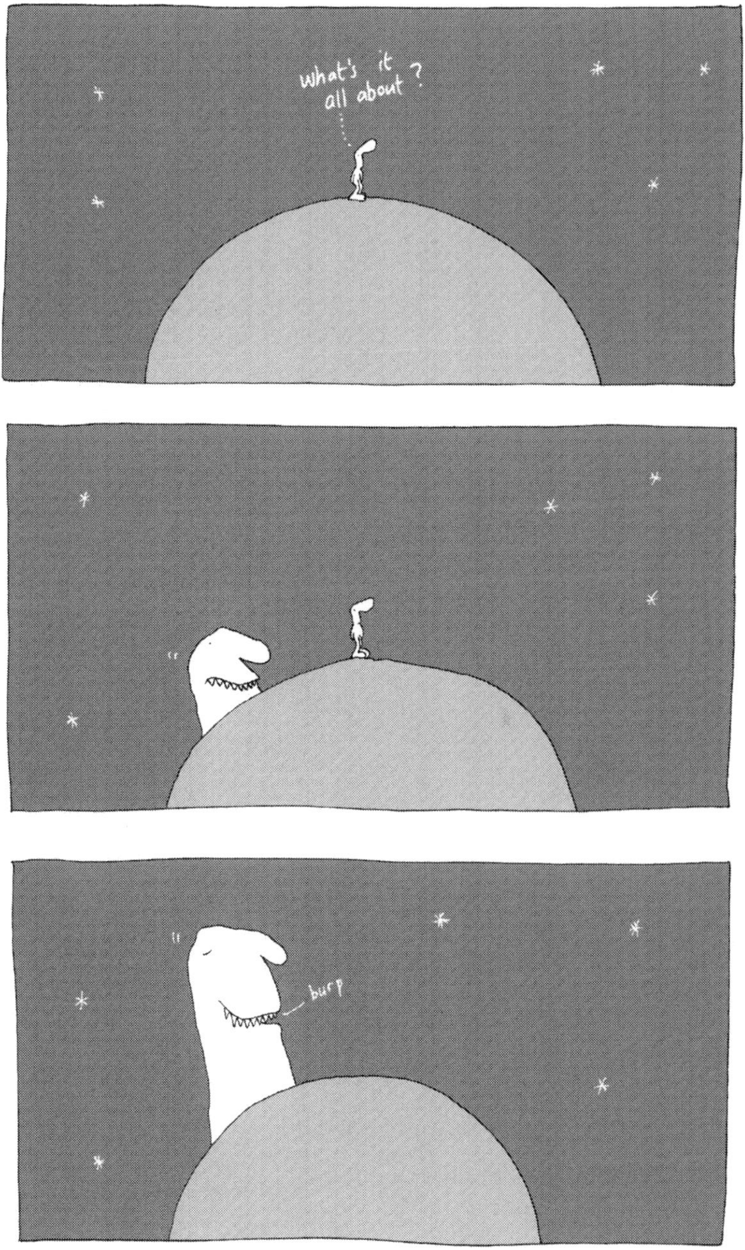
what's it all about ?
burp

2007

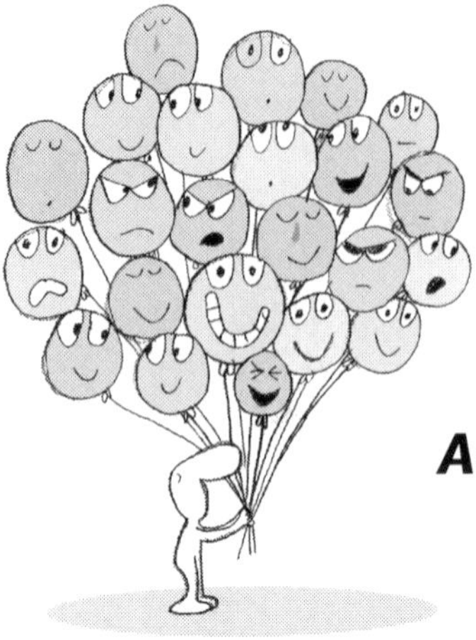

Aaaaaaah Life...

2013

"The foolish man seeks happiness in the distance,
the wise grows it under his feet."

- James Oppenheim -

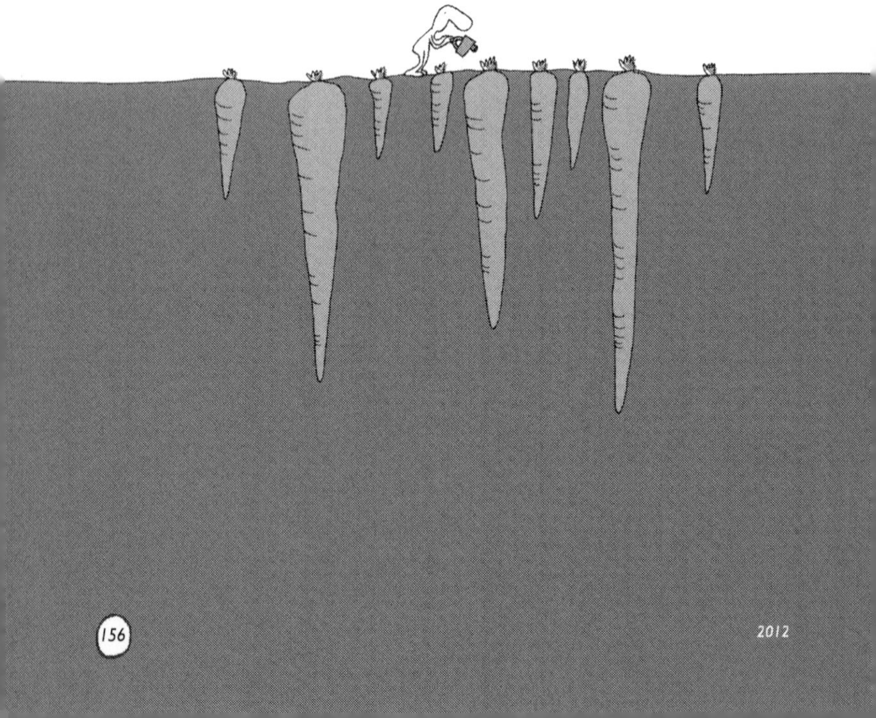

2012

*If I could choose any planet
to be just a small speck on,
I'd still choose this one.*

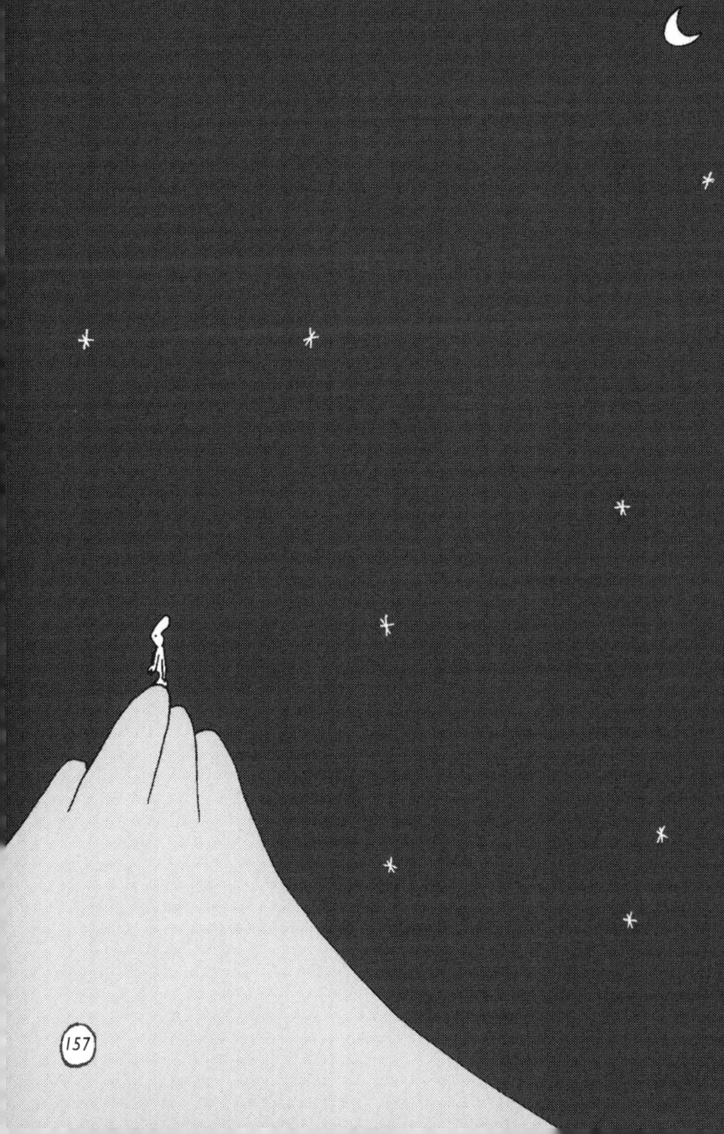

2010

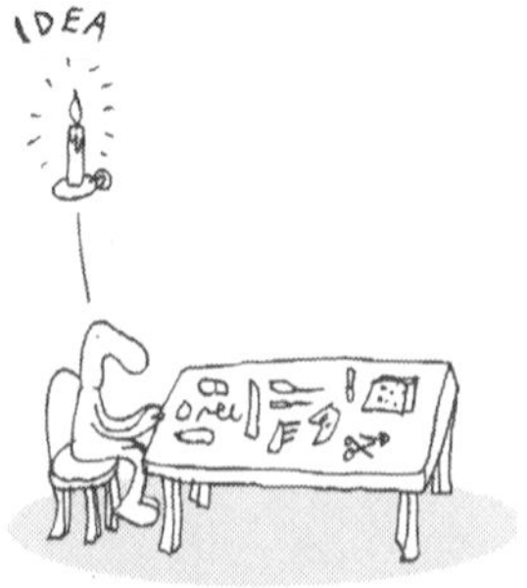
IDEA

Just moments before Edison invented the lightbulb...

2008

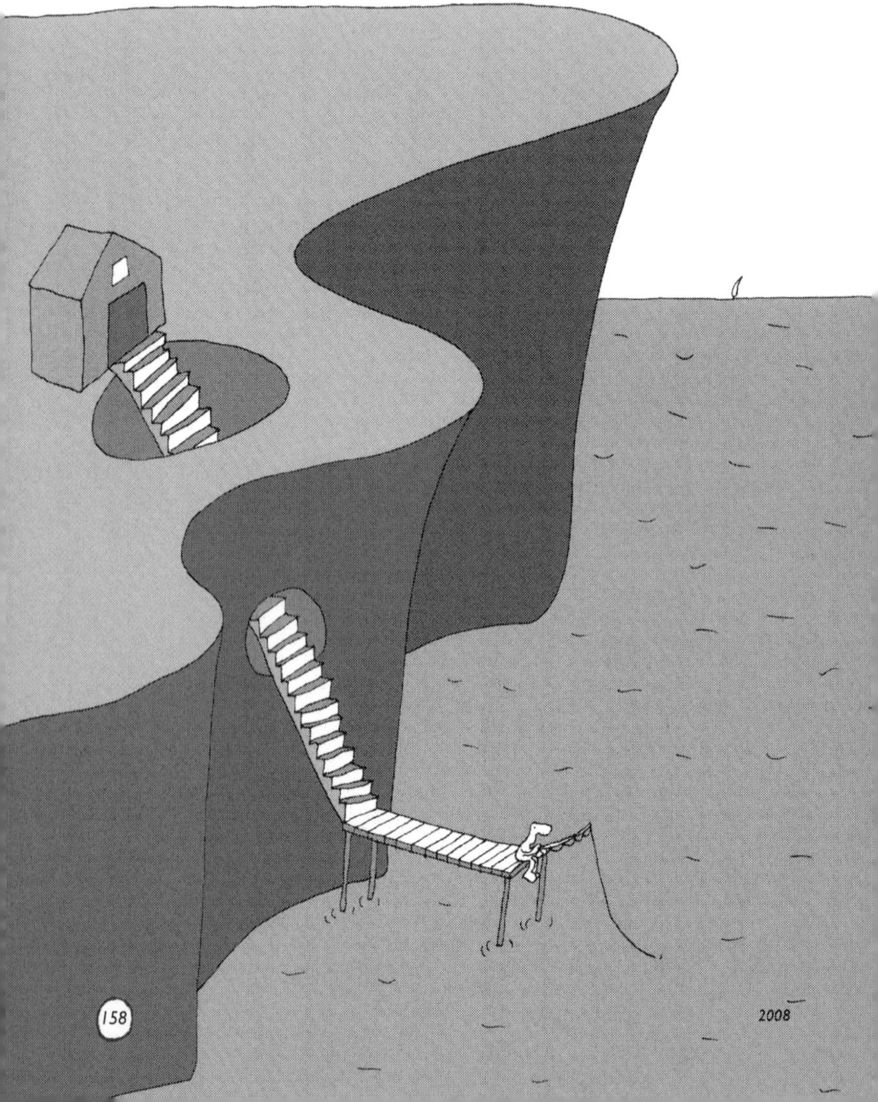

2008

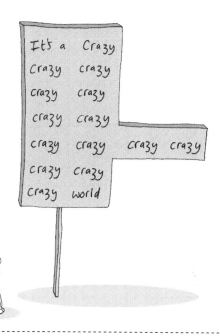

It's a Crazy
Crazy crazy
crazy crazy
crazy crazy
crazy crazy crazy crazy
crazy crazy
crazy world

2008

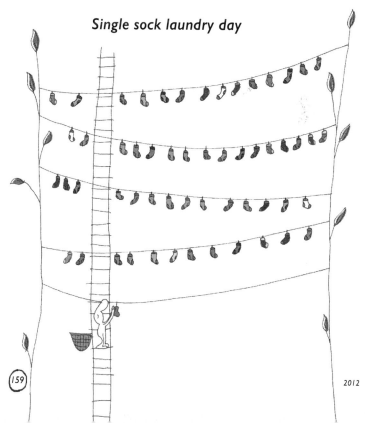

Single sock laundry day

2012

Fiddle Fiddle Fiddle Fiddle Fiddle
Fiddle Fiddle fiddle fiddle fiddle fiddle Fiddle
fiddle fiddle Fiddle fiddle Fiddle fiddle
Fiddle fiddle Fiddle fiddle fiddle Fiddle
fiddle Fiddle fiddle Fiddle fiddle Fiddle fiddle fiddle
Fiddle Fiddle fiddle Fiddle fiddle Fiddle fiddle fiddle
fiddle fiddle fiddle fiddle Fiddle fiddle Fiddle
Fiddle Fiddle fiddle Fiddle fiddle fiddle Fiddle
fiddle fiddle fiddle fiddle Fiddle
Fiddle Fiddle fiddle Fiddle
fiddle fiddle Fiddle fiddle
fiddle fiddle fiddle fiddle
Fiddle fiddle fiddle
Fiddle fiddle Fiddle
fiddle fiddle Fiddle
Fiddle fiddle
fiddle Fiddle fiddle
Fiddle fiddle
Fiddle fiddle

MODERN CIVILIZATION

2008

One man and his fridge

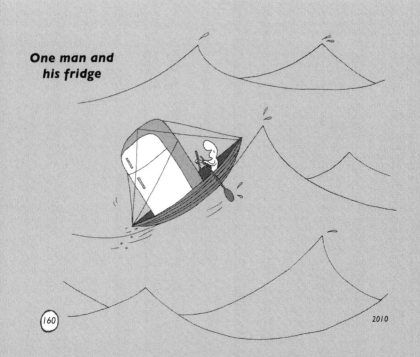

2010

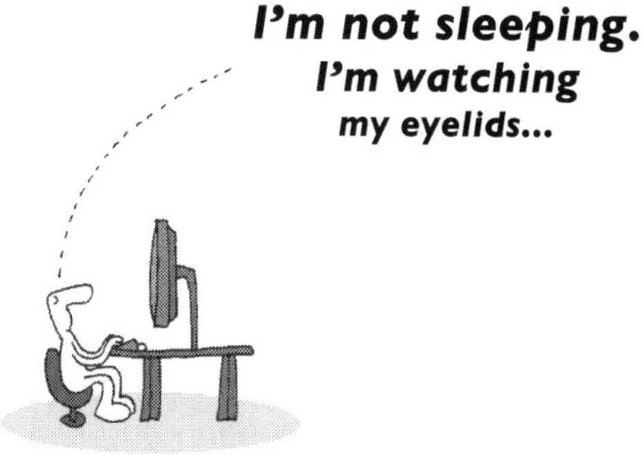
I'm not sleeping.
I'm watching
my eyelids...

2008

The Journey of Life

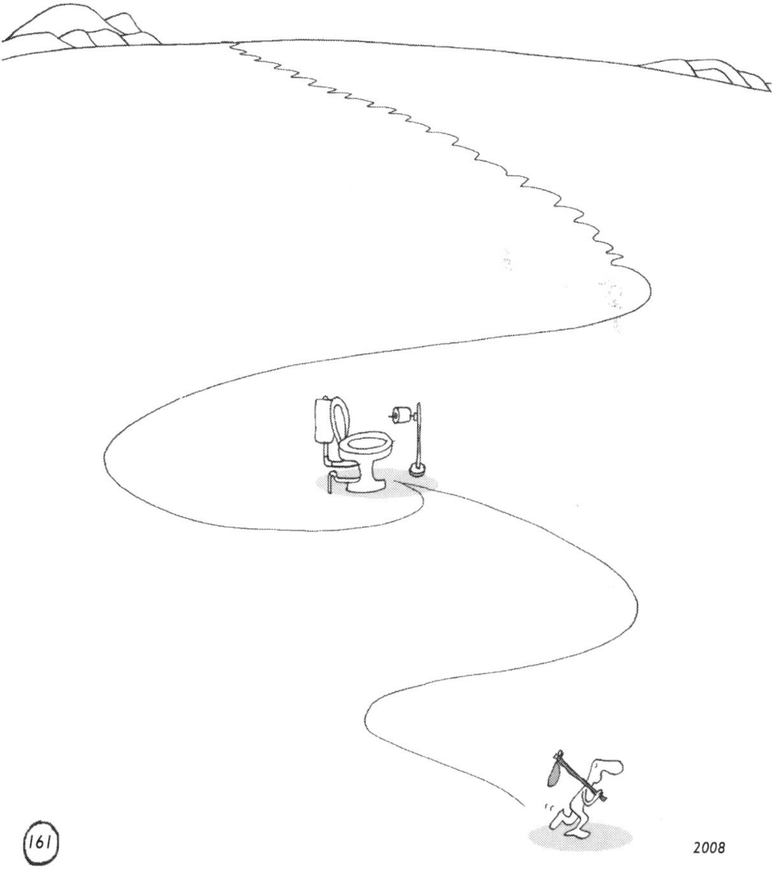

2008

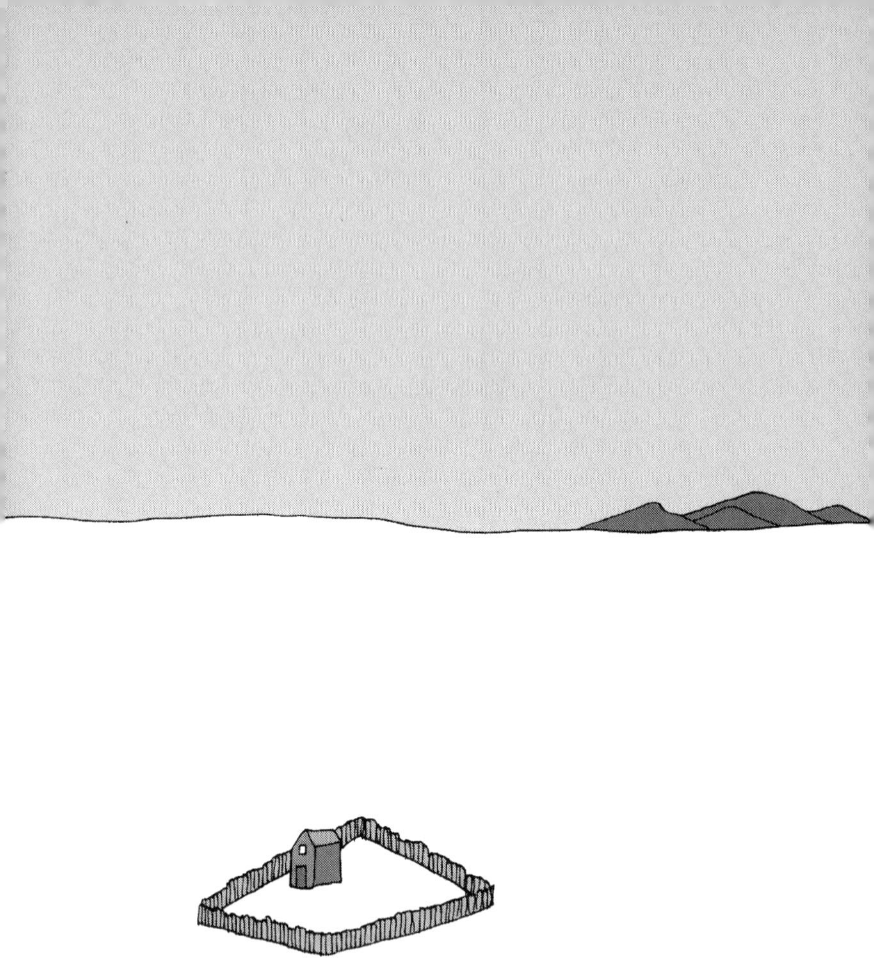

Maybe I should
trademark my nose?

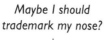

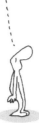

2008

Harnessing Wind Energy #16

Wind-generated wind-generator

aaaaah..

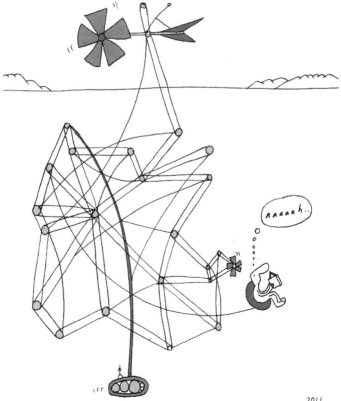

2011

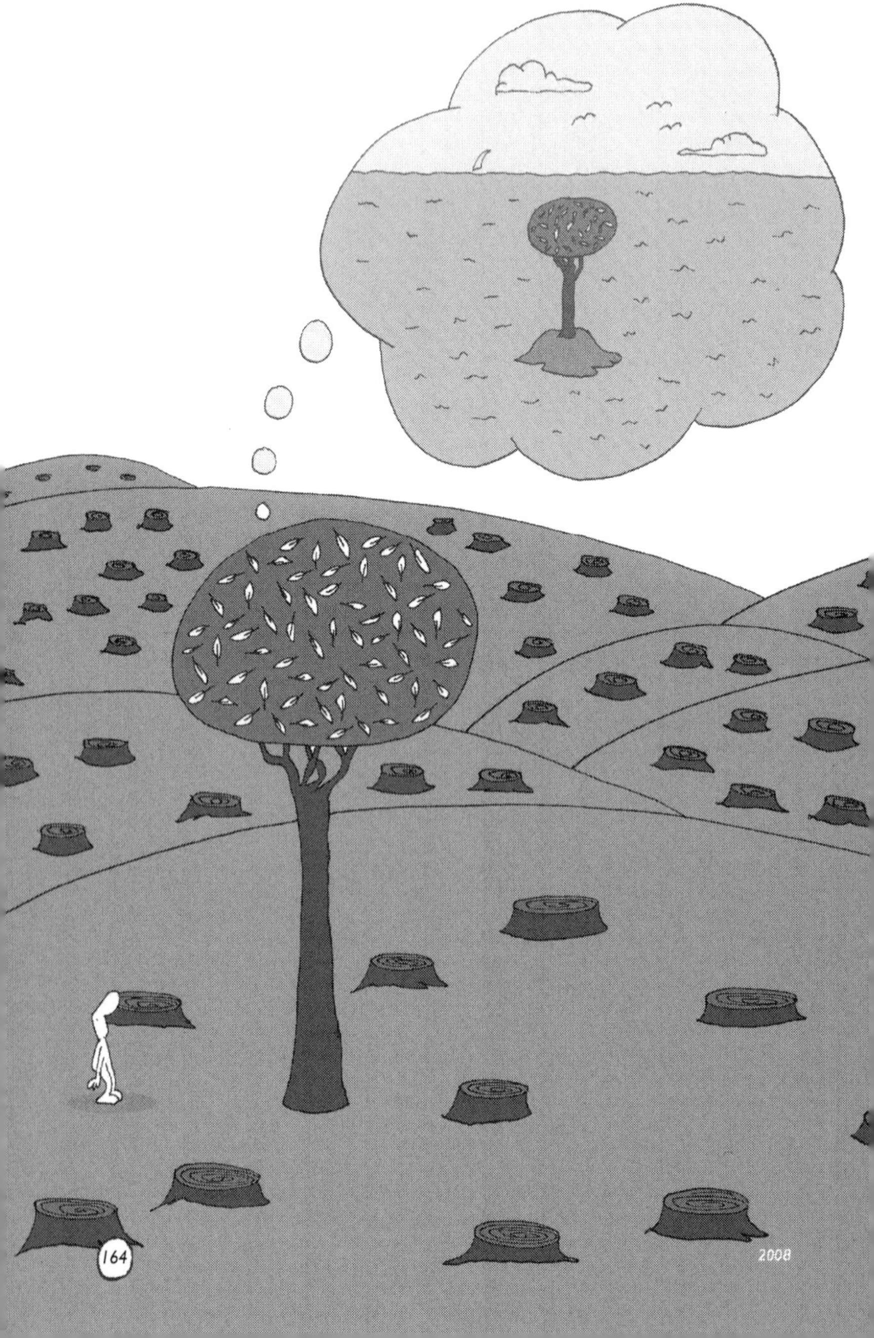
2008

How to Prepare and Eat Chocolate-covered Chocolate

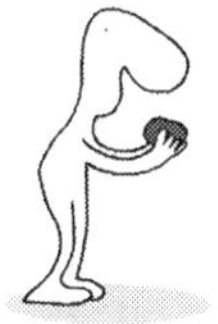

1. Get a chocolate.

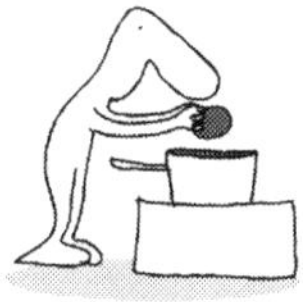

2. Dip it in melted chocolate.

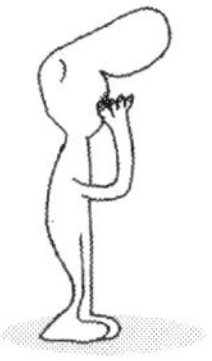

3. Eat it.

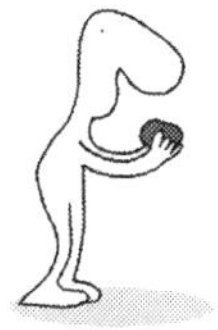

4. Repeat if necessary.
(and if not necessarily necessary).

2013

One day your life will flash before your eyes.

Make sure it's worth watching.

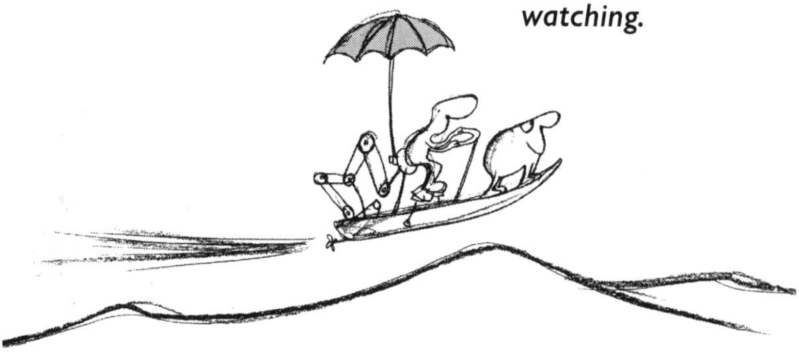

2013

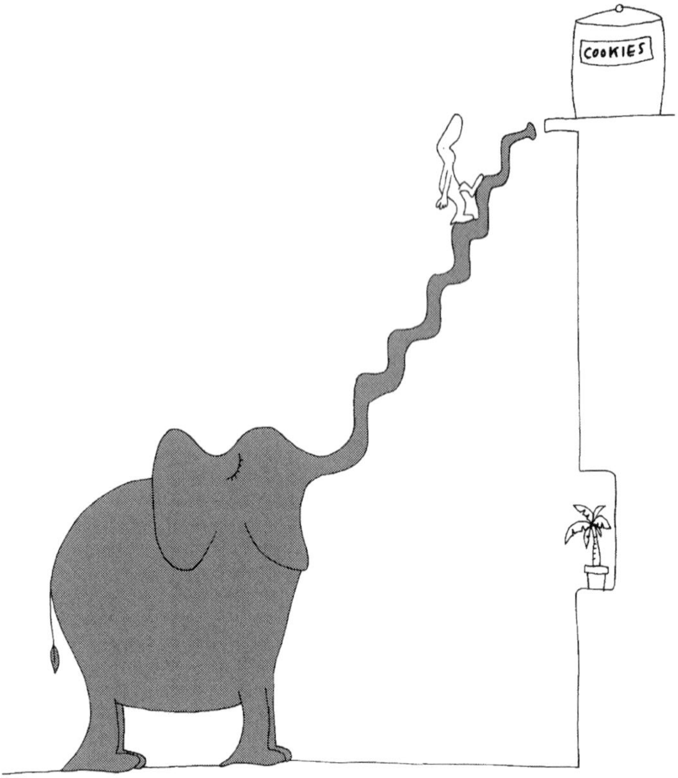
COOKIES

2010

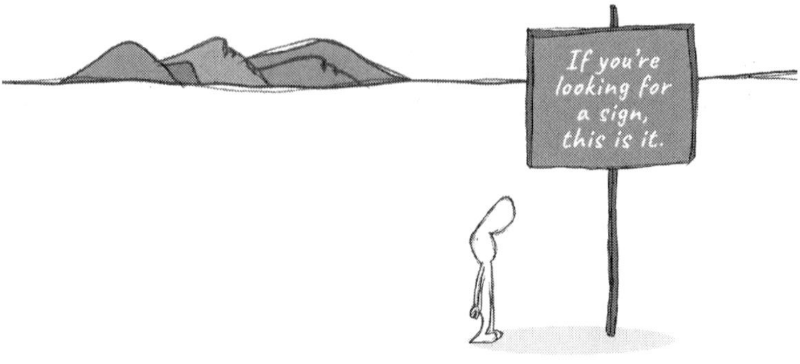
If you're looking for a sign, this is it.

2013

Some people were
***meant* to be**
together...

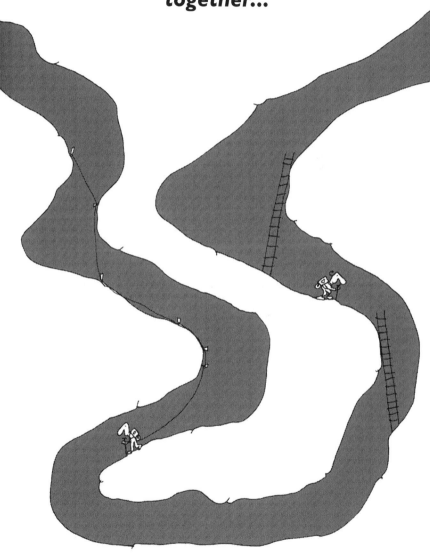

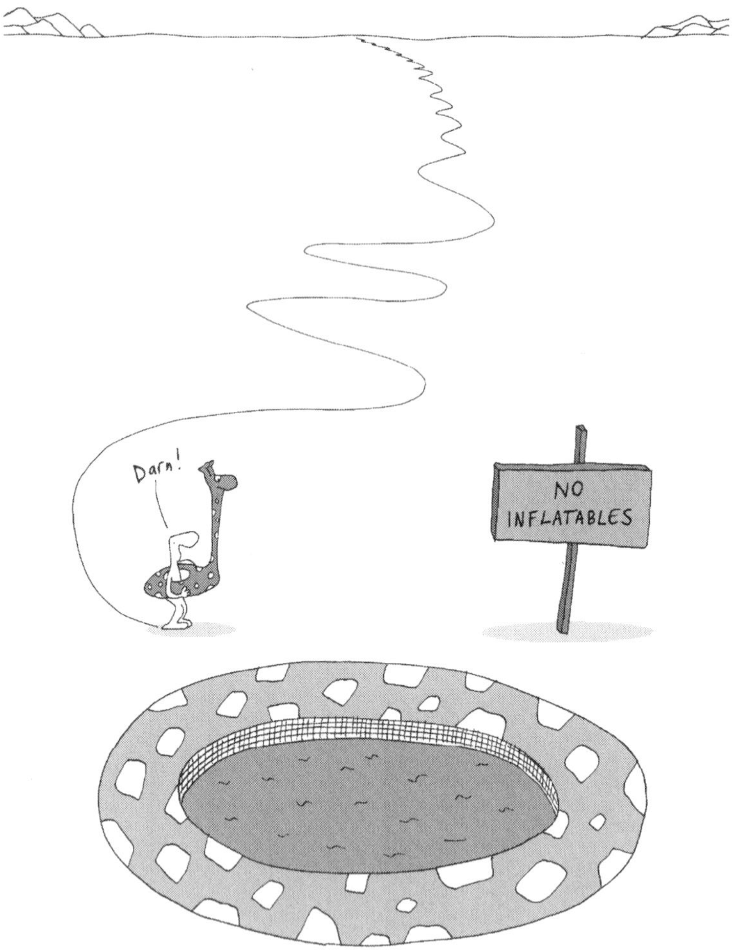
Darn!
NO
INFLATABLES

2008

How to *Deal with Monsters under your Bed*

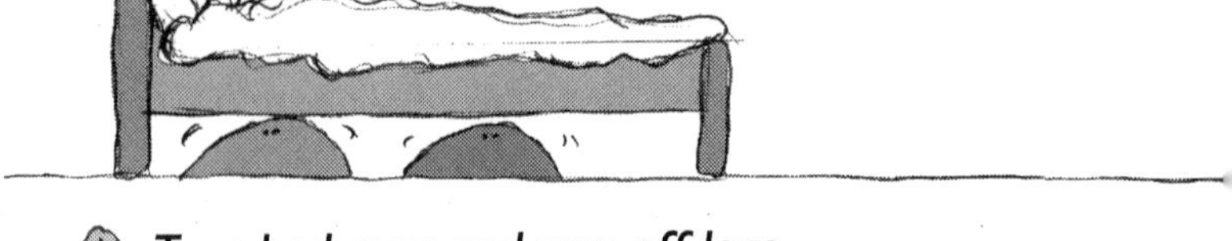

(1) *Turn bed over and saw off legs.*

Time-lapse photo
of housing market

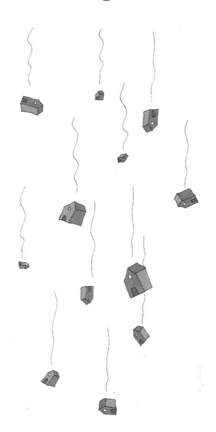

2008

Monsters will have to go elsewhere.

2003

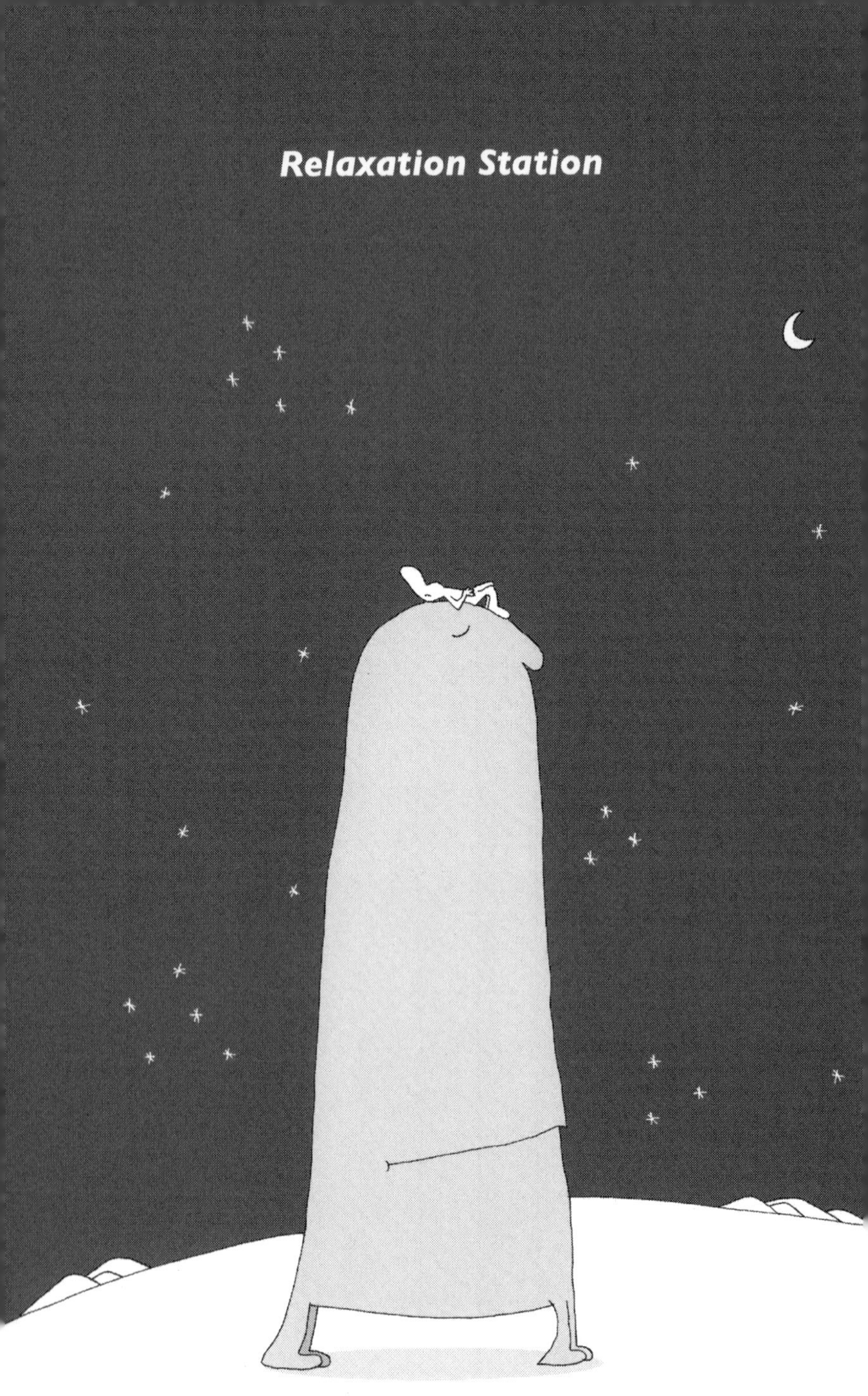
Relaxation Station

2011

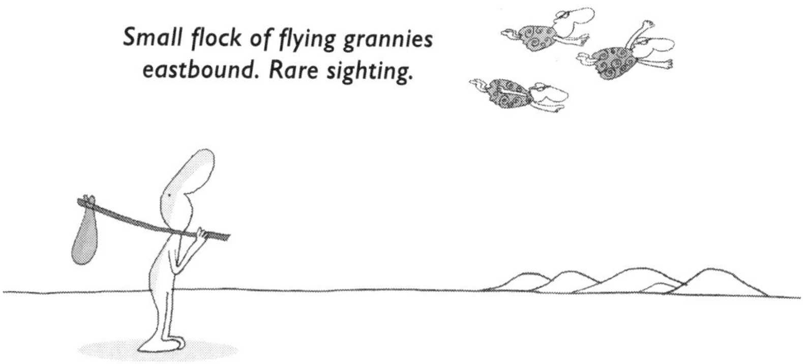

Small flock of flying grannies eastbound. Rare sighting.

2015

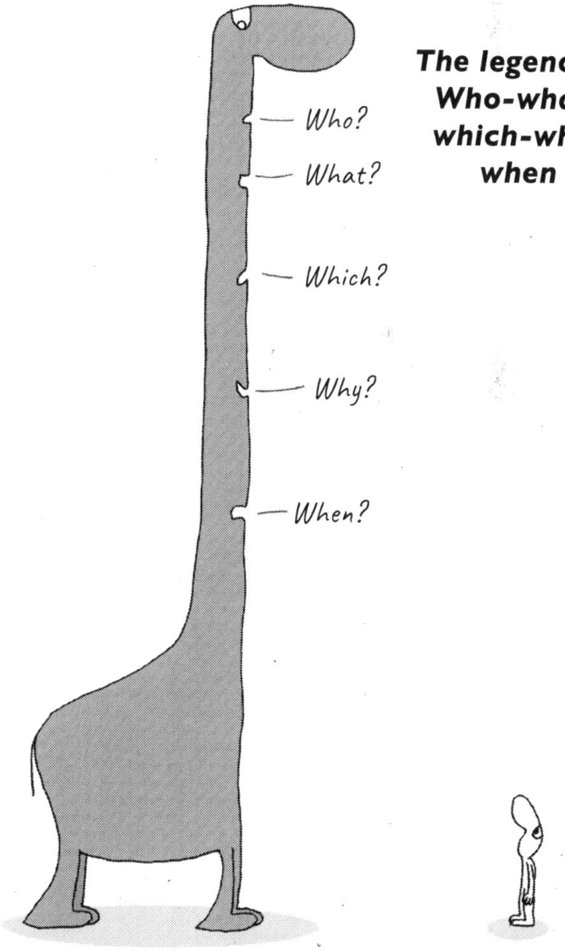
Who?
What?
Which?
Why?
When?

The legendary Who-what-which-why-when

2012

Harold's Indispensible Gadget #12:

DINNER PARTY OPINION GENERATOR

(Can be set in four modes: Impressive, Annoying, Charming or Repetitive)

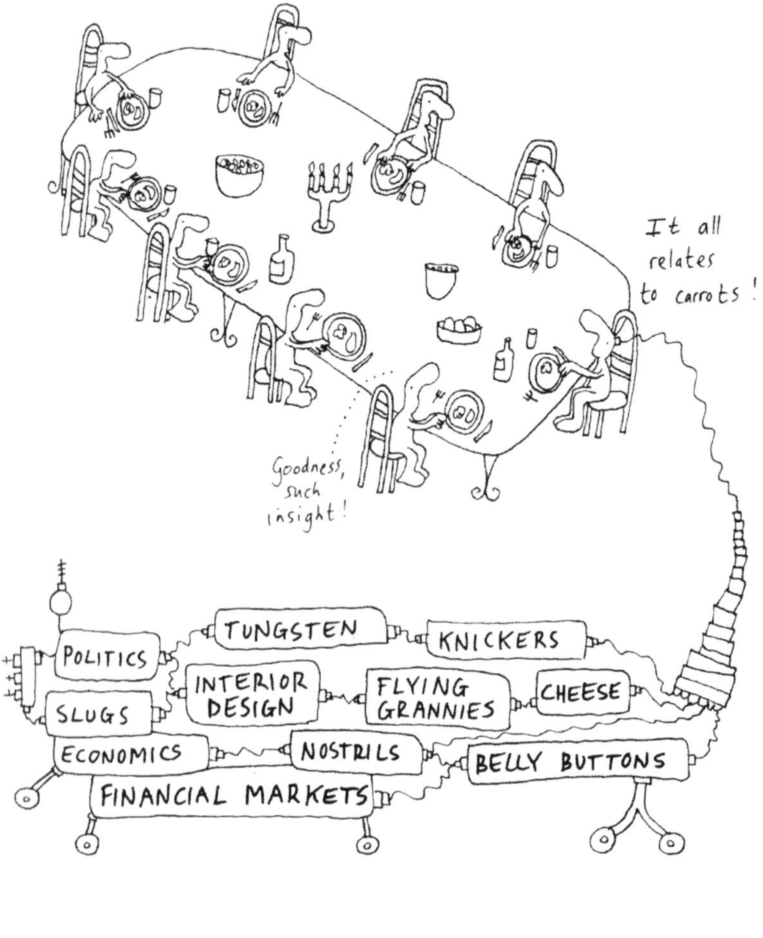

It all relates to carrots!
Goodness, such insight!
TUNGSTEN
KNICKERS
POLITICS
INTERIOR DESIGN
FLYING GRANNIES
CHEESE
SLUGS
ECONOMICS
NOSTRILS
BELLY BUTTONS
FINANCIAL MARKETS

2005

Sweeping
generalizations

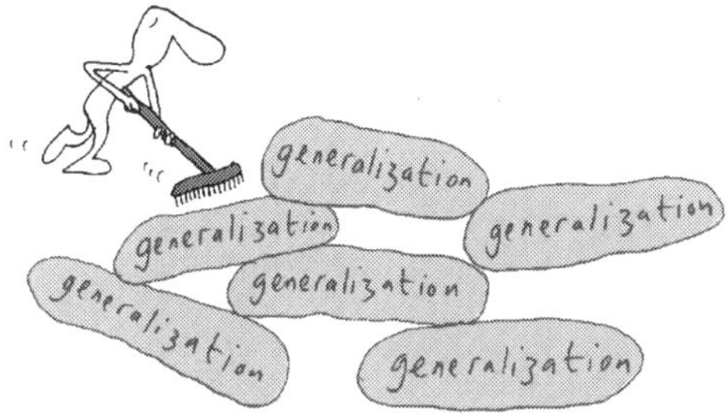
generalization
generalization
generalization
generalization
generalization
generalization

2013

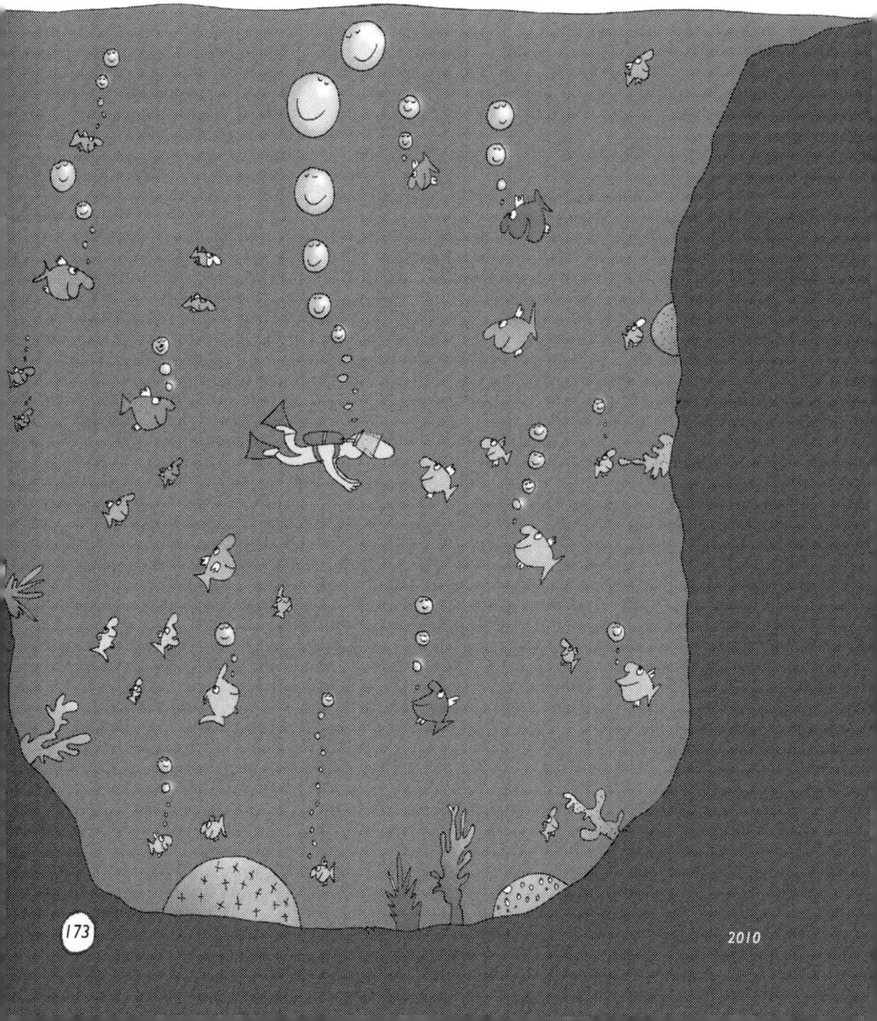

2010

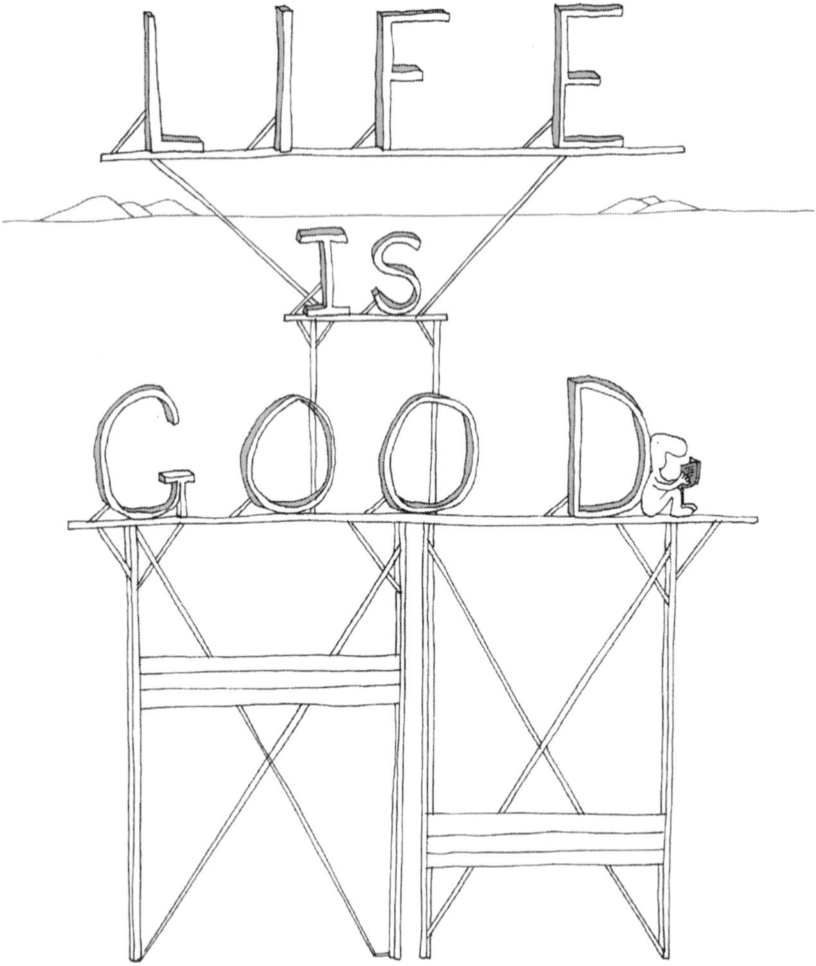
LIFE
IS
GOOD

2010

HOW TO AVOID A COMPLICATED RELATIONSHIP WITH A BOSS

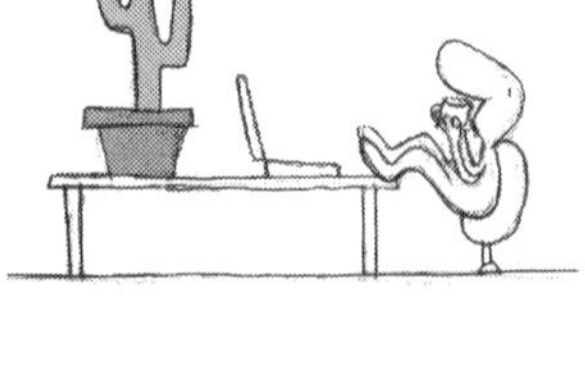

Don't have a boss...

2013

My current thinking

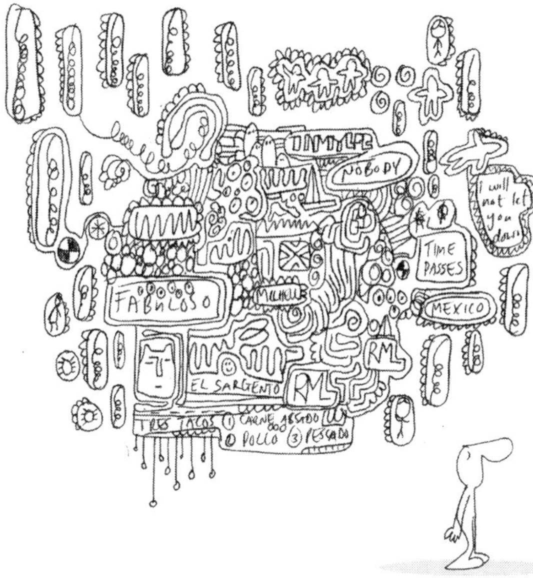
NOBODY
I will not let you down
TIME PASSES
FABULOSO
MEXICO
RML
EL SARGENTO
RML

2015

Brie tree

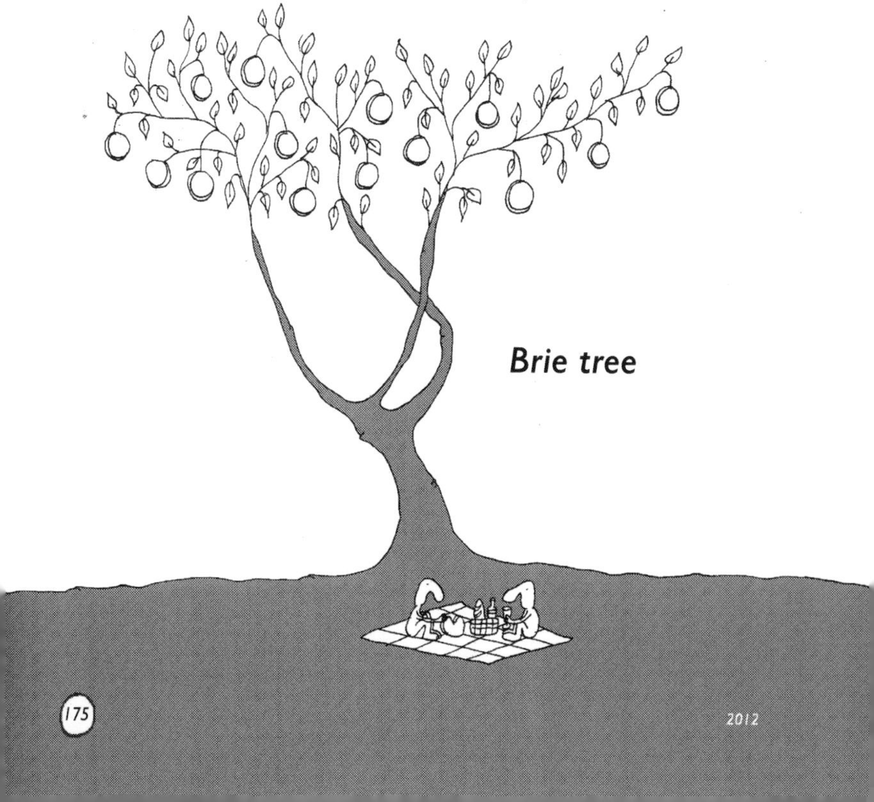

2012

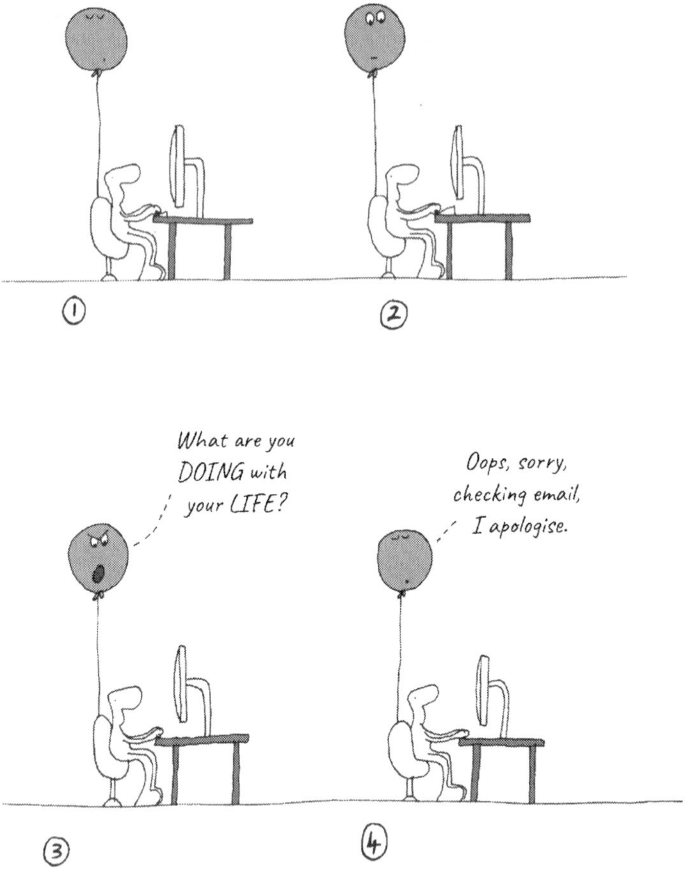
What are you DOING with your LIFE?
Oops, sorry, checking email, I apologise.

2008

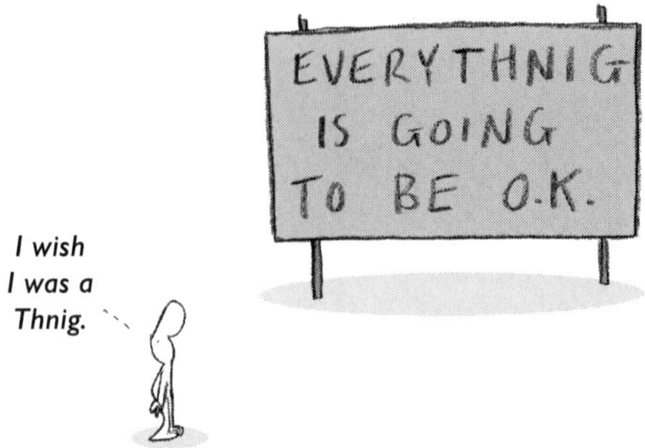
EVERYTHNIG IS GOING TO BE O.K.
I wish I was a Thnig.

2013

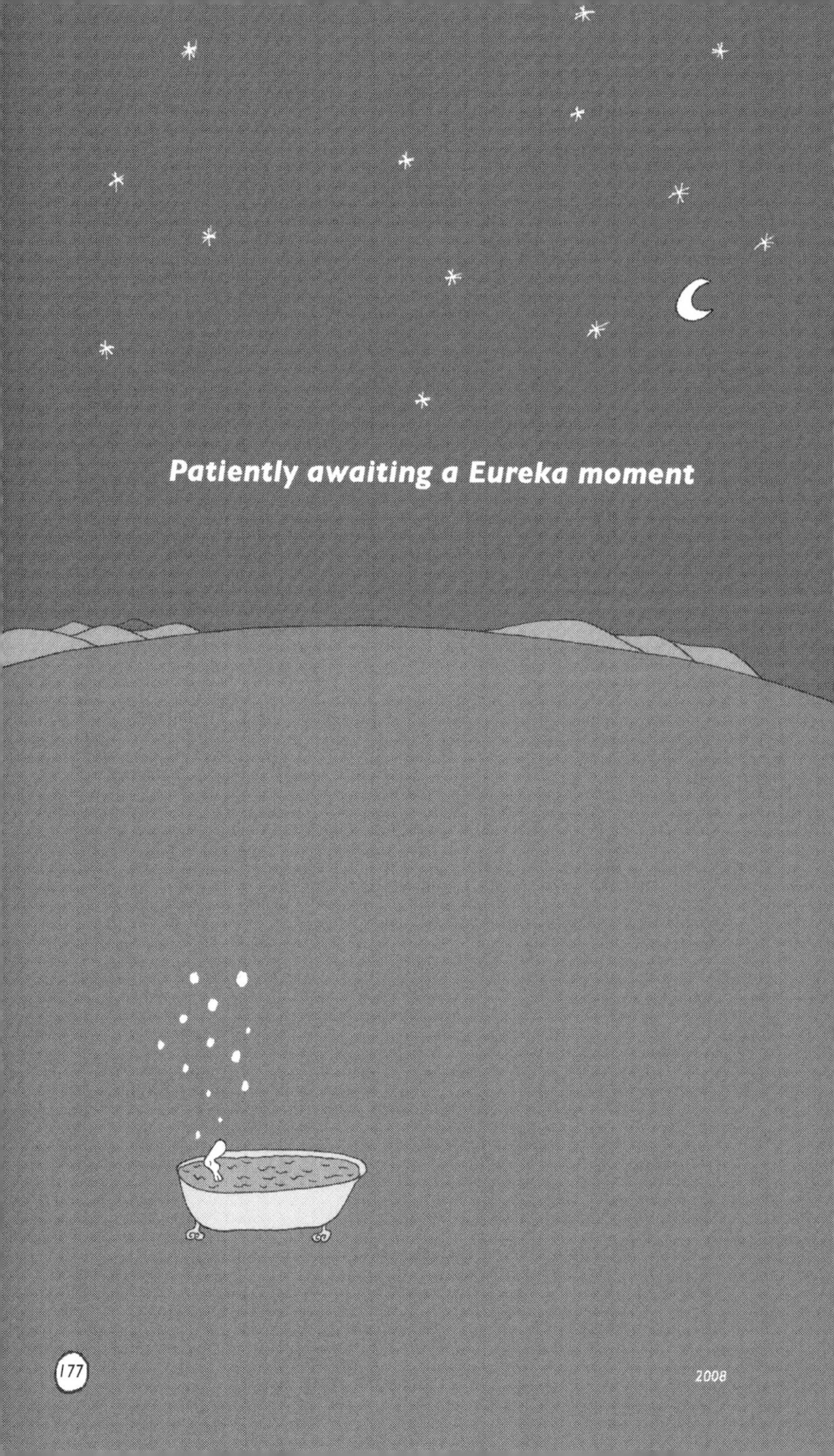

Patiently awaiting a Eureka moment

2008

Worth it for the view...

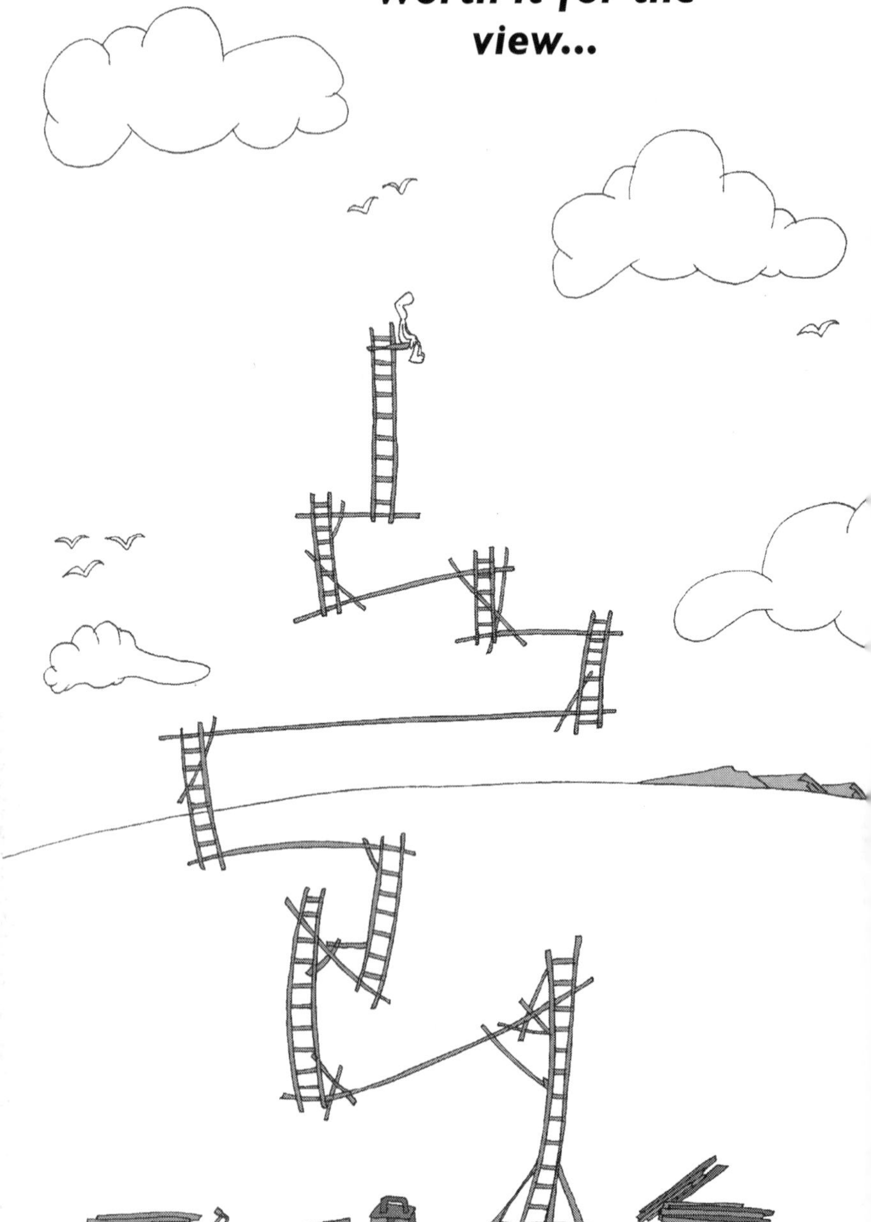

2008

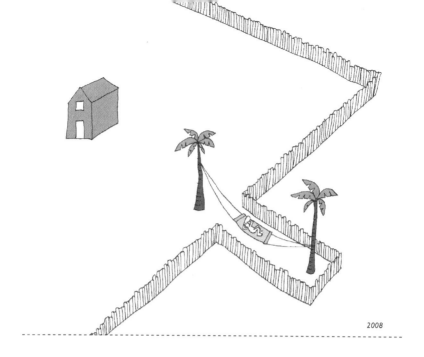

2008

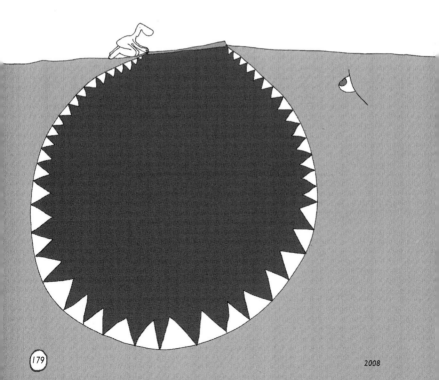

2008

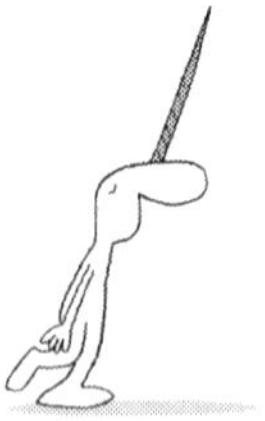

Some days are
just kind of unicornish...

2015

The Gentle Art of **Tweeting**

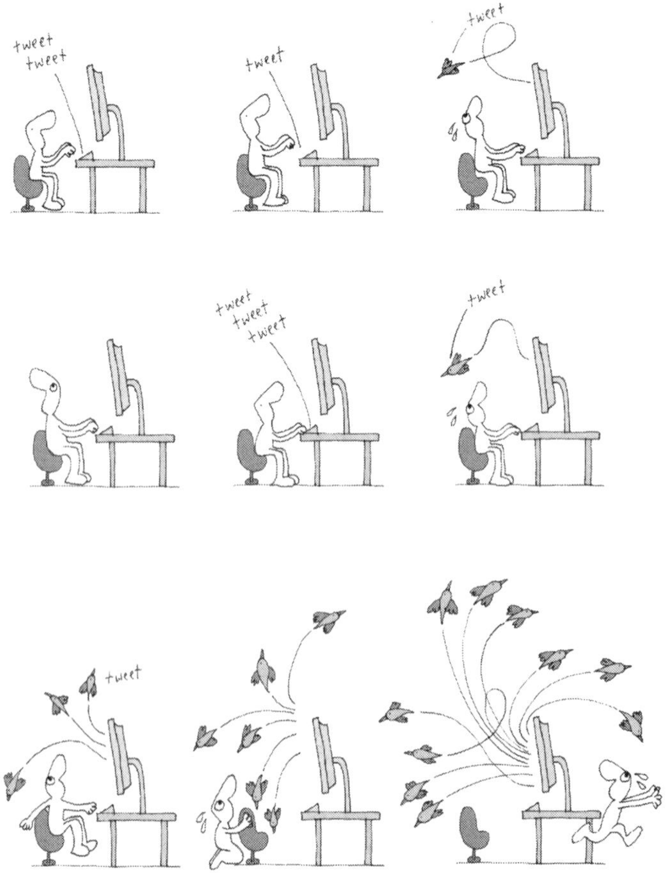
tweet
tweet
tweet
tweet
tweet
tweet
tweet
tweet
tweet

 ALSO AN ANIMATION! **www.lastlemon.com/harolds-planet/animations** 2010

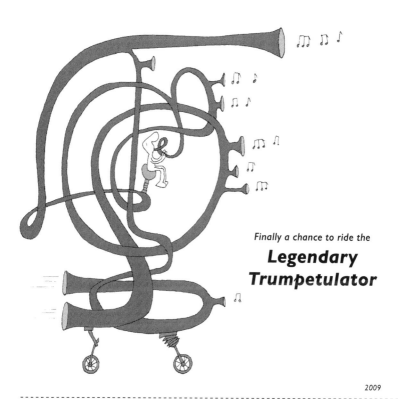

Finally a chance to ride the

Legendary Trumpetulator

2009

Village in search of an idiot

2015

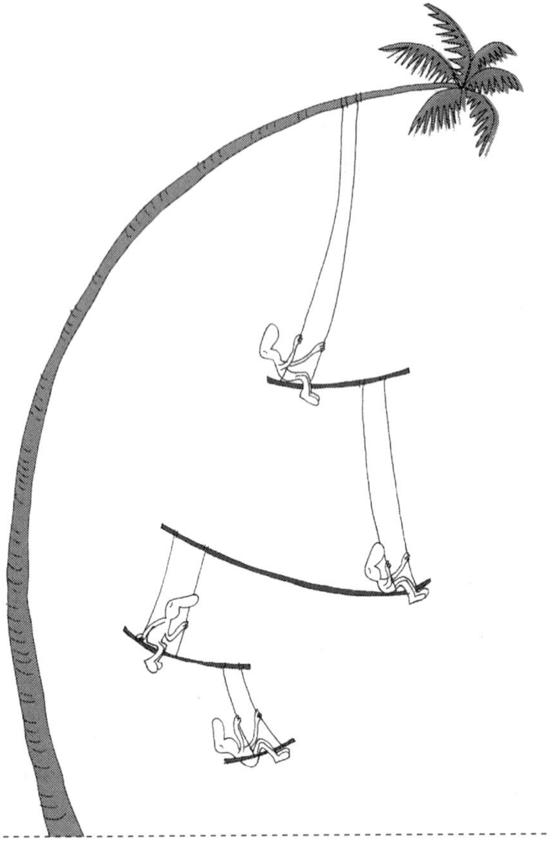

2012

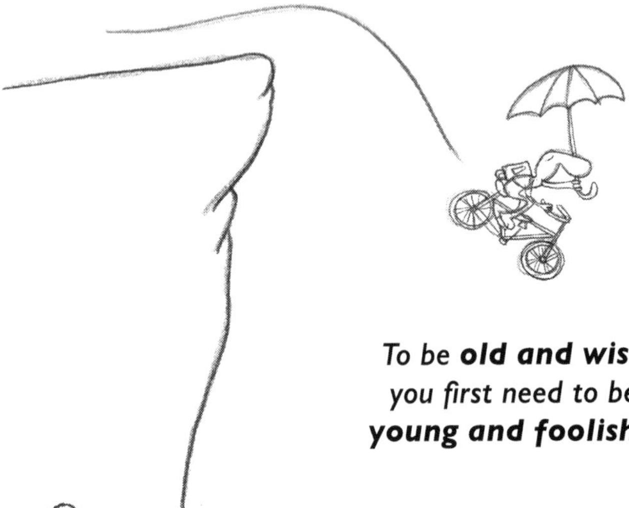

To be ***old and wise***
you first need to be
young and foolish...

2014

On the *Baobab* of Life

may you find the most comfortable branch

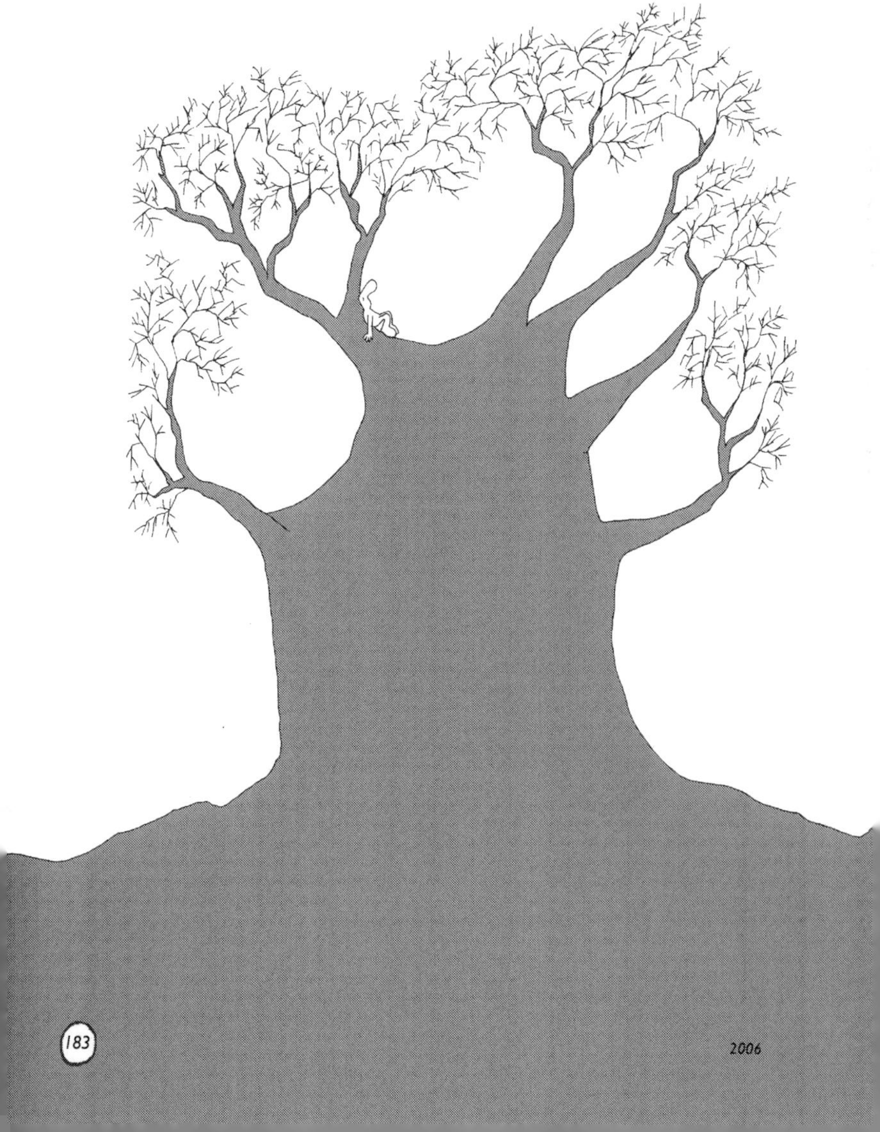

2006

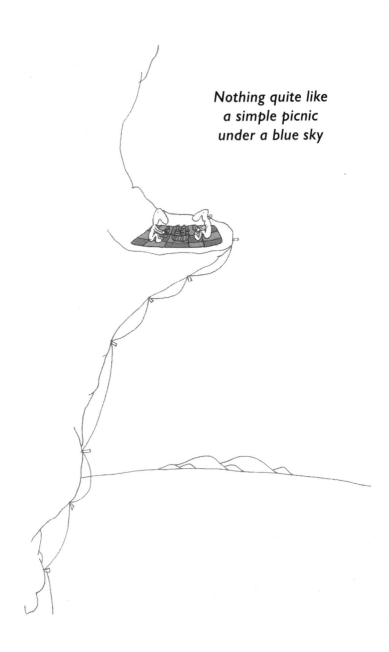

*Nothing quite like
a simple picnic
under a blue sky*

How to *Deal with Life's Hurdles II*

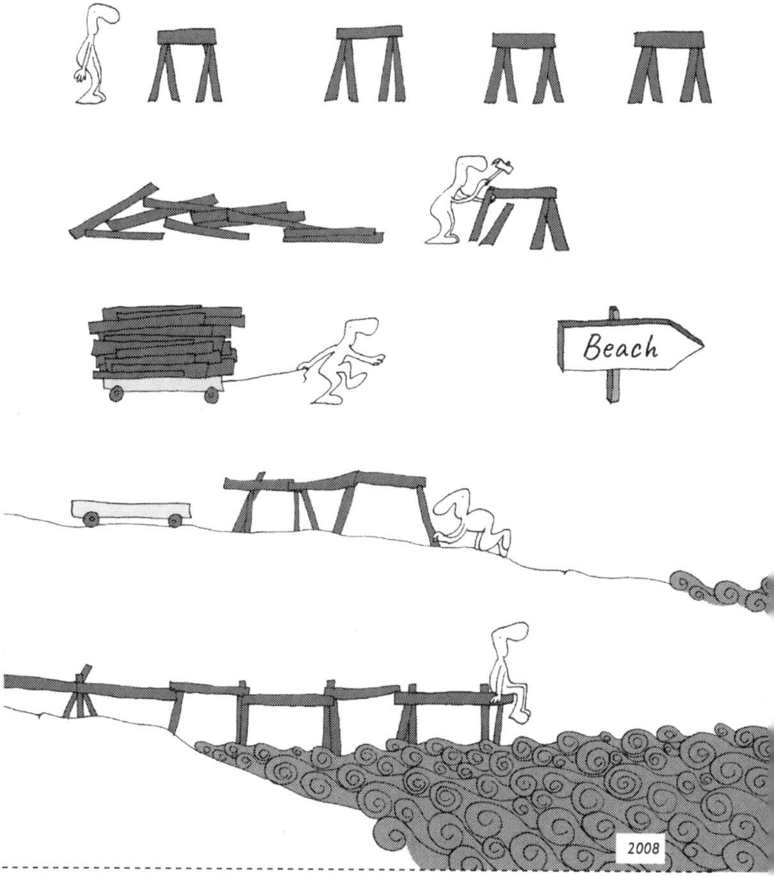
Beach
2008

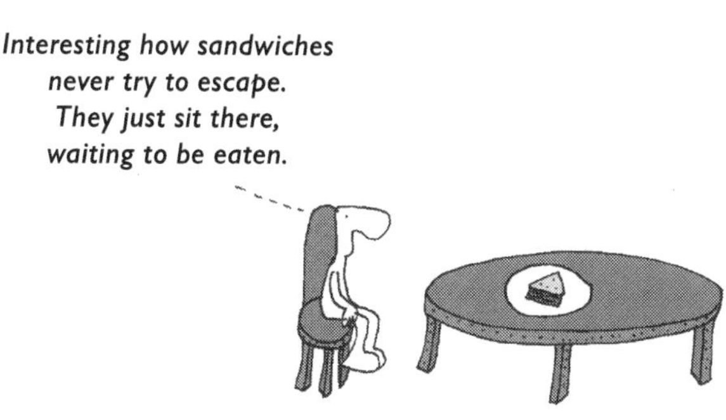
Interesting how sandwiches
never try to escape.
They just sit there,
waiting to be eaten.

2008

How to *Escape Time*

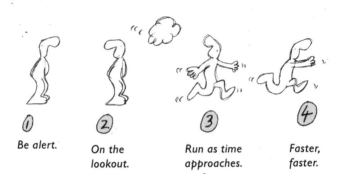

① Be alert.

② On the lookout.

③ Run as time approaches.

④ Faster, faster.

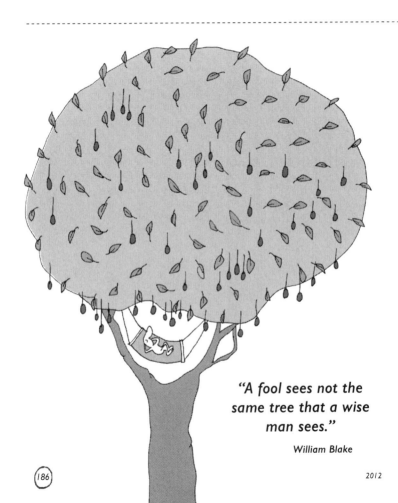

"A fool sees not the same tree that a wise man sees."

William Blake

5 Leap into...

6 ...wheelbarrow.

7 Time passes by.

This concept was made into a tv pilot animation with Gaumont/Xilam, Paris 2003

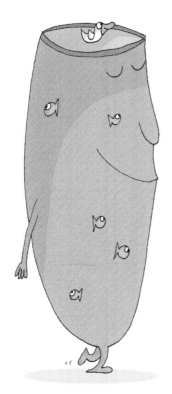

**Some folks are
just way cooler
than others...**

2019

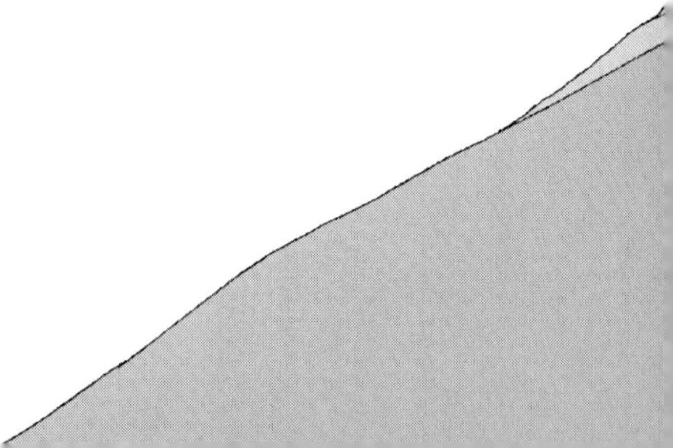

The End

for now

And also back to

The Beginning

and the story of how

it all started...

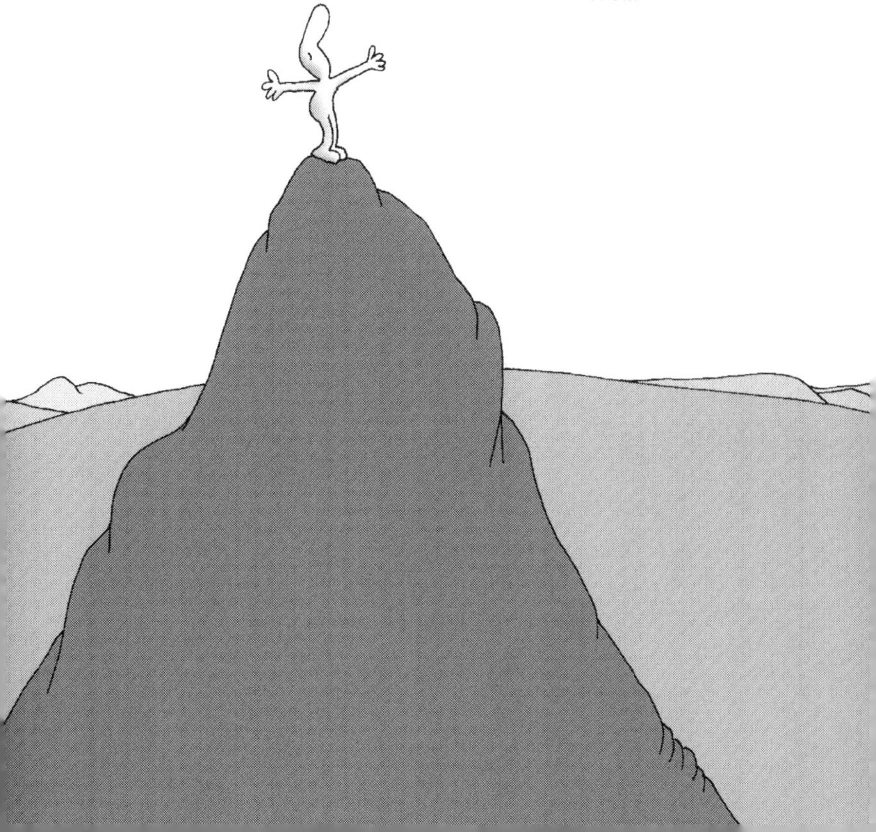

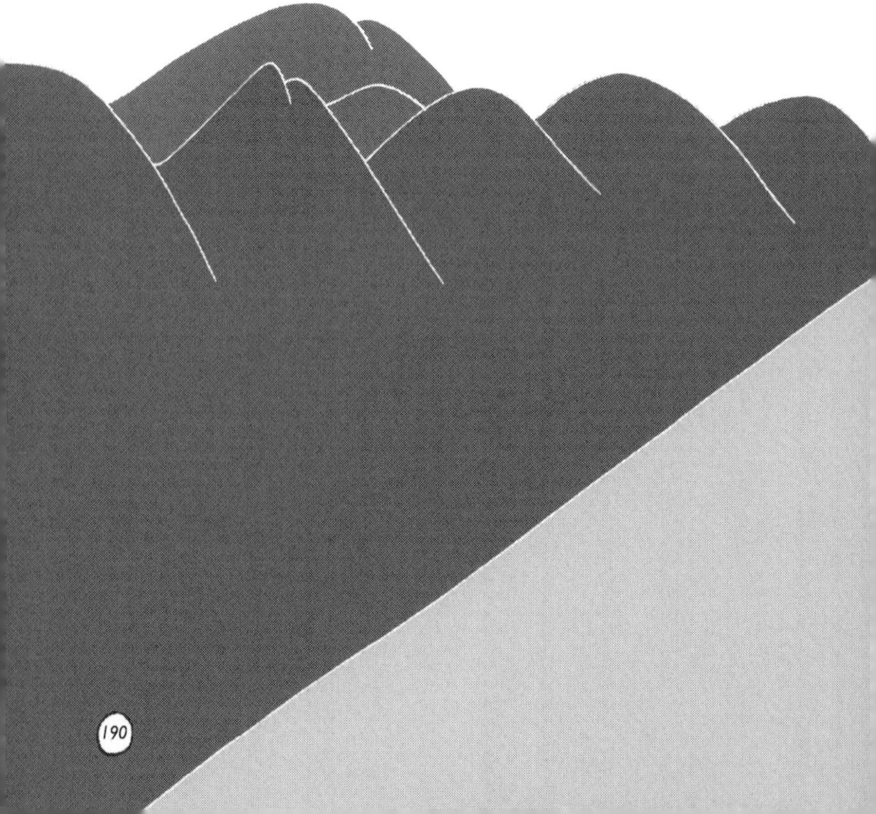

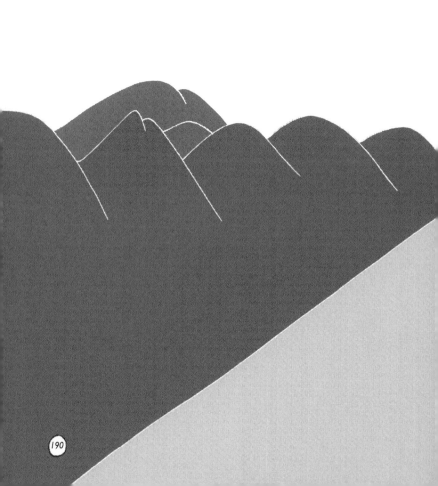

Our Firstborn: Harold

In those early days, Harold had us up all night, his little bobbly-nosed face staring up at us from the pages of dozens of Moleskine sketchbooks and glowing out from our (newly invented) iMacs.

Harold was a most active little being - climbing, digging, sleeping, watching, bathing, inventing, building, but mostly just walking, walking, walking, alone out in the wilderness, at his own distinctively slow pace.

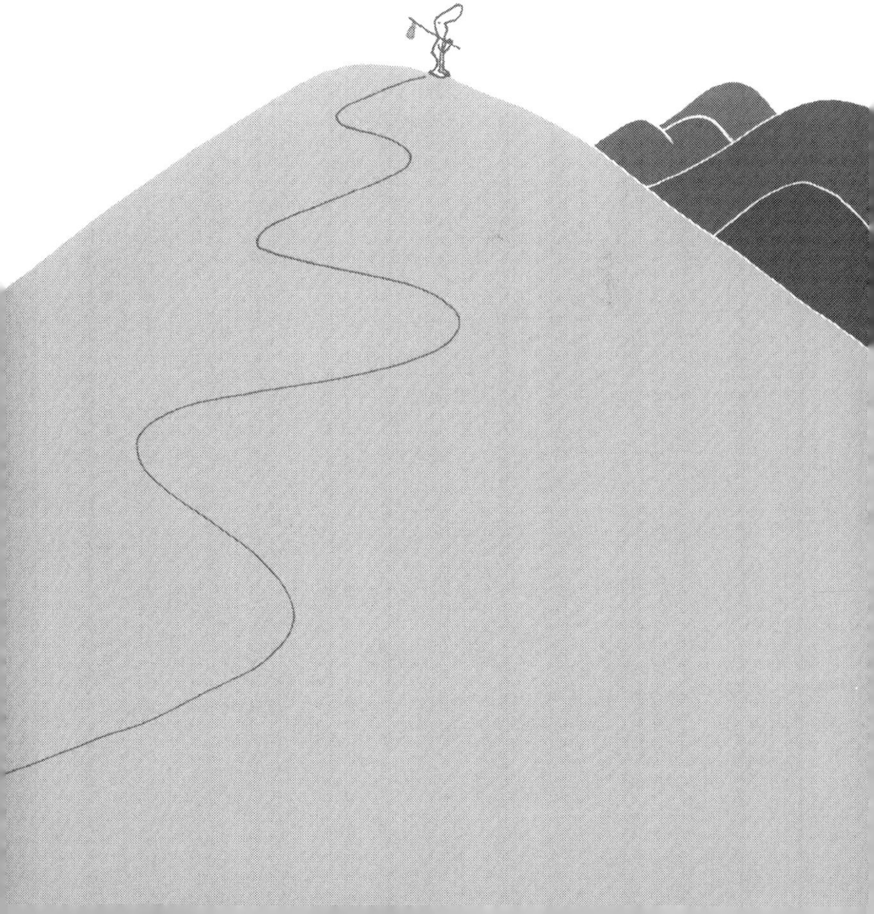

Big Bang

Our creative collaboration started with a bang. Within a year of that fateful Indian meal, we had:

1. Won the *Annecy Animation Festival* Grand Prix in France with a Harold's Planet TV series proposal (*"Tellement naive, si original!"*)

2. Secured representation from *Curtis Brown* literary agency in London (*"It's not a question of whether Harold's Planet is big enough for Curtis Brown, but whether Curtis Brown is big enough for Harold's Planet"* I swear these words were spoken)

3. Signed a TV deal with the giant French production company *Gaumont* (the CEO Marc du Pontavice compared Harold to Voltaire's *Candide*, oh yes indide) to go off to the **Seychelles** for a year to develop an animation series...

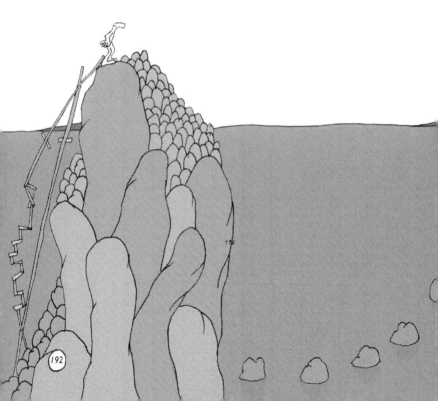

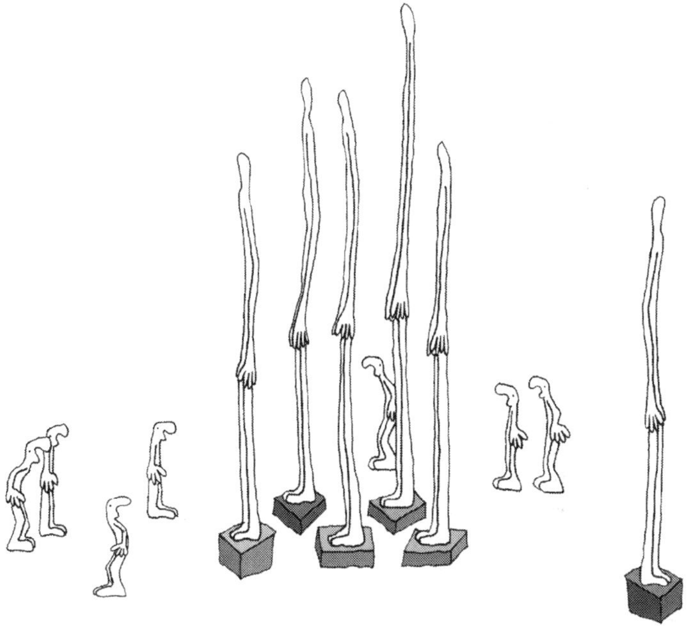

Annecy 'Grand Prix' Project Winner: Harold's Planet "Walks in the Sculpture Park" 1999

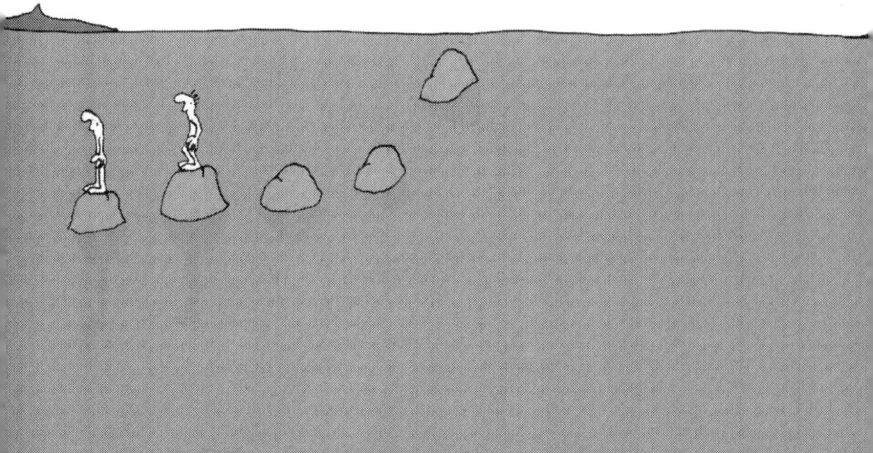

Image from "A Pile of Rocks": Harold's Planet story series for Curtis Brown 1999

Desert Island

So we gave up our day jobs (Ralph worked at an Investment Bank, and I was running my own tiny graphic design agency called Swerlybird) and headed for the small island of Cerf, in the Seychelles in the Indian Ocean.

Inspired by fish, boats, trees and animals - and interspersed always with the beauty and weirdness of the human condition - we invented snerd-drifting in the moonlight, singing grisbiums and migrating grannies, and wrote stories about traveling cactus salesmen, lemons loved to death, hiding from time, and islands set adrift...

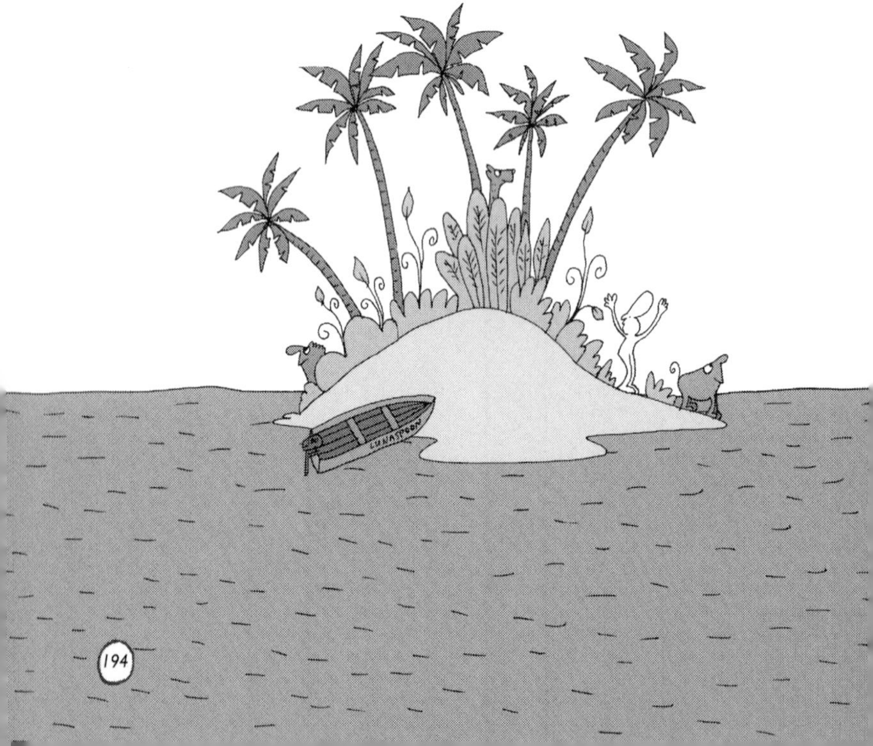
LUNASPOON

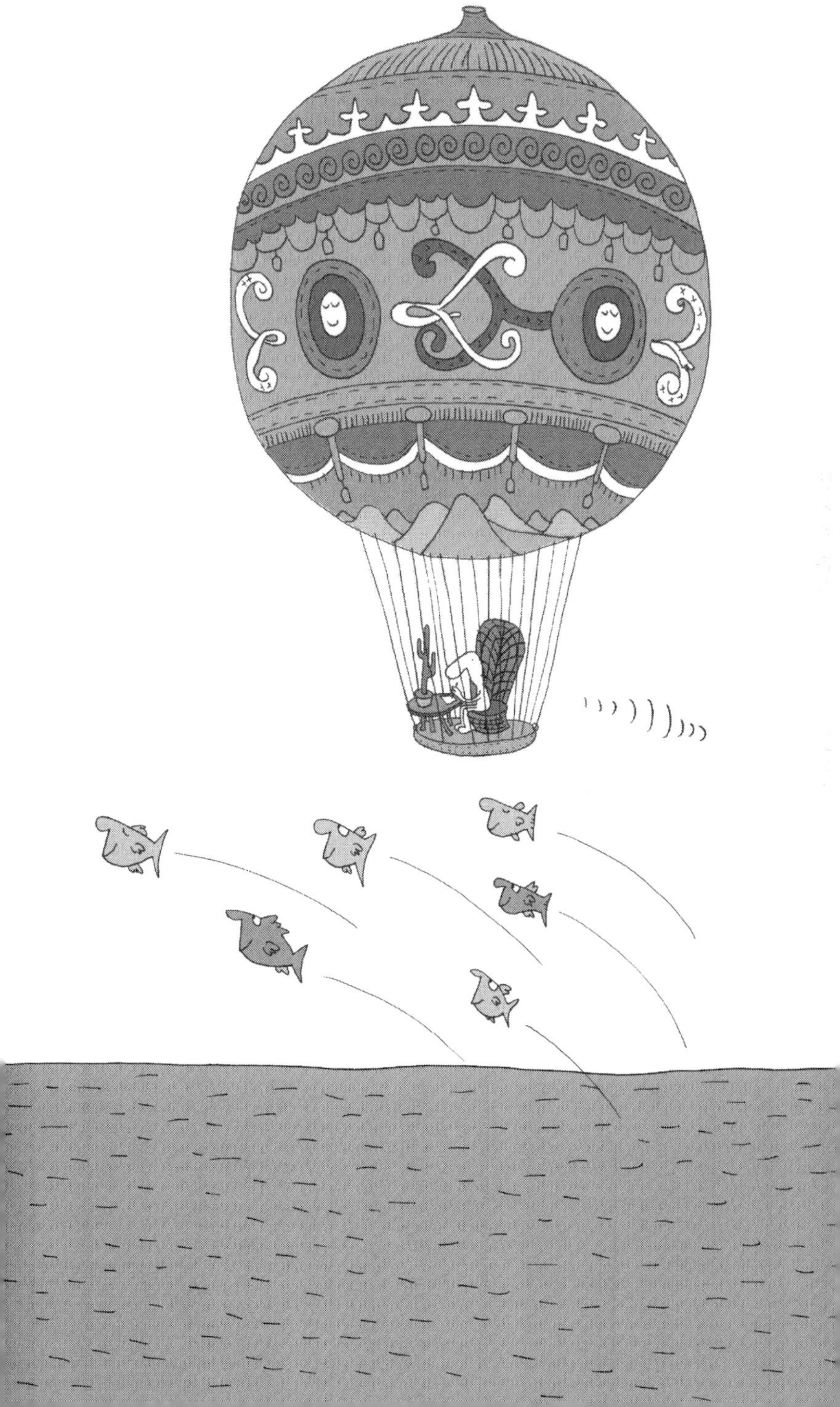

An actual granny, flying

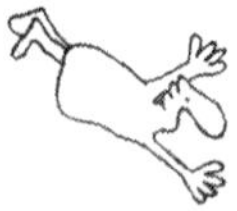

But then...

Not even a year later, we had separated from our hot agent and sadly gone our separate ways with Gaumont. We were back in a small apartment in London, whose only redeeming quality was that Pink Floyd had been formed there. The mould on the walls could probably be carbon-dated back to that era.

But we were young and then, as now, outrageously optimistic and energetic. So we started a creative studio called Last Lemon, named after one of the stories we'd written in the Seychelles - and self-published our first set of greeting cards starring Harold.

On rainbow watch

Contemplating horseness

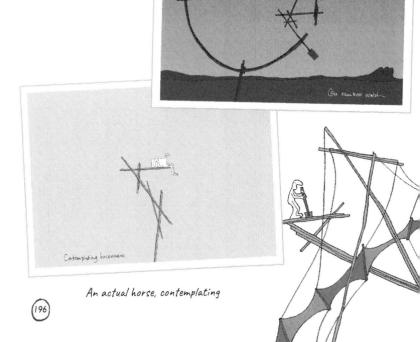

An actual horse, contemplating

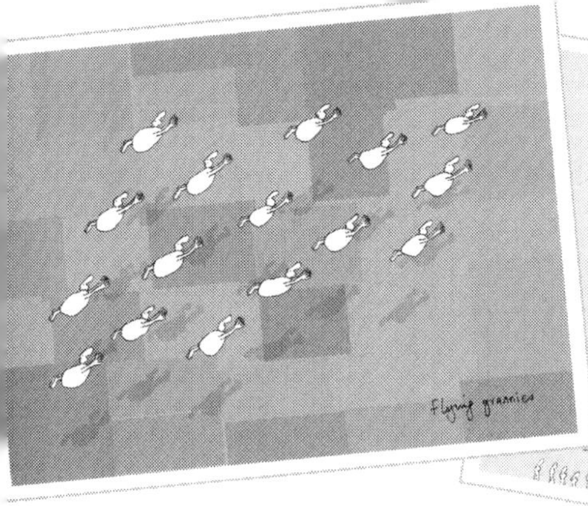
Flying grannies

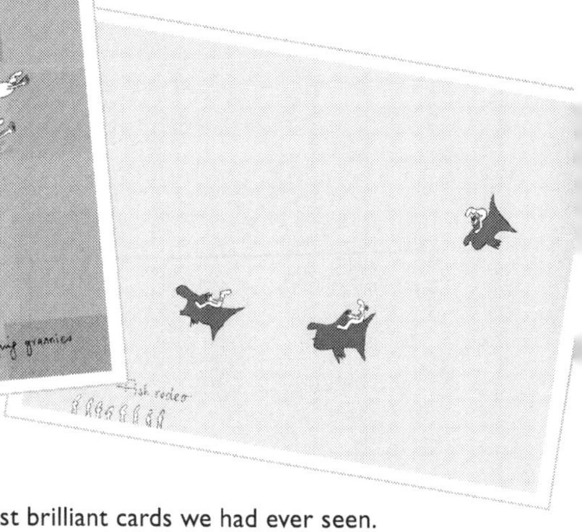
Fish rodeo

They were the most brilliant cards we had ever seen.

We printed 5,000 of each of the 24 designs, to be sure we could keep up with the certain demand. We were both quite sensible and worldly, but when we made the *"Contemplating Horseness"* card, we adored it with an almost religious devotion. *"Flying Grannies"* was the most original and important work coming out of the art world in centuries. *"The Cat Release Mechanism"* would, surely, soon be made into a ride at the inevitable Harold's Planet theme park. (We had actually reserved the rights to the theme park in all our TV dealings.)

You know how it ends.

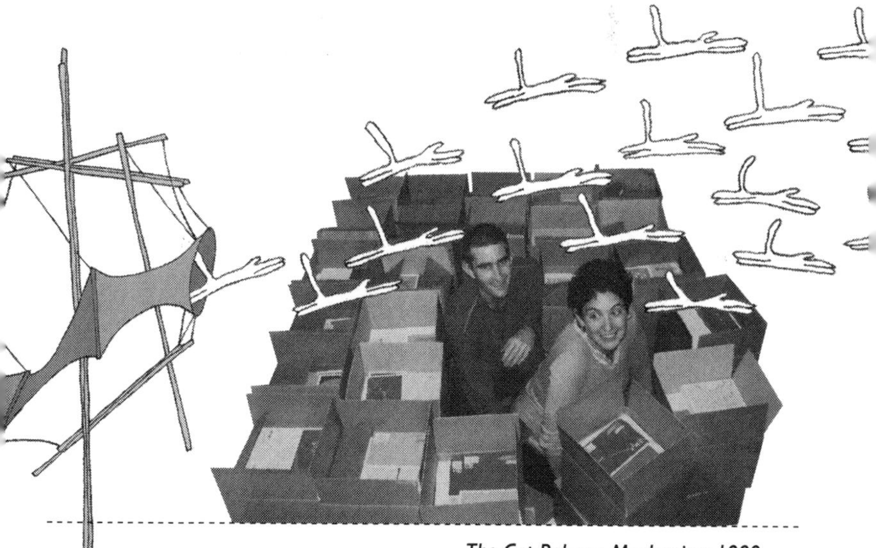

The Cat Release Mechanism 1999

CARDS LEFT TO RIGHT: Contemplating Horseness, On Rainbow Watch, Flying Grannies, Fish Rodeo

Risk and Return

Not only were our first set of self-published cards a spectacular failure, but we also felt unhappily tied to the 'bricks and mortar' side of making and distributing products. We were yearning for a more creative and free way of life.

It was around then that we discovered this thing called **The Licensing Industry** - which is a very inconvenient industry to work in when you are at dinner parties - no-one has heard of it and it's impossible to explain in a sentence.

Basically we began to sell manufacturers the right to stick our designs on their stuff - mugs, t-shirts, stationery. This business model gave us the freedom to focus on the creative side of Harold's Planet and later, other cartoon worlds.

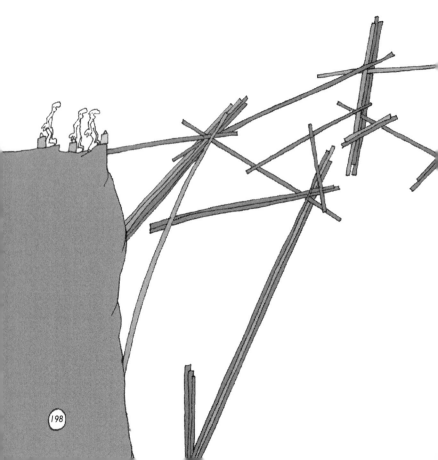

And in the end Greeting Cards turned out to be the perfect platform for Harold's Planet's bold graphics and eye-catching colours, and with a bit of tweeking, we found an audience for our idiosynchratic ideas. We had to move on, a little, from "*Contemplating Horseness*" but not too terribly far.

Licensing greeting cards to *Claire Maddicott Publications* in the UK in 2001 was the first commercially successful adventure for dear old Harold, and, happily, we have sold millions of cards since then.

Most importantly, we were able to work and travel at the same time - with only a couple of laptops, a couple of baby girls, paper, pen and scanner. In fact our scanner has travelled to Brazil, Japan, France, Spain, India, Mexico, the UK and USA, and all over Southern Africa in the back of various Landrover Defenders...

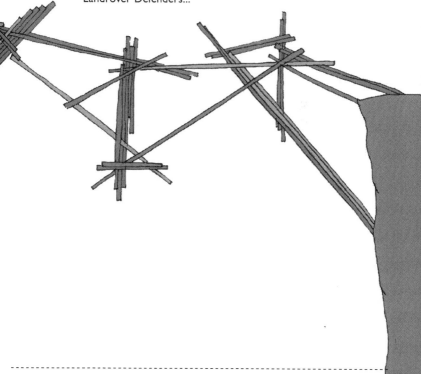

The fine balance between risk and return, 1999

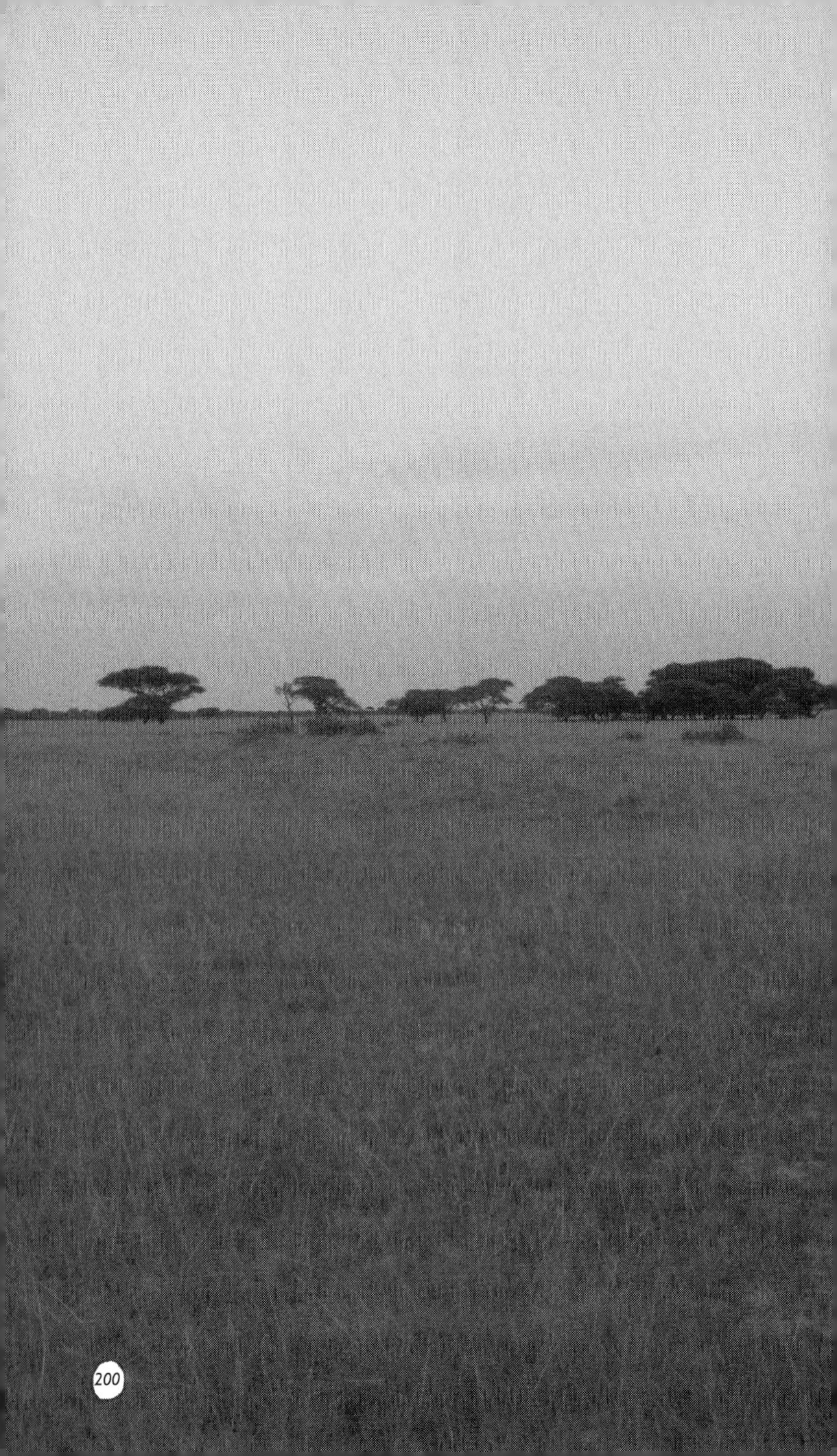

...like this one, Mpandangare the Great, our most beloved and faithful Landy. We travelled for four months atop and inside Mpandangare - through South Africa, Mozambique, Zimbabwe, Botswana and Namibia.

The landscapes of Southern Africa have had a big influence on Harold's Planet, in particular the mountains of the Western Cape and the vast horizons of the Central Kalahari.

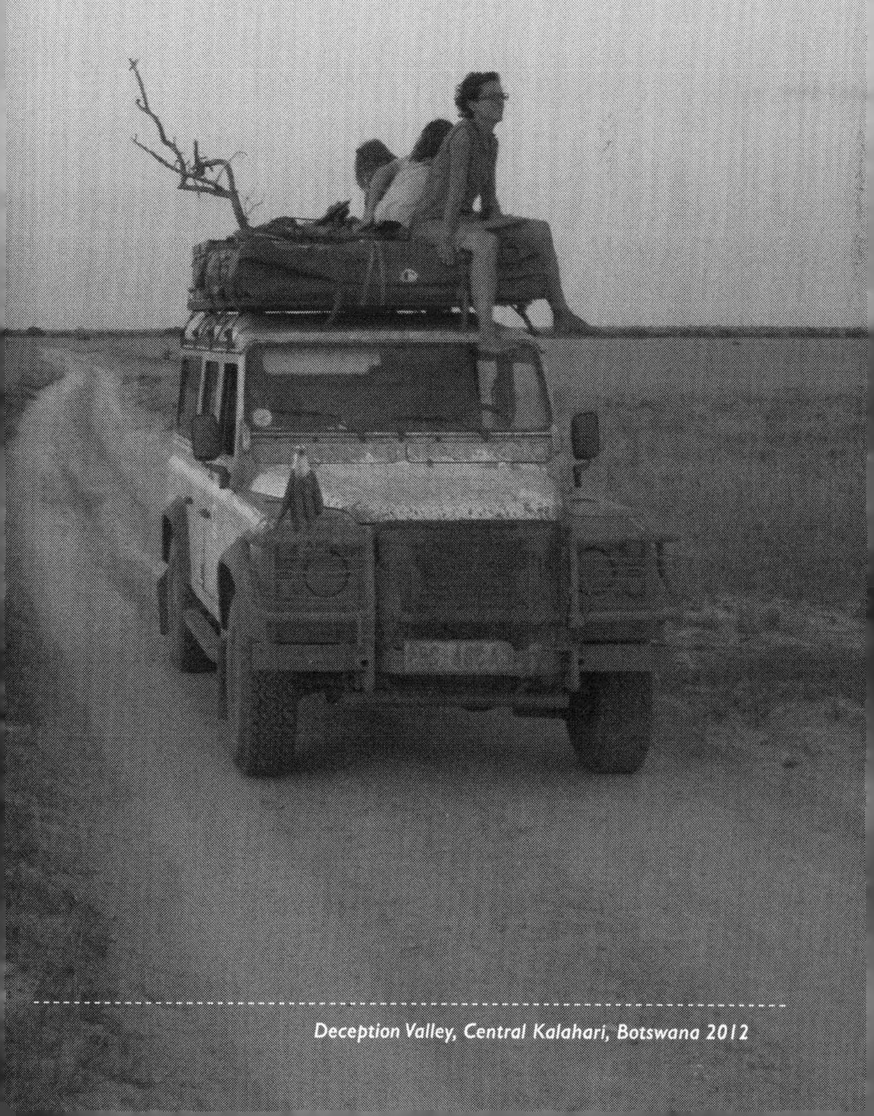

Deception Valley, Central Kalahari, Botswana 2012

Life as Art

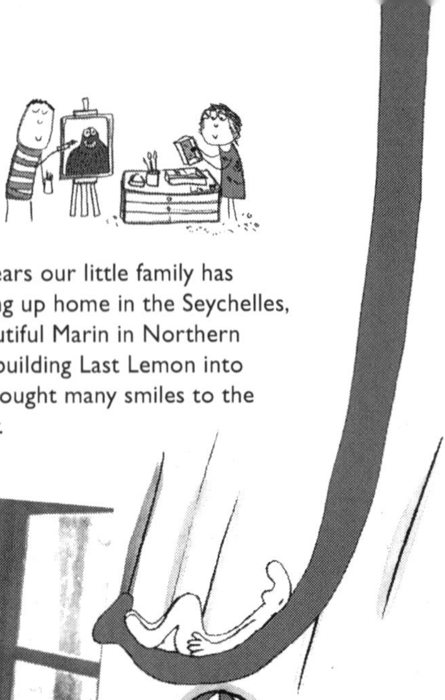

Yes! For the last 20 or so years our little family has traveled and worked - setting up home in the Seychelles, Paris, London, and now, beautiful Marin in Northern California - making art and building Last Lemon into a creative studio that has brought many smiles to the world one way or the other.

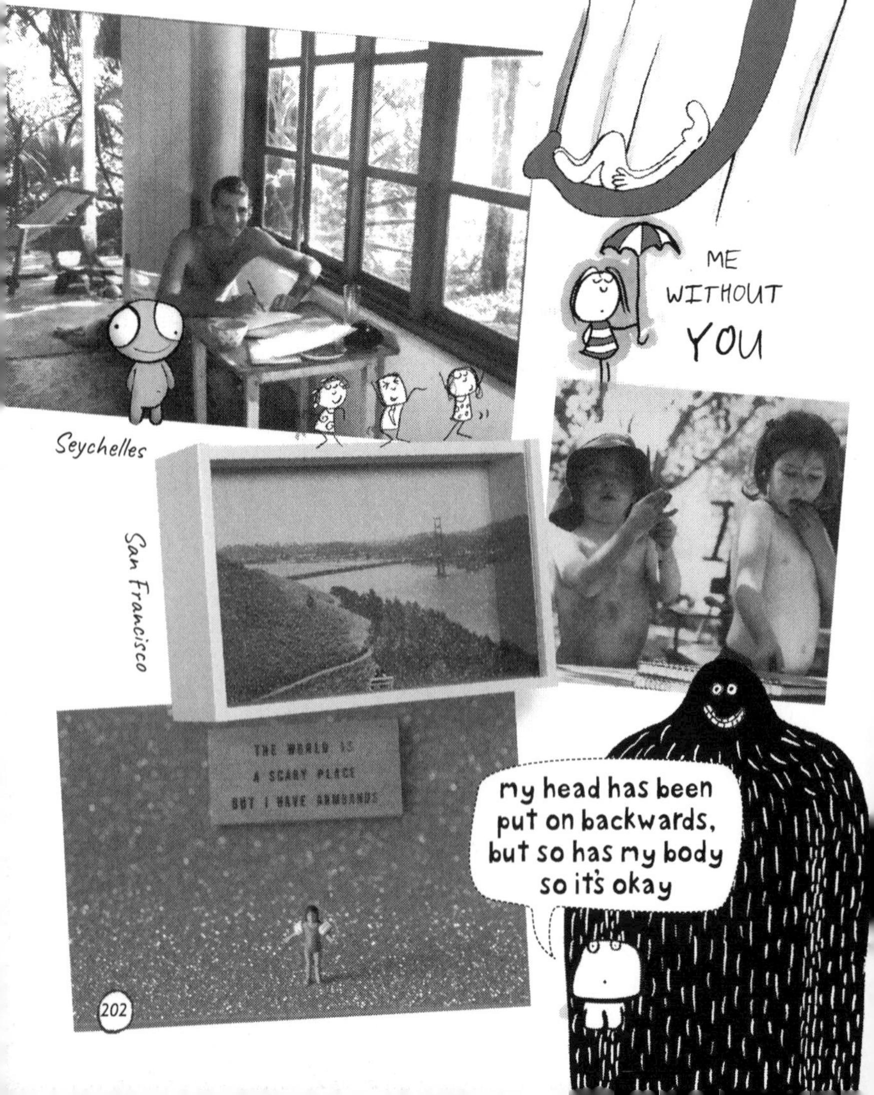
ME WITHOUT YOU
Seychelles
San Francisco
THE WORLD IS
A SCARY PLACE
BUT I HAVE ARMBANDS
my head has been put on backwards, but so has my body so it's okay

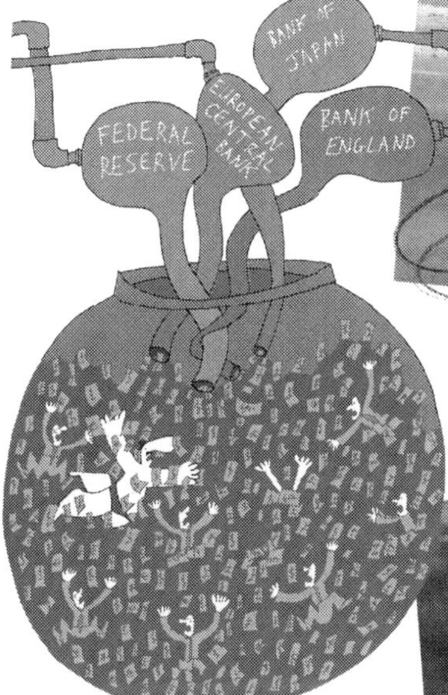
BANK OF JAPAN
EUROPEAN CENTRAL BANK
FEDERAL RESERVE
BANK OF ENGLAND

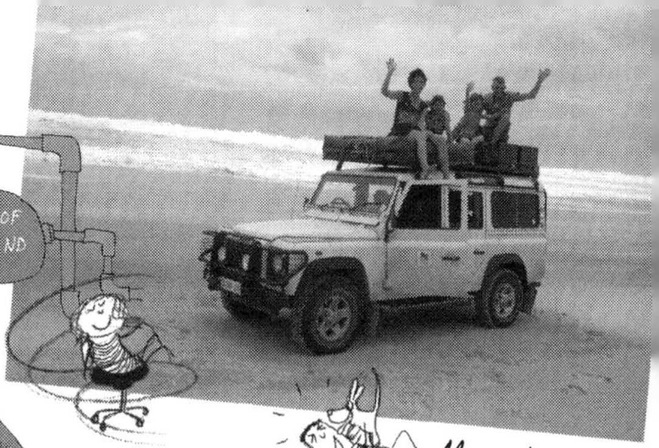

Mozambique

HAPPINESS IS...

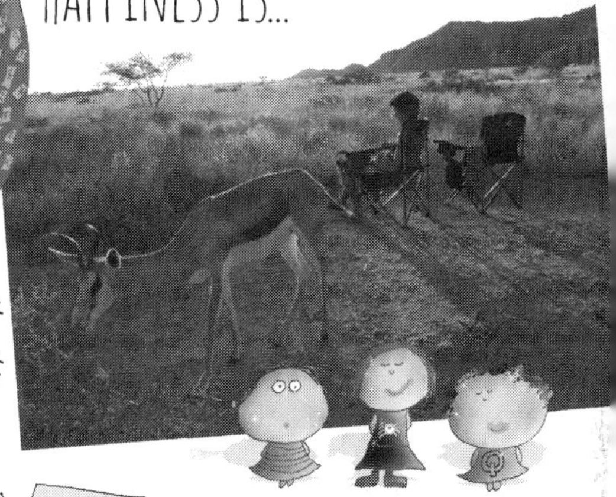

Namibia

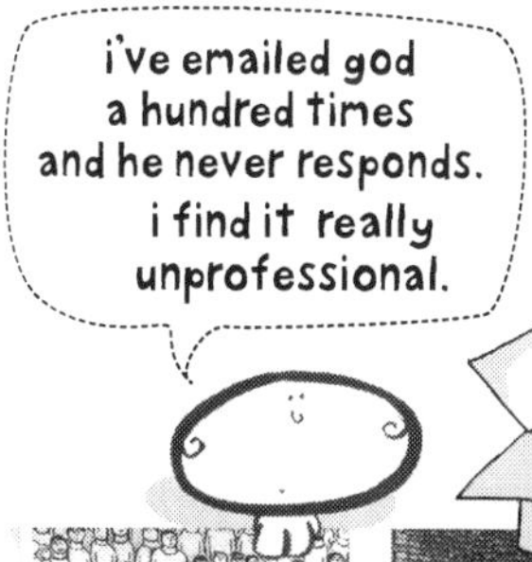
i've emailed god
a hundred times
and he never responds.
i find it really
unprofessional.

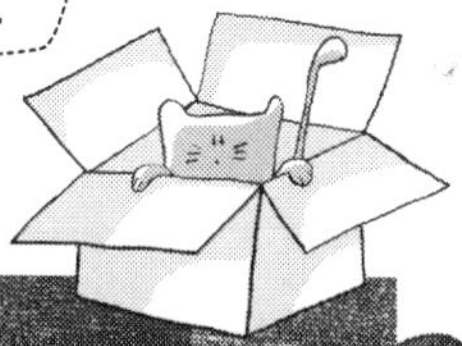

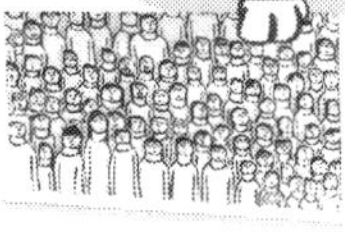

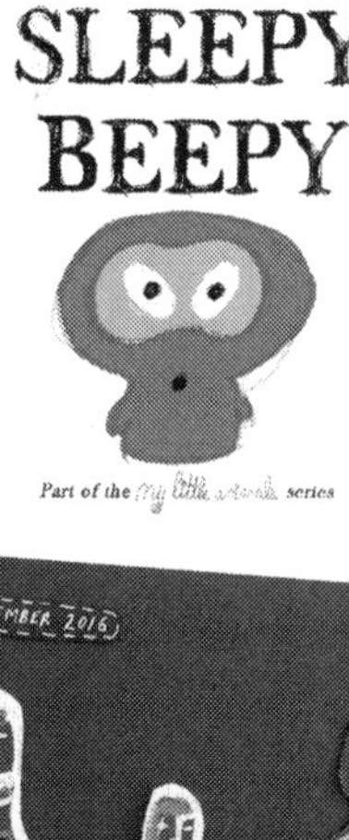
SLEEPY
BEEPY
Part of the my little worlds series

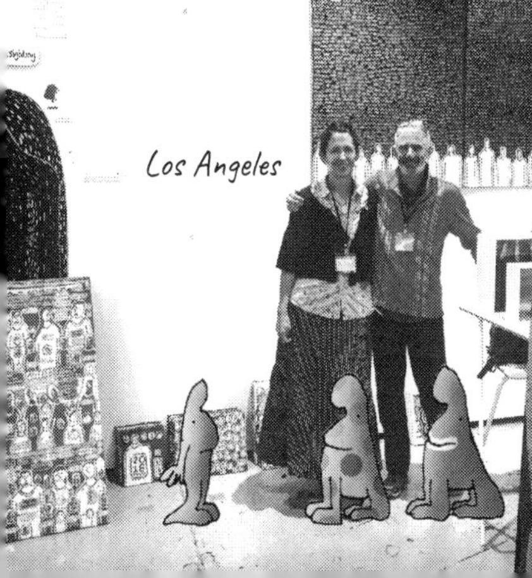

Los Angeles

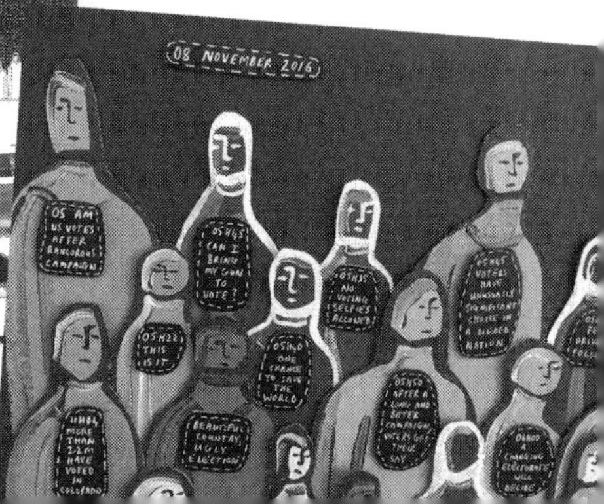
08 NOVEMBER 2016

Onward

Somehow, in all this time, we have never published a Harold's Planet book. So here we are, and you are too.

We're still dreaming and planning our next adventures, more than 20 years later, and we still dearly love Harold. If you have accompanied him along with us for all these years, we give our heartfelt thanks, we feel the love. If you are new to Harold's Planet, welcome - you may just want to stay.

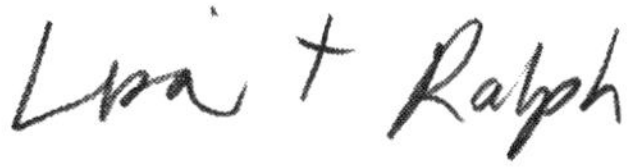

Lisa Swerling and Ralph Lazar
California, July 2019

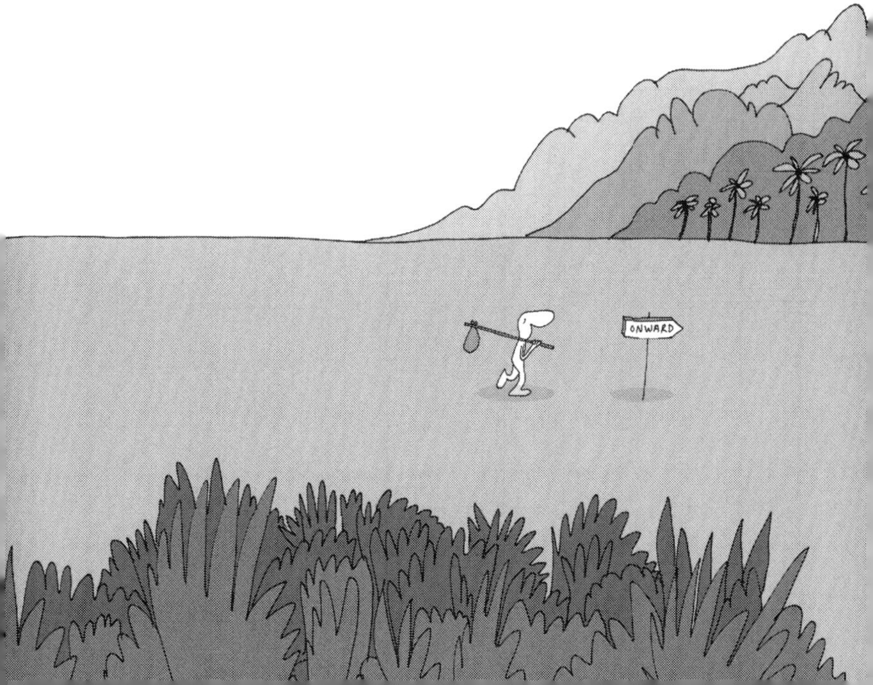
ONWARD

Two other **HAROLD'S PLANET** *books* ***BE AFRAID*** *and* ***Merlot merlittle*** *are also available on Amazon.*

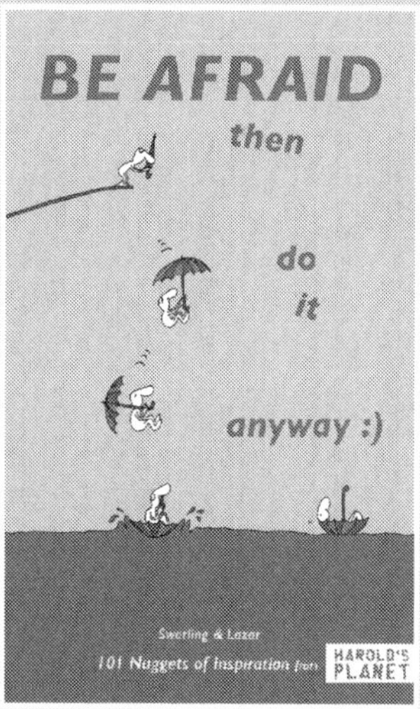
BE AFRAID
then
do
it
anyway :)
Swerling & Lazar
101 Nuggets of Inspiration from
HAROLD'S PLANET

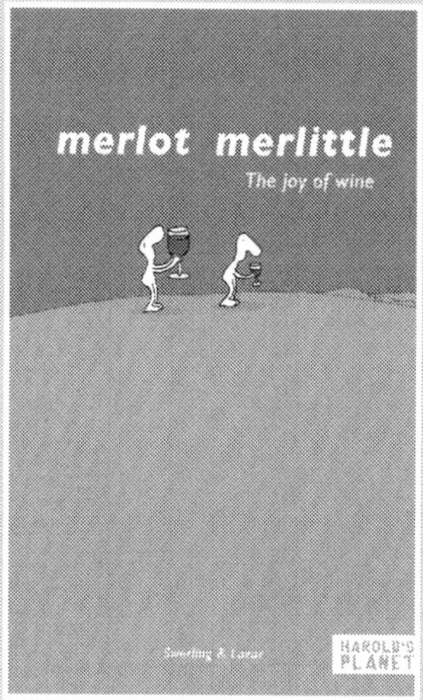
merlot merlittle
The joy of wine
Swerling & Lazar
HAROLD'S PLANET

VISIT HAROLD ONLINE

There is a huge library of Harold's Planet cartoons online at ***www.lastlemon.com/harolds-planet***

facebook.com/itsharoldsplanet
instagram.com/harolds.planet

ABOUT THE AUTHORS

Lisa Swerling & Ralph Lazar live in California.

They are the creators of the popular illustrated project Happiness Is..., which has sold nearly half a million books and has over three million followers online.

They also wrote and illustrated the New York Times bestseller Me Without You.